Using English

Edited by Janet Maybin, Neil Mercer and Ann Hewings

The Open University

Routledge
Taylor & Francis Group

Published by

Routledge
2 Park Square
Milton Park
Abingdon OX14 4RN

in association with

The Open University
Walton Hall
Milton Keynes MK7 6AA

Simultaneously published in the USA and Canada by

Routledge
270 Madison Avenue
New York NY 10016

Routledge is an imprint of the Taylor & Francis Group

First published 2007

Edited and designed by The Open University.

Typeset in India by Alden Prepress Services, Chennai.

Printed and bound in the United Kingdom by CPI, Glasgow.

This book forms part of an Open University course U211 *Exploring the English language*. Details of this and other Open University courses can be obtained from the Student Registration and Enquiry Service, The Open University, PO Box 197, Milton Keynes, MK7 6BJ, United Kingdom: tel. +44 (0)870 333 4340, email: general-enquiries@open.ac.uk

http://www.open.ac.uk

A catalogue record for this book is available from the British Library.

Library of Congress Cataloging in Publication Data
A catalog record for this book has been requested.

ISBN 978 0 415 37681 5 (hardback)
ISBN 978 0 415 37682 2 (paperback)

1.1

Contents

Preface to the series

The books in this series provide an introduction to the study of English, both for students of the English language and the general reader. As Open University course books, they constitute texts for the course U211 *Exploring the English language*. The series aims to provide students with:

- an understanding of the history of English and its development as a global language
- an appreciation of variation in the English language across different speakers and writers, and different regional and social contexts
- conceptual frameworks for the study of language in use
- illustrations of the diversity of English language practices in different parts of the world
- an understanding of how English is learnt as a first or additional language, and of its role as a language of formal education
- introductions to many key controversies about the English language, such as those relating to its position as a global language, attitudes to 'good' and 'bad' English, and debates about the teaching of English
- explorations of the use of English for new purposes and in new contexts, including multimodal texts.

Parts of these books were published previously as:

Graddol, D., Leith, D. and Swann, J. (eds) (1996) *English: History, Diversity and Change*, London, Routledge/Milton Keynes, The Open University.

Maybin, J. and Mercer, N. (eds) (1996) *Using English: From Conversation to Canon*, London, Routledge/Milton Keynes, The Open University.

Mercer, N. and Swann, J. (eds) (1996) *Learning English: Development and Diversity*, London, Routledge/Milton Keynes, The Open University.

Goodman, S. and Graddol, D. (eds) (1996) *Redesigning English: New Texts, New Identities*, London, Routledge/Milton Keynes, The Open University.

The editors for the previously published books were listed in alphabetical order. The list of editors for the present series retains this original order, followed by the additional editors who have worked on the present series. Production of this series, like that of the previously published books, has been a collaborative enterprise involving numerous members of Open University staff and external colleagues. We thank all those who contributed to the original books and to this series. We regret that their names are too many to list here.

Joan Swann and Julia Gillen
Series editors

Biographical information

Book editors

Janet Maybin is a Senior Lecturer in Language and Communication at The Open University. She has written extensively for Open University courses on language, literacy and learning and researches and writes on children's and adults' informal language and literacy practices. Recent publications include *Children's Voices* (2006, Palgrave) and *The Art of English: Everyday Creativity* (co-edited with Joan Swann; 2006, Palgrave).

Neil Mercer is Professor of Education at Cambridge University. He is a psychologist with a special interest in the role of language in the classroom and the development of children's thinking. Recent publications include: *The Guided Construction of Knowledge: Talk Amongst Teachers and Learners* (1995, Multilingual Matters) and *Words and Minds: How We Use Language to Think Together* (2000, Routledge).

Ann Hewings is a Senior Lecturer in the Centre for Language and Communication at The Open University. Her research focus is academic writing in disciplinary contexts, particularly at tertiary level and in electronic environments. Recent publications include: *Grammar and Context* (with Martin Hewings; 2005, Routledge); *Applied English Grammar: Functional and Corpus Approaches* (with Caroline Coffin and Kieran O'Halloran; 2004, Hodder-Arnold).

Additional contributors

Mike Baynham works at the University of Leeds, where he is Professor of TESOL and Director of the Centre for Language Education Research. His book, *Literacy Practices*, published by Longman in 1995, has recently been translated into Greek and published by Metaixmion. His current research interests include adult ESOL, language and migration.

Adrian Beard has taught English in secondary schools and higher education, including at the University of Newcastle upon Tyne. He co-edits the Routledge *Intertext* series, and is editor of the *Routledge A Level English Guides*. His own publications include *The Language of Sport* (1998), *The Language of Politics* (2000), *Texts and Contexts* (2001) and *Language Change* (2004), all with Routledge.

Sharon Goodman is a Lecturer in the Centre for Language and Communication at The Open University, where she has been involved in the writing and production of many of the Centre's undergraduate and postgraduate English Language courses. Her interests include stylistics, media literacy, multimodal communication and academic writing.

Almut Koester is a Lecturer in English Language at the University of Birmingham. She has an MA in Applied Linguistics from the University of Birmingham and a PhD on spoken workplace discourse from the University of Nottingham. In addition to teaching undergraduate and postgraduate university students, she has extensive experience as a teacher and teacher trainer of business English.

Donald Mackinnon is a Lecturer in the Open University Faculty of Education and Language Studies. He is not a linguist, but comes to writing about language from a background in sociology, philosophy and the old-fashioned university study of English (before structuralism, let alone post-structuralism).

Introduction

Ann Hewings

This book is about how the English language is used to get things done in the private and public areas of our lives in both English-speaking countries and in the wider English-using world. English, like Spanish and Cantonese, is a world language, having many millions of native speakers across the globe. In addition, English talk has developed into the dominant language for business and trade between speakers of different languages. The diversity of users of English, the many settings in which it is found and the varied purposes for which it is used have contributed to the richness of the language itself. The English language continues to evolve and is shaped by being adapted to different ends and to suit particular social settings and cultural practices.

The book deals with uses of English in a number of different ways. Some chapters focus on particular contexts and purposes of use such as English at work and English used to persuade. Here the emphasis is on how English is adapted to serve specific communities and purposes and to conform to the conventions that have become associated with particular sites of use. In other chapters, the emphasis is on the social use of English to maintain or convey aspects of personal or cultural identity. Use is seen to vary depending on the meanings that need to be made within particular contexts. Making sense of what is said and written depends on listeners and readers using more information than is provided by the words they see or hear. This joint construction of meaning is a theme brought out in a number of chapters.

Many of the chapters in this book deal with aspects of spoken language use. The spoken word has been transcribed for analysis and is presented here in the form of transcripts. Presenting spoken language in writing involves making choices about what features are considered most significant and which ones can be left out; for example, is it necessary to indicate the rise and fall of the voice, the pauses and hesitations or the overlapping speech? Once decisions on what to include are made, the writer must decide how to lay out the transcript – like a play with standard spelling and punctuation, in columns for each speaker, annotated with comments on nonverbal information? Writers select conventions in order to focus attention on those aspects that are most salient to their arguments. For this reason, a variety of transcription conventions is used, representing the choices of the individual chapter authors or the authors of sources they are quoting.

- Chapter 1 introduces the significance of context in language use – a theme returned to throughout the book – and raises questions concerning the nature of talk. What kinds of linguistic and cultural knowledge do people bring to English conversations and how are these used in dialogues? Ways of analysing different aspects of everyday talk are introduced.

- Chapter 2 concentrates on how English is used to convince or persuade, with a particular focus on political rhetoric and advertising. The range of contexts in which persuasive language is used is considered and both spoken and written data are analysed.

- Chapter 3 moves on from a focus on English to achieve a purpose such as persuasion, to aspects of language use which are 'playful' and do not necessarily have a goal other than to entertain or surprise. However, for such language to be successful it is necessary for those interacting to share elements of the cultural context. Playful uses of English are illustrated with reference to songs, newspaper headlines, graffiti, puns and chat room talk.

- Chapter 4 focuses more on written English and its use across a variety of social and cultural contexts. A distinction is made between characteristic grammatical and lexical features of speech and writing and how this distinction is blurred in electronic communications such as email. The use of English is seen to be affected by the writer's purpose, the relationship between the writer and reader, and the social practices surrounding a particular type of text.

- Chapter 5 turns to language used to 'get things done' – the language of work. Here English is seen as a tool to achieve certain outcomes both in face-to-face communication and in writing between colleagues, customers or clients. The 'discourse community' of a shared language between co-workers is contrasted with the language used to get things done in exchanges with the general public.

- Chapter 6 moves on from the language of work to look at how English is bound up in technological innovation and social change. The growth of consumerism and the global market influences how language is used to effect and influence both producers and consumers. A feature of this is the blending of different genres of text, particularly the increasing informality of public texts.

- Chapter 7 is written by a specialist in English literature and philosophy, not in English language. It examines aspects of English use from a philosophical perspective. How do we make judgements about English language? Are certain uses of language correct or appropriate in one context but not another? When we judge as offensive something someone says, is it the language itself that is offensive, or does the offence lie not in the words used but rather in the speaker's *intention*?

We have tried to ensure that all chapters are of interest to readers from different linguistic and cultural backgrounds. We have selected examples of research and other evidence from different contexts, perspectives and experiences of English. The readings that accompany each chapter, for example, represent ideas and research from Australia, Britain, India, New Zealand, Nigeria, Singapore and South Africa. These readings include accounts of research, reviews of certain topics and arguments for or against certain positions. They are presented not as definitive statements on an issue, but as texts that are open to critical evaluation – as, of course, are the main chapter texts themselves.

Each chapter includes:

activities to stimulate further understanding or analysis of the material

text boxes containing illustrative or supplementary material

key terms which are clearly explained as soon as they appear in order to increase the reader's familiarity with the subject.

1 Everyday talk

Janet Maybin

1.1 Introduction

> Conversation is without doubt the foundation stone of the social world –
> human beings learn to talk *in* it, find a mate *with* it, are socialized *through*
> it, rise in social hierarchy as a result of it, and, it is suggested, may even
> develop mental illness *because* of it.

(Beattie, 1983, p. 2)

What kind of knowledge do you need in order to be able to have a
conversation in English? And how do people actually use conversation to get
things done, pursue relationships and negotiate various kinds of knowledge?
In this chapter I explore the various kinds of linguistic and cultural knowledge
that people bring to English conversations and the ways in which these are
used in dialogues.

English has tended to be described by linguists in terms of its linguistic
structure – its phonology, grammar, and so on. While people use the structural
resources of English to express ideas, they are also simultaneously using
language to express and pursue relationships. The linguist Halliday (1978)
suggests that language has a dual function: it communicates **ideational
meaning**, in terms of the information and ideas expressed, and at the same
time it also communicates **interpersonal meaning**, expressing the degree of
friendliness, or status difference, for instance, between speakers. In addition,
language takes meanings from the context in which it is used, and in spoken
language in particular the distinctions between language and context, and
language and culture, begin to blur.

Some linguists define 'conversation' in the strict sense as informal talk
between equals, but, like Geoffrey Beattie in the quotation above, in this
chapter I use the term more loosely and will draw on a wide range of
examples from different contexts to try to give some sense of the diversity of
ways in which English is used today in everyday talk.

1.2 The structure and function of conversation

In the past, some traditional linguists tended to view informal conversation as
rather disorderly, pointing out its inexplicit use of language, random subject
matter, general lack of planning and high proportion of 'errors'. More recently,

especially with the rise of the subdiscipline of **conversation analysis** (Psathas, 1995; ten Have, 1999), linguists have come to appreciate the intricate patterns evident in the management of conversation. Furthermore, when we look closely at actual examples of talk, we find that what is said draws meaning from a vast amount that is left unsaid because of the way language is embedded in social activities and relationships. Language alone does not make meaning: it is used to invoke a whole range of shared knowledge and experience between speakers, from aspects of a joint physical activity, to past conversations together, to shared cultural values. Thus, the very aspects of talk that might be seen as incoherent are in fact an important part of the way talk is used to bind people together and to enable them to negotiate shared understandings about the world. In order to understand the meaning and significance of talk, therefore, we need to look at its function in specific contexts.

Openings, small talk and social binding

ACTIVITY 1.1

Allow about
15 minutes

Here are two examples of informal talk. Notice points where the talk is inexplicit, but the speakers' shared knowledge makes it comprehensible. What might be the function of the talk in each case?

1   In a university in the south of England, Julie has come to her tutor's office to receive comments on an assignment.

[Knocks on door]

Tutor   come in

Julie   hallo

Tutor   hallo (.) have a seat (.) better this time

Julie   yeh (.) tired (.) I'm (−) dead now (.) I can't wake up I'm thinking of going back to bed (.) ohh God (.)

Tutor   first to ar first to arrive (.) that's a (.) I wonder if anybody else a I always get a ⌈ bit worried

Julie   ⌊ somebody after me

Tutor   yes I know that there's somebody, there's somebody all day

(adapted from Cheepen and Monaghan, 1990, p. 199)

Transcription conventions

- (.) means a brief pause
- (–) represents inaudible speech
- deep brackets [indicate overlapping speech

2 A group of people in New Zealand are waiting to start a meeting.

[*The Maori is in italics*. THE TRANSLATION IS IN SMALL CAPITALS]

Sarah   I think everyone's here except Mere.

John   She said she might be a bit late but actually I think that's her arriving now.

Sarah   You're right. *Kia ora Mere. Haere mai. Kei te pehea koe?*
                          [HI MERE.   COME IN.   HOW ARE YOU?]

Mere   *Kia ora e hoa.*   *Kei te pai.* Have you started yet?
         [HELLO MY FRIEND,   I'M FINE]

(Holmes, 2001, pp. 34–5)

Comment

Let's look first at the talk between Julie and her tutor. Informal talk is of course largely unplanned because it arises spontaneously out of fluid and changing everyday activities and relationships. Talk in this example certainly contains inexplicit references (e.g. *better this time* and *somebody after me*), as well as unplanned and overlapping utterances which look nothing like whole grammatical sentences, but they are a completely normal part of the spoken language. One of the key points about talk is that it is **dialogic**. In other words, people constantly refer implicitly to what previous speakers have said, anticipate what they might say next and assume a large amount of shared experience. The tutor's *better this time* is perfectly comprehensible to Julie, who seizes the opportunity to let her tutor know she still isn't feeling too good. Similarly, Julie's *somebody after me* is immediately understood by the tutor to mean another student who has booked the next time slot, and we can use our knowledge of the context to interpret the tutor's rather enigmatic *yes I know that there's somebody, there's somebody all day* as referring to his own busy tutorial timetable.

What about the function of the talk? This is the beginning of what may be a rather stressful session for Julie, and after the exchange of greetings the tutor is probably showing he remembers Julie's previous health problems as a way of putting her at ease. One function of this kind of 'small talk' before getting down to business is to bind people together (what the anthropologist

Malinowski, 1923, called **phatic communion**) and establish an interactional framework for the encounter. Here the tutor, as the higher status speaker, is the one who asks the personal questions and leads the conversation.

In the second extract, in contrast to the first, the speakers are more explicit, but there is still a lot of assumed shared knowledge, for instance about why they are gathered together, who else they are expecting and why it is important for everyone to be there before they start. This extract also illustrates the common practice in multilingual communities of **codeswitching**, in this case between English and Maori. Although the rest of the meeting will be in English, Sarah greets Mere in Maori. Multilingual speakers often switch to another language to signal shared group membership and ethnicity with the person they are addressing. In this brief extract, we cannot tell whether Sarah is Maori, or Pakeha (European New Zealander); if the second, she may be signalling a positive acknowledgement of Mere's ethnic identity, and solidarity with Maori speakers through her own use of the language. Like the first example, this is also talk leading into a scheduled event; Sarah and Mere's exchanged greetings are another example of phatic communion, where the primary purpose is not so much the content of the talk as its function in binding people together. The talk between Sarah, John and Mere also sets up a relatively egalitarian interactional framework, as well as checking if they are ready to start on the business of the meeting. You may have noticed from your own experience that more formal language events such as meetings are often preceded by this kind of 'binding' social small talk.

Closings, face and politeness

In the extracts above, we saw speakers establishing and confirming interactional relationships at the beginning of a conversation. There are also important rituals for closing a conversation and withdrawing from the relationships it involves. In the next example, P and C are English women in their thirties who became friends because they both had children at the same school. P has been spending the afternoon at C's house.

> P   I must go (.) taking up your time (.) have a nice day tomorrow
>
> C   oh thanks and thanks again for the things (.) this is lovely (.) cyclamen isn't it (.) cyclamen
>
> P   yeh (.) cyclamen (.) I think it is
>
> C   's gorgeous (.) have a lovely time

P   all this evening to look forward to (.) oh *[squeak]*

C   enjoy it

P   I will

C   have a lovely time and thanks again

P   thanks (.) bye

C   bye

P   bye

(adapted from Cheepen and Monaghan, 1990, p. 41)

Transcription convention

- (.) means a brief pause

In terms of language structure, conversation endings are usually highly repetitive: people repeat their own and each other's utterances, and sometimes refer back to topics from earlier in the conversation (*all this evening to look forward to*) which necessitates a quick sidetrack of conversational turns before the speakers can continue with the closing and reach their final exchange of goodbyes. This repetition is part of the emphasis on solidarity at the closing point of an encounter. Before parting, speakers express positive evaluations of their time together, using phrases such as *thanks again*. It is important for them to guard against any possible loss of face or apparent rejection, and the person initiating the closing often cites an external reason for needing to go or effaces her- or himself in some way (e.g. *taking up your time*). There may well also be reference (though not in this example) to a future meeting.

Social interactions like those in the examples above involve the constant management of one's own and other people's **face**, a term used by the American sociologist Erving Goffman (1967) for people's public self-image. Loss of face for any speaker disrupts the conversation and may need to be repaired, for instance by the rephrasing of a comment, or an apology. Thinking back to the examples in Activity 1.1, Julie's remark about feeling tired may be a pre-emptive face-saving move, in case her performance at the tutorial doesn't come up to scratch. Face work is related to the status of the speakers, both inside the encounter and in terms of their more permanent status – their socio-economic class, gender, and so on. The aspects of status most relevant to the goal of an encounter (e.g. teacher–student in Julie's case) tend to be given most attention in the talk.

Politeness

Face needs

Building on Goffman's work, the British linguists Penelope Brown and Stephen Levinson (1987) define politeness in terms of positive and negative face needs. **Positive face** needs relate to the desire to be liked and admired, and are supplied through greetings, compliments and other direct expressions of approval. **Negative face** needs relate to the desire not to be imposed on, and are fulfilled by accompanying requests with apologies, hedging expressions (like *kind of* or *I think maybe*) and using other indirect forms to avoid a **face-threatening act**: for example, saying *there seems to have been a bit of an accident in here* rather than *how the hell could you have been so stupid!* Generally speaking, we try to satisfy the face needs of others, while protecting our own. Brown and Levinson suggest that particular cultures may stress one kind of politeness more than others; for instance, they see the UK as a 'negative politeness' culture.

Relationship constraints

Politeness involves using appropriate terms of address, and appropriate degrees of directness and formality, according to a person's relationship with you in terms of **social distance/solidarity** and **relative status**. For example, *Eat up your lunch, dear!* might be an appropriate command to a child, or even to an intimate friend, but not to one's boss at work, and possibly not to one's grandmother, depending on the formality of status relationships within the family. Generally speaking, people in a lower status position pay more attention to face needs than those in a higher status position, and women use more polite forms than men.

Social and cultural context

Being linguistically polite also involves sensitivity to the formality of the occasion and to sociolinguistic rules about behaviour: how to accept or refuse an invitation, the appropriate language practices around giving and receiving hospitality, greetings formulae, terms of address, taboo terms, and so on. These conventions vary in different English-speaking communities, as do the values governing the way formality, social distance and status are expressed.

So far, the examples we have looked at show people assuming an amount of shared knowledge, and communicating easily and amicably. It can of course happen that people are mistaken in their assumptions, and misunderstanding may lead to an embarrassing loss of face for at least one of the speakers. Again, a remark may be misinterpreted in conversation and speakers have to backtrack, or change the topic, in order to get the conversation running smoothly again. But, in general, people are remarkably adept at interpreting the inexplicit references, the subtle nuances and the unspoken implications which abound in conversation, so that accounts of experience become essentially collaborative affairs.

Turn taking

Within this collaborative process, the turn taking which is taken so much for granted is in fact accomplished through the complex management of a range of linguistic and social cues and signals. Like the previous examples, the next extract involves a negotiation, but a less amicable one.

ACTIVITY 1.2

Allow about
10 minutes

Look at the conversation below between a mother (Anna) and her teenage daughter (Jess) about the thorny subject of money. Notice the face work which is going on. Even in this quite tense situation, how do they manage the turn taking so smoothly?

	Anna	How much is it going to cost you tomorrow?
	Jess	Tomorrow? A couple of pounds. Nicola said just take a fiver and you probably won't have to use it all
	Anna	Well you'll have to find it
5	Jess	Yes well what am I going to spend tonight?
	Anna	I can't afford for you to go to the pub, and I'm not going to
	Jess	Yeah well I'll give you the money back once I've spoken ⌜ to Dad
	Anna	⌞ I don't *want* you to spend this much money on sitting in a pub
10		drinking
	Jess	Well drinking ⌜ (–)
	Anna	⌞ Fifteen pounds you've spent already and you'll spend another ⌜ five pounds
	Jess	⌞ I haven't spent fifteen pounds mum. OK just give
15		me a pound then
	Anna	What for?
	Jess	*[Exasperated sigh]* God, you don't listen at all!

Transcription conventions

- (–) represents inaudible speech
- deep brackets [indicate overlapping speech

You may have noticed Anna's face-threatening comments in lines 9–10 and 12–13, and Jess's face-protecting vagueness about the amount of money she needs in lines 2–3 and her use of *Yes well*, to signal acceptance of Anna's point and soften the force of her own.

Linguistic knowledge about turn taking in English has been strongly influenced by the work of Sacks et al. (1974), early conversation analysts with a particular interest in the management of everyday encounters. They suggest that English speakers conform to basic turn-taking rules which mean that only one person speaks at a time, and instances of overlap (e.g. lines 8–9 and 13–14 above) are quickly repaired. People have shared cultural knowledge about the kinds of 'script' used in particular kinds of speech event (e.g. parent–teenager argument), so the content of some turns can be roughly predicted. Sacks and his colleagues, however, were particularly interested in the way people use their intuitive knowledge of the structure of English in managing turn taking. A considerable amount of conversation, they suggest, is based on **adjacency pairs**, where particular kinds of utterance and response tend to occur together. For instance, one of the obvious ways in which Anna and Jess allocate turns is through the use of question and answer. Other adjacency pairs in English include greeting–greeting, invitation–acceptance/rejection, complaint–denial, request–accedence/denial.

In addition to knowledge about adjacency pairs, speakers unconsciously use their grammatical knowledge of English and respond at the end rather than in the middle of a grammatical unit. Such units range from sentences (*I can't afford for you to go to the pub, and I'm not going to*) to single words (*Tomorrow?*). At the end of each unit is what Sacks et al. call a **transition relevance place**, which is where the speaker may pause for a response, or other speakers come in, sometimes slightly overlapping the previous speaker (e.g. lines 9 and 14 above). Breaking in before a transition relevance point, as Anna does in line 12, counts as an **interruption**.

The Sacks et al. model has provided an important baseline for the study of how conversations are managed, and for the development of conversation analysis, which focuses on the structure and management of interactions, highlighting the predictable patterns of turn taking, conversational openings and closings, and how topics are developed. This approach has, however, also been criticised for not giving much attention to how conversation management is affected by:

- the relative status of the participants, which may not be directly referred to but still influences the management of turns
- the cultural knowledge required to recognise what counts as an invitation, request, and so on, particularly when these are expressed indirectly (e.g. *what am I going to spend tonight?*)
- intonation and body language – the use of voice pitch and rhythm, eye contact, gesture and posture. These are all important both for conversation management and for the communication of meaning and feelings.

Let's draw together the main points about the structure and functions of conversation covered in this section.

- *Structure*
  If we apply criteria from written English, the language used in everyday talk can seem hesitant, ambiguous and full of half-finished sentences and interruptions. It may include codeswitching (and local varieties of grammar and vocabulary) which would not be acceptable in formal written texts. In spontaneous everyday interactions, however, this kind of language use is perfectly appropriate; an utterance makes sense in relation to its cultural and social context. Elliptical structures, which assume a considerable amount of shared knowledge and experience between speakers, also signal solidarity and intimacy. We have seen how there are predictable structures in conversation around turn taking, and openings and closings (these will vary depending on the cultural background of the speakers).

- *Function*
  The examples above show the close intertwining of the ideational and the interpersonal functions of language. For example, we have seen that talk about tiredness is also managing a tutor–student relationship, and that a language choice can express solidarity. There is constant feedback between these two functions; relationships constrain the content of what is said, but what is said can also build or change a relationship. The meanings communicated in a particular conversation depend partly on the actual words used, but they are also shaped by the negotiation of relationships between the participants, and by other aspects of the social and cultural context.

I consider this issue of context in the next section.

1.3 Context and meaning

I have already touched on the importance of context in using and interpreting language appropriately in conversation, and the importance of cultural conventions in the expression of politeness. In a broad sense, **context** can include the following (overlapping) elements, all of which will influence the use and interpretation of particular words and phrases:

- the physical surroundings
- the relationship between speakers
- their past shared experience, and current conversational goals
- the social events of which the conversation is a part
- broader cultural values and expectations.

In addition, language also creates its own context, even as it is being used, in two different ways. First, the meaning of a word or utterance is shaped by other words or utterances which have gone before; for example, when Anna says *Well you'll have to find it* in the example in Activity 1.2, we know that she is talking about money, because of the preceding comments. Second, words evoke nuances and associations from our experience of them in other contexts; they gather a collection of contextual associations which reflect the history of their use.

Anthropologists have demonstrated that, in order to use and interpret language, we draw on a considerable amount of cultural as well as linguistic knowledge (e.g. see the 'Politeness' box in Section 1.2). Within any single community there will also be a range of ways of speaking: different uses of language associated with legal, educational and religious institutions, with particular relationships and with particular social events. In order to understand the function and meaning of any conversational exchange, we need to know the values and expectations about language held by those speakers in that particular cultural context.

Bearing all this in mind, let's look at one particular practice in English, to see what kinds of factors influence the use and interpretation of language.

Terms of address

In some languages the relationship between speakers is encoded grammatically; for example, the *tu/vous* distinction between informal and formal 'you' in French, the choice of high or low Javanese in Java depending on whom you are addressing, and in Japanese the addition of particular **morphemes** (the smallest part of a word that carries its own meaning, e.g. 'hopeful' consists of two morphemes: 'hope' and 'ful') to the terms you are using to signify respect to the listener. In English, however, relationships between speakers are not so immediately obvious. One has to look across a whole conversation to gather clues from the way language is used to see how particular relationships are being marked, negotiated or contested. However, one way in which relationships are quite explicitly marked in English is in the terms people use to address each other – whether one is 'on first name terms', for instance.

ACTIVITY 1.3

Allow about 10 minutes

Jot down all the names or terms that people use to address you. What are the reasons for people calling you one name rather than another? And would it be appropriate for you to address them in a similar manner?

Comment

My own list for this activity includes variations on my first and last names, together with *Miss, Ms* or *Mrs*, nicknames, *mum, mother, aunty, madam* (in shops), *love* and the local variant *me duck* (in markets), *miss* (in schools), and various terms of endearment and abuse. Some of these names are kinship terms (with some variation between more and less formal versions); while *miss* used by children in schools signals a particular work role (like *doctor* or *your honour*). Honorific terms, like *madam*, mark not just formal respect, but also certain genteel politeness conventions – hence the difference between the ways in which I am addressed in smart department stores and in the local market. A male colleague who carried out this activity commented on the large number of terms there are in Britain for men addressing each other (e.g. *mate*, *guv*, *chum*, *pal*, *squire*) and how these can be used to play up, or play down, class differences between the speakers. In addition to identifying a large number of different terms, you may have found that the same term can mean rather different things in different relationships; for instance, a woman may be addressed as *love* (though she may not always use the same term back) by her mother, her husband, an older male colleague and the local butcher.

By way of illustration, consider the response to Activity 1.3 from Lo Wing Yu, a student in Singapore.

Lo Wing Yu, aged 21

Terms of address	Explanation
Debbie	Although this name is not included on my birth certificate, it was given to me at the age of three. Most of my friends, except my primary school classmates, know me by that name. I'm also known as Debbie in my various workplaces.
Deb	Reserved only for my best friend of seven years. An indication of our 'closeness'.
Wing Yu	Used by almost all my primary school classmates. At that time, all teachers called me that because I was registered in school with that name. Anyway, it wasn't that 'fashionable' to have English names then.
Wing Yu (pronounced in Cantonese)	Used by my family members, except my elder sister.
Yingyu (Mandarin pronunciation version)	Used mostly by my Mandarin teachers in school and a seamstress whom I always go to.
Lo Wing Yu	My full name is occasionally used when I am either at some government departments such as the Immigration Department, at the hospital/clinic, or somewhere where strangers happen to be holding my IC [identification card] or some information about me.
Ah Mui (pronounced in Cantonese, meaning 'little sister')	Used by my family members, especially my elder sister. Also used by my friends to disturb me because they find that term of address very funny (if they happen to hear that being used to address me, e.g. when they call and my family members call for 'Ah Mui' to answer the phone).

Xiao mei mei ('little girl/sister' in Mandarin)	Used by older guys who are trying to be funny, or older women who think that I am actually very, very young.
Jie Jie ('older sister' in Mandarin)	Used by children, or parents of little children whom I meet at the clinic. I hardly ever use this term to address strangers. If it is someone I know, I might call her by her name followed by Jie Jie.
Aunty	Used by children, or parents of little children, whom I meet at the clinic where I am working. I may use the same form of address for female adults who are very obviously older than me.
Xiao jie ('Miss' in Mandarin)	Mostly used by strangers or patients in the clinic where I work part time. I would use the same term for Chinese strangers who are female and young.
Miss	Usually used by strangers. I would use the same term to address other female strangers who do not look that old.
Miss Lo	Usually used in a more formal context e.g. during the job interview which I went for during my vacation. Also used by shop assistants or waiters/waitresses if I happen to use my credit card.
Ma'am	Used by counter staff at fast-food restaurants. Also used more in formal contexts when people/strangers are trying to be polite.
Sweetheart/honey	Used by some of my closer friends for fun. Sometimes used by myself to them as well.
Woman	Usually used by closer girl friends. Sometimes used by myself to them.
Girl	Often used by strangers older than me who are trying to catch my attention, or ask me to do something.

So are there sociolinguistic rules that tell us who has the right to use which terms to whom? **Terms of address** are a part of politeness, and will depend on:

- difference in status between the speakers: for example, in relation to age, gender, class, work role (hence the asymmetrical use of many terms)
- social distance between speakers: how well they know each other
- formality of situation: some contexts mark particular roles, for instance *miss* in school, and *your honour* in court; also, you would probably not wish to embarrass a dear one by using a special private nickname in a more public formal situation
- the cultural and linguistic context: notice, for instance, the variety of personal names from different languages used for Lo Wing Yu above. In Singapore, older family members tend to be addressed by a kinship term rather than by a personal name, and the word *aunty* is frequently used as a friendly term of respect for an older woman.

Although terms of address are sensitive to status, social distance and context, they also have a particular force of their own which can mark, construct or change some aspect of a relationship. Notice the way Lo Wing Yu feels positioned by certain people calling her *little sister.* In Britain, people have commented on estate agents' alacrity in adopting rather informal terms of address for their clients, presumably to try to establish a close, trusting relationship as rapidly as possible. Conversely, an irate parent who addresses their child as *James* rather than *Jamie* symbolically increases the social distance between them as part of the reprimand.

As the famous example in the box overleaf shows, terms of address are powerful ways of expressing and asserting relationships. We have already seen how in some communities speakers have access to terms from a number of languages, and there may be a particular reason why a term from one of these is used rather than another. For example, Indian English speakers often use Indian language kinship terms to signal that they want to invoke Indian conventions, rather than those associated with British culture (Pandharipande, 1992). In Indian languages kinship terms, as in Singapore, are extended beyond biological relations. So, for instance, an Indian English speaker may address a listener who is not a blood relative as *didi* or *di* (elder sister), to indicate a particular relationship of respect and affection; someone addressed as *didi* then has the right to behave as if she were the speaker's elder sister, advising them, or interrupting their speech. Indian English speakers may also address a wider range of people as *aunty* and *uncle* than do British English speakers. This extension of English kinship terms is common in many of the new Englishes (e.g. Hawaiian English, Singaporean

English, Nigerian English), reflecting the greater social importance of kinship for these speakers in comparison with most British speakers.

> In the 1960s, a black man was stopped and questioned on a public street in America:
>
> > 'What's your name, boy?' the policeman asked ...
> > 'Dr Poussaint. I'm a physician ...'
> > 'What's your first name, boy? ...'
> > 'Alvin.'
>
> The policeman manages to insult Dr Poussaint three times in this short exchange; once by his initial use of the term 'boy' which denies adult status on the grounds of race, secondly because he ignores the doctor's stated preference for how he should be addressed, and thirdly by repeating the denigrating term 'boy' even when he knows the doctor's name. Dr Poussaint's own experience of the encounter was 'profound humiliation' – 'For the moment, my manhood had been ripped from me.'
>
> (Ervin-Tripp, 1969, pp. 93, 98)

1.4 Communicative strategies and conversation style

In its broadest definition, **style** refers to a combination of features relating to meaning and management of conversation: prosody (rhythm and intonation), overlapping, repetition, use of laughter, tolerance of noise and silence, and ways of using anecdotes, asking questions, linking topics and expressing particular emotions (Tannen, 1984). At the individual level we all may be said to have our own particular style of talking – the way we use stories, for instance, or how much personal information we tend to reveal, or how we express politeness. Aspects of our style can be traced to where we have come from, our class, our age and our gender.

How do conversational styles vary?

There can be a remarkable diversity of styles within one social group, as Deborah Tannen showed when she analysed the conversation of five friends and herself during a Thanksgiving dinner party. These friends came from different geographical backgrounds: two were Californian men, three (two men and Tannen) were New Yorkers, and there was one English woman.

Tannen was intrigued by the striking difference between the New Yorkers and the rest when she asked them afterwards how much they had enjoyed the conversation during the meal. Whereas the New Yorkers remembered it as lively and satisfying, the others had found it 'all over the place and frenetic', and had felt bulldozed and marginalised.

In contrasting the New Yorkers' conversational style with those of the others, Tannen highlights the following differences:

- expectations about what it is appropriate to talk about; for example, whether topics should be 'personal'
- how turn taking is managed; for instance, whether pauses and silence are tolerated, and whether interruptions are meant to encourage or stop the other speaker
- the degree of directness in questions and whether these are perceived as supportive or off-putting
- use of intonation and voice quality (to signal enthusiasm, the punch line of a story, and so on)
- willingness to enter ironic routines or story rounds, and expectations about what constitutes a joke or story worth telling.

Some of the differences in communication strategies that Tannen identifies between her friends are also highlighted in studies of different cultural groups and in studies of gender and talk. In the next two subsections, questioning strategies, ways of seeking and expressing personal information, and the role of pauses and silence crop up again as important aspects of communication style that can have quite far-reaching effects if they are not used in the same way by people trying to talk to each other.

Aboriginal English

Diana Eades, an Australian linguist, has studied the 'ways of speaking' of Aboriginal English speakers and the effects these have on their experience of communicating with white Australians. She suggests that Aboriginal ways of using English are closely related to their lifestyle and culture, and to their beliefs about how people should relate to each other.

ACTIVITY 1.4

Read the extract from 'Communicative strategies in Aboriginal English' by Diana Eades (Reading A). Try to keep a mental note of the features of Aboriginal communicative style she identifies. What kinds of misunderstanding arise between speakers of Aboriginal English and white Australians?

Comment

Eades suggests that the lack of personal privacy in the Aboriginal lifestyle is balanced by an indirect verbal style. Aboriginal people are reluctant to express personal opinions, supply information or account for actions directly. Indirectness is often achieved through the 'multifunctional' nature of utterances. Whether a question is also a request, for instance, can be negotiated between the speakers concerned. Responses to the directness of white interactions often include 'gratuitous concurrence' (agreeing with whatever they say), which can cause misunderstanding whenever direct questions are used in legal, medical and educational settings.

Gender and style

If one way of identifying significant aspects of style is to compare different cultural groups, another is to compare different genders. Research in this area has tended to be carried out among middle-class, white British or American women, but, as we shall see, ideas developed in this area are beginning to be applied to other contexts and cultures.

ACTIVITY 1.5

Allow about
10 minutes

Spend a few moments noting down your personal experience of any differences between men's and women's talk – the way they interact, their choice of words and phrases, the topics they like to discuss. Why might these differences exist? My comments follow.

A number of researchers have found that, in mixed company, women usually talk less than men (contrary to popular belief), and that in most situations they are less competitive, more cooperative and work harder to make things run smoothly; for instance, encouraging others to talk and using more face-saving politeness strategies. One explanation for this is that women are brought up to occupy a less powerful position in society, and to display deference towards men, which they do through being more hesitant and indirect. In 1975, Robin Lakoff suggested that women use more tag questions (e.g. *isn't it? don't you think?*) and more indirect polite forms (e.g. *could you possibly?*), intensifiers (e.g. *I'm so glad*), euphemisms and what she sees as generally weaker vocabulary (e.g. words such as *lovely, nice* and *Oh dear*).

Lakoff's observations were largely intuitive and anecdotal; they received elements of both challenge and support in later studies (see Coates, 1996; 2003). Some studies have borne out Lakoff's point about women's deference, showing how men tend to dominate the topics and management of mixed gender conversation, interrupting more and giving less feedback and support.

An alternative explanation is that men and women speak differently, not because of an asymmetrical power relationship between them, but because they are socialised into different gender subcultures as children through play. For instance, Goodwin (1990), who studied African-American children playing in the street, found that, while boys played in groups with hierarchies and those higher up issued clear directives such as 'Gimme the pliers', the girls organised in more cooperative groups and made more indirect suggestions, such as 'Let's do it this way'. Boys' arguments, which challenged the group hierarchy, were sorted out straight away through direct competition and verbal confrontation, while girls who organised friendship around inclusion and exclusion tended to have protracted discussions about other girls in their absence. Here then might be the seeds of a non-confrontational, collaborative speech style for women, with an interest in topics concerning people's motives and feelings, and a more directly competitive style for men, with a focus on the physical world.

These two approaches have been referred to as the 'dominance' and the 'difference' approach. Other researchers, however, have pointed out that neither of these approaches seriously addresses the ways in which men and women use language differently in different contexts, or the considerable range of speaking styles within each gender group. More recently, there has been a shift in the study of gender and language, away from simply matching up particular language features to men or women, to examining how people 'do' or 'perform' gender through language. The performance of gender involves what is said as well as how it is said. For instance, Deborah Cameron (1997) showed how gossip between a group of young men had both cooperative and competitive elements, including the features signalling solidarity that some researchers have associated with 'women's talk'. She argues that gender is expressed here, in this private conversation among male friends, not so much through their speaking style as through the content: their references to sexual exploits with women and their complaints about the repulsiveness of gay men. Cameron suggests that, through what they say, the young men define themselves *against* these other groups (women and gay men), in a performance of the gender identity of 'red-blooded heterosexual males'.

Individual language features on their own, then, are not enough to **index** (point to) a particular gender identity. But particular combinations of features, together with the content of talk, communicate messages about gender identity. Eckert and McConnell-Ginet (2003) suggest that this behaviour is also tied in with other aspects of personal style. They describe how style and performance are part of the formation of identity:

> ... working within the constraints imposed by a gender order and by the linguistic practices of their communities, [people] assemble the various resources in [their] linguistic toolbox to fashion selves that they can live with. ... Each person uses the toolbox in their own way, mixing and matching linguistic resources such as lexical items, grammatical gender marking, syntactic constructions, metaphors, discourse markers, speech acts, intonation contours, segmental variables. And the toolbox also includes other communicative resources such as pregnant pauses, overlapping speech, rhythm and speed, tone of voice, gaze and posture, facial expression. Some of these uses may be automatic – the product of long-ingrained habit – some of them may be quite consciously strategic. The outcome is a communicative style, which combines with other components of style such as dress, ways of walking, hairdo, and so on to constitute the presentation of a persona, a self. This presentation may place the individual squarely within a well-known category, or it may constitute a claim to a somewhat novel identity. Communicative style is sometimes thought of as the external wrapping inside which the meaningful substance is found, the how it is said as distinct from what is said. But this picture is profoundly misleading. What and how are inextricably linked, and the styles people develop have as much to do with what they (typically) say and do as with how they say it. ... Style ... is not a façade behind which the 'real' self stands but it is a manifestation of a self we present to the world.
>
> (Eckert and McConnell-Ginet, 2003, pp. 305–6)

ACTIVITY 1.6

Read 'The role of compliments in female–male interaction' by Janet Holmes (Reading B). How might Holmes's findings relate to the various arguments about gender and speech style discussed above? How does what she has to say about giving compliments relate to your own experience? Notice how Holmes combines the two dimensions of cross-gender and cross-cultural comparison.

Comment

In research among mainly white middle-class New Zealanders, Holmes found that compliments were used most frequently by women to other women, who also used more intensifiers in their compliments, and terms such as *lovely* and *nice*. Her finding that the women gave and received many more compliments than the men could be seen as supporting the argument that women's linguistic behaviour, at least in this social group, is affiliative and facilitative, rather than competitive or control oriented (and this seems to be Holmes's own position). The women's affiliative behaviour could be explained using either the 'difference' or 'the dominance' positions. However, an alternative argument is that, while being apparently supportive, there may be a competitive edge to the giving of compliments, and an implicit exercise of control over what counts as admirable and compliment-worthy. Cameron (1997) points out that women's display of appreciation of others can also be a way of gaining popularity and status for themselves, within the 'egalitarian norms' of female friendship groups. She would see the content and focus of the compliments as also important, in relation to cultural expectations about what women are like. Interestingly, the most common topics for compliments in Holmes's research, especially for women, were clothes and hair, important aspects of personal style. Eckert and McConnell-Ginet would see this kind of complimenting as a speech act which signals being a woman, a styled performance which girls may learn in the course of taking on a particular kind of female identity. Complimenting another woman about her appearance with words such as *lovely* and *nice* appears to be a particularly strong way of performing femininity for the middle-class white New Zealanders in Holmes's research. However, as Holmes points out, complimenting reflects cultural conventions as well as gender expectations. Although compliments in English have a simple predictable linguistic structure, they carry a wealth of social significance, and knowing how to use them requires sophisticated sociolinguistic knowledge.

To summarise, early research on language and gender suggested that there is a particular women's speaking style in English which involves more hesitations, indirectness, qualifiers, polite forms and tag questions. Some researchers relate this to women's inferior social position and claim that men dominate cross-gender talk through their control of the topic, interruptions and lack of supportive feedback. Other researchers describe women's use of English as not weak, but different; such differences have been related to boys' and girls' socialisation in different gender subcultures. While both the dominance and difference arguments provide useful explanations for certain language behaviour patterns, more recent research studies show how style, function and meaning vary across different contexts, and suggest that there may be more complex reasons underlying the patterns of women's (and men's) language use (Coates, 1996; 2003). Particular language features and communicative strategies may be used more often by some men or women in certain contexts.

1.5 Stories, accounts and identity

One aspect of style that we mentioned in the discussion above is people's use of storytelling. Eades (Reading A) described how Aboriginal people may respond indirectly to questions, using a narrative. In fact, a large amount of informal talk in English seems to take the form of narrative. Bruner suggests that conversational storytelling is the major way in which we account for our actions and the events we experience and that 'our sensitivity to narrative provides the major link between our own sense of self and our sense of others in the social world around us' (Bruner, 1986, p. 69).

Storytelling and voices

Stories told in conversations can range from the briefest of anecdotes to long, detailed accounts of experiences or incidents, and from the mundane to the extraordinary. An important element of every story is the way in which narrators convey (or try out) their own evaluation of the events and people involved. This evaluation is the point of the story – why the narrator has chosen to tell it – and it also conveys social and moral values which are an important part of the narrator's personal identity.

ACTIVITY 1.7

Allow about 15 minutes

We pick up the following narrative after an American man announced to a friend that he had just pulled off an excellent deal on a house purchase. The friend asked 'How come?' and the man explained that the house he wanted belonged to an elderly sick widow, who had moved into a nursing home and had been trying to sell her house for some time. Snyder was the estate agent.

What kinds of evaluative comment is the narrator making, either directly or indirectly, of the events and people involved?

> [W]hen I went to see it, the guy says to me, says, 'We got a bid for thirty-three – thirty-four,' says, 'If you bid thirty-five,' he says, 'You'll get it.' I said, 'Okay, let me think it over.' And I went home and called up my wife's cousin who's a realtor. Well, his partner knows Snyder very well, so he called him up. The bid was for twenty-seven, five! So I figured they could do the same thing I was going to do ... So he calls me the next day and I told my wife exactly what to say. So he gets on the phone and so my wife says, 'Look, we're not talking land, we're talking house. The house isn't worth it and it needs a lot of work.' You know, and we made up a lot of things ... So she says, 'Yes, we have to lay

down new floors, the rugs are no good (the rugs happen to be in good shape), we have to- -there's too much shrubbery, we have to tear out some of the shrubs.' (The shrubbery around the house is magnificent if it's done right, if it's done right.) So really we made up everything. So he says to my wife, he says, 'Well, what would you bid?'. So she says, 'It's stupid for me to talk,' she says ... 'Why should I even talk to you? It ain't gonna be anywheres near.' So he says to her, he says, 'Well,' he says, 'the person at thirty-four backed out.' So she says, 'Oh, yeah?' He says, 'Yeah,' he says, 'What would you bid?' So she says, 'Twenty-eight.' He says, 'Oh,' he says, 'No, that she'll never go for.' So she says, 'Okay, that's my bid, Mr Smith. You want it, fine; you don't, fine.' Got a call that afternoon. It was accepted!'

She finally went – we settle at November 18th. And I got to sell my house now – three weeks now.

(adapted from Wolfson, 1982, pp. 25–7)

My comments are in the following text.

Some of the ways in which storytellers convey particular evaluations of the events they are relating are not visible in the transcription; for instance, their use of prosody, sound effects, facial expressions and gestures. But there are two important ways of communicating evaluation which are clearly present in the example above.

- Narrators step outside the story at particular points to bring in important additional information, or to justify their actions. For instance, the narrator here tells us that, in spite of what his wife claims on the phone to the estate agent, the house and garden are actually in very good condition: *the rugs happen to be in good shape* and *The shrubbery around the house is magnificent.* He makes sure that the listener appreciates the cleverness of the trick by explaining. *So really we made up everything*, and guards against his strategy being condemned as dishonest by his remark near the beginning of the story, *So I figured they could do the same thing I was going to do.*

- Many conversational narratives use reported speech, particularly when it gets to the key part of the action. But we hardly ever report someone else's exact words when we are relating an incident or anecdote; we paraphrase and reframe them to make a specific point and to show ourselves in a particular kind of light (Volosinov, 1973; Tannen, 1989). One can sense the narrator's triumphalism behind the confident, no-nonsense voice he has constructed for his wife, and the clear evaluation of his actions as pulling off a great deal rather than, for instance, how he cheated a sick elderly widow.

Evaluation strategies are tied in with the structure of conversational stories, as Labov (1972) demonstrated in his influential US research.

The structure of conversational narrative using Labov's 1972 categories

- *Abstract: what is the story about? (How the narrator had just pulled off an excellent deal.)*

- *Orientation: who, when, what, where? (She's a widow; she put the house on the market some time ago.)* This section is often more grammatically complicated than when the action gets going, because the teller wants to sketch out what was happening before, or alongside, the main narrative events.

- *Complicating action: then what happened?* This is the main action part of the story, the account of significant events, with switches in and out of the present tense; it often includes plenty of reported speech.

- *Evaluation: so what?* In order to make sure the listener gets the point of the story, the narrator may step outside the story at particular points to bring in additional important information (*the rugs happen to be in good shape*), to make evaluative points (*So I figured they could do the same thing I was going to do*), or to use sound effects and gestures. Evaluation is also conveyed through the voices the narrator creates for the characters, and through devices to increase suspense and strengthen emphasis.

- *Result: what finally happened? (It was accepted!)* This resolves the story, and often again emphasises the point of telling it.

- *Coda (And I got to sell my house now.)* An additional remark or observation usually bridges the gap between story time and real time, bringing the teller and listener back to the present.

In conversation, stories are often told collaboratively. Notice in the next example how eleven-year-old Karlie provides an evaluation right at the beginning for her friend Nicole's story, which they told together. I had just asked Nicole who else lived at her house and Karlie mentioned that Nicole's sister Terri had recently had a baby.

JANET	So does your sister live quite near you?
NICOLE	She lives with us
KARLIE	Cause she's only quite young

NICOLE	She's young, she's sixteen
JANET	Ah right
KARLIE	She did the best thing about it though, didn't she, Nicole?
NICOLE	She didn't tell a soul, no one, that she was pregnant
KARLIE	Until she was due, when she got into hospital, then she told them
NICOLE	On Saturday night she had pains in her stomach, and come the following Sunday my mum was at work and my sister come to the pub and my aunt Ella was in it and my sister went in there and said 'I've got pains in my stomach!', so my aunt Ella went and got my mum, and took her to hospital, and my mum asked her if she was due on and she said 'No, I've just come off' and when they got her to hospital they said 'Take her to Maternity!' My mum was crying.
JANET	Your mum didn't realise she was pregnant?
NICOLE	No. And my mum slept with her when she was ill!
	...
KARLIE	/My dad said she did, Terri did the best thing about it. Her sister's Terri
NICOLE	Or if she did tell, as she's so young, she weren't allowed to have him

(Maybin, 2006, pp. 117–18)

Transcription conventions

- ... indicates omitted talk
- / indicates where another speaker interrupts or cuts in

This story is actually introduced by Karlie's evaluation *She did the best thing about it*, before Nicole and Karlie together give the abstract of the story: *She didn't tell a soul, no one, that she was pregnant – Until she ... got into hospital, then she told them*. Nicole provides additional information which emphasises the extraordinary nature of the story in her comment *and my mum slept with her when she was ill* (i.e. 'and still didn't notice that she was pregnant').

Interestingly, although Karlie's initial evaluation is presented as her own, later in the conversation we learn that it is in fact her father's: *My dad said she did, Terri did the best thing about it*. Karlie seems initially to have taken on her father's voice, and presented his judgement of Terri's actions as if it were her own. Mikhail Bakhtin (1981) suggests that this direct taking on of other people's voices (in addition to reporting them) is a common feature of all spoken language, that we are forever using words and phrases from other people's mouths. He argues that whenever we take on a voice, we also take on an evaluative stance (as Karlie obviously does here). In fact, our taking on of voices and their attitudes is part of 'the ideological becoming of a human being' (Bakhtin, 1981, p. 341).

Codeswitching

As we saw in Activity 1.1, speakers who speak a number of languages or dialects may switch between them within a conversation. They may also switch codes to create voices for different characters in stories and anecdotes.

The following example, from research carried out in London, shows Andrew (A), a fifteen-year-old of Jamaican parentage, in conversation with Barry (B), a friend aged sixteen with parents from Barbados and the southern USA. Andrew switches between London English, a London variety of creole based on Jamaican Creole, and Standard English with a near Received Pronunciation accent, to create different personae in the story he is telling Barry.

1   A   yeah man, I was on the till on Saturday (.) and this this black
        man *come* in (.) and you know our shop, right, they u:m give
        refund on Lucozade bottles

    B   m:

5   A   a black man *come in an' im b(h)u::y* a bottle (.) of *Lucozade*
        while 'e was in the shop ⌈an'

    B   ⌊free p- e's e got free pee [3p] off is it?

    A   yeah

    B   small ones or big ones?

10 A   big ones and 'e drank the bottle in fron% of us an then ask(d)
        for the money back (see man) *'me want me money now'*

    B   ⌈heheh

    A   ⌊he goes (pnk) (I'm on) the till guy hhh (I jus) I jus' look
        round at 'im I said well you can't 'ave it (.) I said I 'ave
15   to open the till (w) wait till the next customer comes (.) *'now!*
        open it now and give me the money' I said I can't (.) the man *just*
        thump 'is fist down an' (screw up dis for me) (s no man) the
        manager just comes would you leave the shop before I call
        the security: hh the man *jus' take the bottle an' fling it at me an* (I)
20   jus' catch it at the (ground)

(Sebba, 1993, pp. 119–20)

Transcription conventions

- (.) means a brief pause
- switches to Creole (accent or dialect) are in italics
- : indicates a lengthened consonant or vowel
- % indicates glottal stop
- deep brackets [indicate overlapping speech
- words in brackets ( ) indicate uncertain transcription

Sebba comments:

> Andrew's own reported speech, like most of his narration, is in London English. The customer's is mostly in Creole, cf. lines 11 and 16, where the boundaries of the Creole stretches correspond with quotation marks. However, there are other Creole stretches of talk in this narrative, especially lines 5, 17 and 19. (Note that 'thump' [tomp] and 'fling' are characteristically Creole words.) These Creole stretches are just those parts of the narrative where the customer himself and his actions are described: *come in an' 'imb(h)u::y, just thump 'is fist down, jus' take the bottle an' fling it at me*, all of which have 'the man' as subject.
>
> Although the correspondence between the use of Creole and the description of the customer's action is not perfect, what the narrator seems to be doing is creating a persona for his character 'the difficult customer' by linking him to Creole. The impersonation of the shop manager at lines 19–20, done in a near-RP 'posh' voice, is an even clearer evocation of a persona, but this time using maximally Standard style.
>
> (Sebba, 1993, p. 120)

Like the house buyer and Nicole and Karlie in the earlier examples, Andrew uses animated voices not just to replay an event, but to convey a particular evaluation of his own and the customer's actions. Andrew's representation of his own courageous stand, and of the customer's unreasonable and violent behaviour, is accomplished almost entirely through the ways in which he reports the voices.

Codeswitching in conversation is also tied up with the transmission of complex messages about identity and allegiance. One study illustrating this is Roger Hewitt's account of white working-class teenagers in south London who on certain occasions switch to using London Jamaican Creole (Hewitt, 1987). Hewitt found that many black adolescents, particularly boys, spoke more Jamaican Creole as they got older, and that it had come to be a prestigious symbol of group solidarity and resistance within black youth culture. For the white boys Hewitt studied, creole signified toughness, street credibility and adolescent solidarity, and they also increased their use of it in adolescence. The white boys, however, had to carefully negotiate their right to use creole within established cross-race friendships. This taking on of language associated with another social or language group is termed 'language crossing' by Ben Rampton (2005). Rampton found, in his research in a multi-ethnic British urban community, that white monolingual teenagers would sometimes use Panjabi or Creole words or expressions to momentarily project a different kind of identity (sometimes ironically). He suggests that this kind of voice styling among adolescents, which can also include 'talking posh' and 'talking Cockney', sometimes affirms particular kinds of stratification by race, ethnicity, class, gender and sexuality, but can also be used to destabilise accepted categories and suggest new kinds of solidarity which (as Hewitt found) cut across racial or class divides.

1.6 Conclusion

Talk is a central part of most of our lives; through it we carry out activities, negotiate relationships, try to construct understandings about the world around us and develop our own sense of identity. In this chapter we have looked at the structure of informal talk, both at the level of language, where we discussed reasons for its frequent inexplicitness and apparent incoherence, and at the level of conversational management, where there are predictable structures around openings, closings and turn taking. Particular language practices within conversation also have predictable structures – for instance, storytelling, or paying compliments. But we found that structure is closely tied up with both the ideational and interpersonal functions of language. As well as conveying and negotiating ideas, talk is used to pursue social relationships; through it intimacy and status are negotiated, and people position themselves, and are positioned, in various ways. Face work and politeness are enormously important, but are expressed differently in English across different cultural settings.

We have seen how people and groups may vary in conversational style, but that these differences are also cross-cut by social and contextual factors. Not only do people speak differently according to the context, but the forms they use may have different significance and meaning depending on where and when they are used. Practices to do with questioning, the disclosure of personal information and the use of silence vary across cultures, gender and even individuals, depending on the context of the talk and the relationships involved.

An important aspect of relating experience is negotiating how this should be evaluated, and the way we convey or try out evaluations in stories and accounts is an important part of developing our own beliefs and values about the world. There also exist, in any community, patterned ways of using language to represent and talk about experience which encode particular evaluations and positions. We inevitably invoke these, as part of our cultural linguistic repertoires and through the voices we take on and reproduce. The English language provides a variety of resources for pursuing individual purposes, but it also shapes those purposes, and ourselves, even as we use it.

READING A: Communicative strategies in Aboriginal English

Diana Eades
(Diana Eades is Honorary Fellow, School of Languages, Cultures and Linguistics, University of New England, Australia.)

Source: adapted from Eades, D. (1991) 'Communicative strategies in Aboriginal English' in Romaine, S. (ed.) *Language in Australia*, Cambridge, Cambridge University Press, pp. 84–93.

Sociocultural context of Aboriginal English

Varieties of Aboriginal English are spoken as the first language of Aboriginal people living in most areas of Australia, primarily in urban and rural parts of 'settled' Australia (as opposed to remote Australia). The majority of speakers of Aboriginal English are of mixed descent, and many are undeniably biculturally competent, increasingly participating in mainstream Australian institutions, such as education and employment.

Irrespective of the language spoken, Aboriginal people throughout Australia today belong to overlapping kin-based networks sharing social life, responsibilities and rights, and a common history, culture, experience of racism and ethnic consciousness. Social relations are characterised by on-going family commitments within groups, and the highest priority is placed on the maintenance and development of these commitments (rather than, for example, on financial security, employment, or individual fulfilment). Moreover, Aboriginal social life is very public. In towns and cities the openness of traditional Aboriginal camp life has been replaced by the openness of frequently overcrowded housing and vehicles. Much of the business of day-to-day living occurs in open outside areas, for example, in parks and other public places, on the main streets of towns, and on verandahs of houses. Because people have on-going commitments to a wide network of kin (far beyond the nuclear family) virtually every aspect of their lives is shared in some way with a number of relatives.

While Aboriginal societies place a high priority on constantly maintaining and developing social relations, there is also provision for considerable personal privacy. This personal privacy is ensured not in terms of physical privacy as it is, for example, in mainstream Australian society, where walls, an indoor lifestyle and a strong prohibition on directly observing many of the actions of others, are all essential factors in the maintenance of personal privacy. It is through their indirect style of verbal interaction that Aboriginal people experience much personal privacy, as is shown below.

Figure 1   The public nature of social life in an Aboriginal community

Indirectness in Aboriginal English

Seeking information

While questions are frequently used in Aboriginal English in certain contexts and functions, there are constraints on their use which protect individual privacy ... Direct questions are ... used to elicit orientation information, for example in a typical greeting such as 'Where you been?' Frequently, however, the orientation question takes the form of a statement uttered with rising intonation, e.g. 'You been to town?' Rather than asking directly, the speaker presents known or supposed information for confirmation or denial.

This strategy of seeking information by presenting information is also seen clearly in the ways in which English is used by Aboriginal speakers to seek substantial information, such as important personal details, a full account of an event, or the explanation of some event or situation. In these situations questions are not used, but the person seeking information contributes some of their own knowledge on the topic, followed often by silence. This strategy serves as an invitation (or hint) for another participant to impart information on this topic. There is no obligation on the knowledgeable person to respond, and, further, it is rare for silences to be negatively valued in Aboriginal conversations. Important aspects of substantial information seeking are the two-way exchange of information, the positive, non-awkward use of silence, and the often considerable time delays (frequently of several days) between the initiation of substantial information seeking and the imparting of such information.

Making and refusing requests

Aboriginal people rarely make direct requests. A question frequently serves to make an indirect request, as well as to seek orientation information. For example, a typical Aboriginal way of asking for a ride is to ask a car owner a question, such as 'You going to town?' or 'What time are you leaving?' Such questions can be interpreted as information seeking of a kind common in Aboriginal conversations, but they can also be interpreted as a request for a ride, depending on the relationship between speakers. Even if speakers understand questions such as these as requests for a ride, the ambiguity enables a person to refuse a request in a similar indirect fashion, for example, 'Might be later', 'Not sure'. In this way Aboriginal people can negotiate requests and refusals without directly exposing their motives (see Eades, 1988).

Seeking and giving reasons

Research with Aboriginal speakers of English in south-east Queensland reveals that the questioning of a person's motives or reasons for action is always carried out indirectly through the use of multifunctional linguistic forms (Eades, 1983).

Thus, for example, an orientation question such as 'You went to town yesterday?' would be used to seek information concerning a person's movements, but this answer might also provide evidence of the reasons behind some of their actions. The use of multifunctional forms makes the requests for reasons indirect and ambiguous, and it gives people considerable privacy; they are never confronted with an inescapable request for a reason (e.g. 'Why didn't you visit us yesterday?').

Just as the seeking of reasons relies on the use of multifunctional forms, so too does the expression of reason. There is frequently no unambiguous linguistic marker of reasons (cf. Standard Australian English *because, in order to, so*). Speakers rely on the non-linguistic context for their interpretation of a statement as a reason. Specifically, it is shared experiences and knowledge which provide the evidence that a multifunctional statement is intended as a reason ...

Expressing opinions

A number of studies of Aboriginal communicative strategies provide evidence that it is important for Aboriginal people to present opinions cautiously and with a degree of circumspection. Von Sturmer first discussed the use of disclaimers as a strategy of 'not presenting oneself too forcefully and not linking oneself too closely with one's own ideas'. Examples of such disclaimers are 'might be I right or wrong' (Von Sturmer, 1981, p. 29), and 'this is just what I think' (Eades, 1988) ... Many Aboriginal people in south-east Queensland do not express a firm or biased opinion, even if they hold one. A common strategy involves general discussions on a topic, while speakers gauge each other's views gradually, before a definite presentation. When speakers realise a difference between their views and those of others, they tend to understate their own views. This style of gradually and indirectly expressing an opinion is a significant factor in cross-cultural miscommunication, and will be discussed below.

Also relevant here is the widespread Aboriginal notion of 'shame', which is a combination of shyness and embarrassment occurring in 'situations where a person has been singled out for any purpose, scolding or praise or simply attention, where he/she loses the security and anonymity provided by the group' (Kaldor and Malcolm, 1979, p. 429).

Aboriginal communicative strategies in cross-cultural communication

Aboriginal people have developed a number of ways of accommodating the directions of non-Aboriginal interactions but some of these ways of accommodating can actually lead to further misunderstanding. For instance, one way in which they respond to the much more direct communication style of white speakers is through the use of '**gratuitous concurrence**' (Liberman, 1981; 1982; 1985), where Aboriginal speakers say 'yes' not necessarily to signal agreement with a statement or proposition, but to facilitate the on-going interaction, or to hasten its conclusion. Occasionally, Aboriginal people switch to a vociferous, confrontational style which they perceive as appropriate to interactions with Whites. In some situations the Aboriginal participants are, in fact, more direct and confrontational than the White participants.

Aboriginal speakers' use of gratuitous concurrence has serious implications for all cross-cultural situations in Australia where direct questioning is used, in particular in police interviews, law courts, employment interviews, medical consultations, classrooms at all levels, and government consultations. Differences in degrees of directness lead to misunderstandings in many settings. In meetings, for example, Aboriginal people are often offended and feel dominated by the White participants, who express forceful opinions, often in direct opposition to those expressed by a previous speaker. On the other hand, White people often mistakenly assume Aboriginal agreement with a particular viewpoint after listening to the initial statements of an Aboriginal speaker, and not allowing time for the expression of a different opinion. If asked directly whether they agree with a particular issue Aboriginal speakers may frequently respond with the 'yes' of gratuitous concurrence. The indirect and roundabout Aboriginal style requires a non-linear meeting organisation and a much longer time span than is typical of White meetings, before participants can express important contradictory viewpoints. Thus, in meetings of Aboriginal organisations, for example, the lengthy discussion of issues often causes non-Aboriginal participants to become frustrated with the seeming lack of organisation and inability to make decisions.

My current research with Queensland Aboriginal students at University and College indicates that the bicultural competence of many, but not all, of these students includes the ability to participate successfully in the mainstream strategies of information seeking, which are so central to the western education system. For some Aboriginal students, however, the direct interrogative style used in tutorials is quite unsuccessful in involving them in discussion, and in assessing the extent of their knowledge of a topic. These students are often uncomfortable and annoyed about views expressed by non-Aboriginal students, and the forceful manner of their expression, but are unable to respond in the same manner. Without the Aboriginal students' feedback, non-Aboriginal students continue in the direct expression of opinions upsetting to Aboriginal students, who in their turn become more resentful of the non-Aboriginal students.

Such situations of miscommunication, potentially disastrous in a cross-cultural setting, are being constructively approached by discussions between Aboriginal students, fellow students and staff (some of whom are Aboriginal and some of whom are non-Aboriginal, with some bicultural competence). The resulting processes of in-group discussion and analysis, and particularly the support and responsibility assumed by the successfully bicultural Aboriginal students, is an important factor in the on-going positive resolution of such challenges.

References for this reading

Eades, D.M. (1983) 'English as an Aboriginal Language in South-east Queensland', PhD thesis, University of Queensland.

Eades, D.M. (1988) 'They don't speak an Aboriginal language, or do they?' in Keen, I. (ed.) *Being Black: Aboriginal Cultural Continuity in Settled Australia*, Canberra, Aboriginal Studies Press.

Kaldor, S. and Malcolm, I.G. (1979) 'The language of the school and the language of the Western Australian Aboriginal school child – implications for education' in Berndt, R.M. and Berndt, C.H. (eds) *Aborigines of the West: Their Past and Their Present,* Nedlands, University of Western Australia Press, pp. 407–37.

Liberman, K. (1981) 'Understanding Aborigines in Australian courts of law', *Human Organization,* vol. 40, no. 3, pp. 247–54.

Liberman, K. (1982) 'Intercultural communication in Central Australia', *Working Papers in Sociolinguistics*, 104, Austin, TX, South West Educational Development Laboratory.

Liberman, K. (1985) *Understanding Interaction in Central Australia: An Ethnomethodological Study of Australian Aboriginal People*, Boston, MA, Routledge & Kegan Paul.

Von Sturmer, J. (1981) 'Talking with Aborigines', *Australian Institute of Aboriginal Studies Newsletter* 15.

READING B: The role of compliments in female–male interaction

Janet Holmes
(Janet Holmes is Professor of Linguistics at Victoria University of Wellington, New Zealand.)

Source: Holmes, J. (1994) 'Case study 1: the role of compliments in female–male interaction' in Sunderland, J. (ed.) *Exploring Gender: Questions and Implications for English Language Education*, London, Prentice Hall, pp. 39–43.

Compliments are positive speech acts which are used to express friendship and increase rapport between people, as the following example illustrates.

CONTEXT	Two good friends, meeting in the lift at their workplace.
COMPLIMENTER	Hi, how are you. You're looking just terrific.
RECIPIENT	Thanks. I'm pretty good. How are things with you?

A range of studies, involving American, British, Polish, and New Zealand speakers, have demonstrated that compliments are used more frequently by women than by men, and that women are complimented more often than men (Nessa Wolfson, 1983; Janet Holmes, 1988; Barbara Lewandowska-Tomaszczyk, 1989; Robert Herbert, 1990.)

My own analysis of New Zealand patterns was based on a corpus of 484 compliments collected by students using an ethnographic approach (Holmes, 1988). In this corpus of compliments between mainly middle-class Pakeha [European origin] New Zealanders, women gave and received significantly more compliments than did men.

Women gave two-thirds of all the compliments recorded and received three-quarters of them. Women in fact complimented each other twice as often as men complimented them. Compliments between males were much less frequent, and even taking account of females' compliments to males, men received considerably fewer compliments than women. Research in other places confirms these patterns, though the differences between women and men are not always so dramatic (Herbert, 1990).

In general, then, complimenting appears to be a speech act used much more by women than by men. This is consistent with extensive research which suggests that women's linguistic behaviour can be broadly characterised as affiliative, facilitative and co-operative, rather than competitive or control oriented, concerned with 'connection' rather than status (Philip Smith, 1985; Holmes, 1990; Deborah Tannen, 1991). If compliments are considered expressions of rapport and solidarity, the finding that women give more compliments than men illustrates the same pattern.

Topics of compliments

Mostly compliments refer to just a few broad topics: appearance (especially clothes and hair), a good performance which is the result of skill or effort, possessions (especially new ones), and some aspect of personality or friendliness (Joan Manes, 1983; Holmes, 1986; Herbert, 1990). In the New Zealand data the first two topics accounted for 81.2 per cent of the data.

Women tend to receive most compliments on their appearance, and they compliment each other most often on aspects of their appearance. Over half of all the compliments women received in the New Zealand data related to aspects of their appearance, and 61 per cent of all the compliments between women related to appearance, compared to only 36 per cent of the compliments between males.

New Zealand men do receive compliments on their appearance (40 per cent of all compliments they receive). It is interesting to note, however, that the vast majority of these (88 per cent) were given by women. According to Wolfson (1983), the American pattern is different. Though men rarely compliment each other on appearance in either community, the appearance of American men seems not to be an appropriate topic of compliments from men or from women. Wolfson comments that only when the male is much younger than the female does this occur at all, and in general she says 'there seems to be a rather strong if not categorical constraint against the giving of appearance-related compliments to higher-status males, especially in work-related settings' (1983, p. 93). A further interesting feature of the New Zealand data was a distinct male preference for complimenting other men on their possessions rather than women on theirs.

Vocabulary and grammatical patterns

Compliments are remarkably formulaic speech acts. Most use a very small number of lexical items and a very narrow range of syntactic patterns (Wolfson, 1984; Holmes, 1986; Herbert, 1990). A small range of adjectives, for instance, is used to convey the positive semantic message in up to 80 per cent of compliments. In Wolfson's American data 'two-thirds of all adjectival compliments in the corpus made use of only five adjectives: *nice, good, beautiful, pretty* and *great*' (1984, p. 236). In the New Zealand data, the five most frequently occurring adjectives were *nice, good, beautiful, lovely* and *wonderful*. Most of the non-adjectival compliments also depended upon a very few semantically positive verbs (*like, love, enjoy* and *admire*) with *like* and *love* alone accounting for 86 per cent of the American data and 80 per cent of the New Zealand data.

The syntactic patterns used in compliments are also drawn from a remarkably narrow range. Four syntactic patterns accounted for 86 per cent of the 686 compliments in Wolfson's American corpus, for example, and 78 per cent of the New Zealand corpus. While many of the syntactic patterns used in compliments seem to be pretty equally distributed between women and men, there are some patterns which differ, as Table 1 illustrates for the New Zealand data.

Women used the rhetorical pattern *what (a) (ADJ) NP!* (e.g. *what lovely children! what a beautiful coat!*) more often than men, while men used the minimal pattern *(INT) ADJ (NP)* (e.g. *great shoes; nice car*) more often than women. [These abbreviations are explained beneath Table 1.] The former is a syntactically marked formula, involving exclamatory word order and intonation; the latter by contrast reduces the syntactic pattern to its minimum elements. Whereas a rhetorical pattern such as pattern 4 can be regarded as emphasising the addressee- or interaction-oriented characteristics of compliments, the minimal pattern represented by formula 5 could be regarded as attenuating or hedging on this function. It is interesting to note that there are no examples of pattern 4 in male–male interactions, providing further support for the association of this pattern with female complimenting behaviour.

In another study of American English, Herbert (1990, p. 206) found that only women used the stronger form *I love X* (compared to *I like X*) and that they used it most often to other women. And in students' written reviews of each other's work, Donna Johnson and Duane Roen (1992) noted that women used significantly more intensifiers (such as *really, very, particularly*) than men did, and that they intensified their compliments most when writing to other women.

Cross-cultural differences in complimenting behaviour

... Paying compliments and responding to them appropriately is an aspect of learning English which can be troublesome for those from different cultural backgrounds. Indonesians in the United States, for instance, comment on the very high frequency of compliments between Americans (Wolfson, 1981). Malaysian students in New Zealand are similarly surprised at how often New Zealanders pay each other compliments, while for their part New Zealanders tend to feel Americans pay far too many compliments and, judging by their own norms, assume that American compliments are often insincere. South Africans apparently respond similarly to American complimenting norms (Herbert, 1986; Herbert and Straight, 1989).

Table 1 Syntactic patterns of compliments according to speaker sex

Syntactic formula		Female		Male	
		No.	%	No.	%
1a	NP BE (INT) ADJ	121 ⎫	42	51 ⎫	40
b	BE LOOKing e.g. *That coat is really great* *You're looking terrific*	19 ⎭		13 ⎭	
2	I (INT) LIKE NP e.g. *I simply love that skirt*	59	18	21	13
3a	PRO BE a (INT) ADJ NP e.g. *That's a very nice coat*				
or		38	11	25	16
b	PRO BE (INT) (a) ADJ NP e.g. *That's really great juice*				
4	What (a) (ADJ) NP! e.g. *What lovely children!*	26	8	2	1
5	(INT) ADJ (NP) e.g. *Really cool ear-rings*	17	5	19	12
6	Isn't NP ADJ! e.g. *Isn't this food wonderful!*	5	2	1	1
Total		285	86	132	82

Note:
NP = noun phrase
BE = the verb be
INT = intensifier
ADJ = adjective
PRO = pronoun

The patterns of cross-sex complimenting behaviour described above obviously compound the potential for miscommunication and offence. Women from cultures where compliments are rare, experience them as embarrassing. They often respond inappropriately to compliments from native speakers of English by disagreeing or rejecting them. On the other hand, they may not offer enough compliments, by the standard of native speakers, especially to their English-speaking women friends. Conversely, men from different cultures may embarrass their English-speaking male friends by the frequency of their compliments.

Wolfson (1983, p. 90) suggests that in America the safest compliments to offer to strangers relate to 'possessions (e.g. *That's a beautiful car*)' or to 'some aspect of performance intended to be publicly observed (*I really enjoyed your talk yesterday*)'. This advice appears to be particularly useful when complimenting male addressees. But it would not be appropriate in some Polynesian cultures, as the following example illustrates.

CONTEXT	Pakeha New Zealand woman to Samoan friend whom she was visiting.
COMPLIMENTER	What an unusual necklace. It's beautiful.
RECIPIENT	Please take it.

The complimenter was very embarrassed at being offered as a gift the object she had admired. This was perfectly predictable, however, to anyone familiar with Samoan cultural norms with respect to complimenting behaviour.

The exchange in this example occurred in New Zealand where there is a relatively large Samoan population. When sociopragmatic norms differ, cross-cultural misunderstandings involving compliments are perfectly possible between ethnic groups within one country. There is abundant anecdotal evidence, for instance, of embarrassment experienced by Maori people in New Zealand by what they perceive as compliments from Pakeha people which go 'over the top'. The relative strength of what Geoffrey Leech (1983, p. 132) calls the Modesty Maxim may differ quite markedly between groups.

As illustrated in this paper, most compliments are formulaic: they draw on a very restricted range of vocabulary and a small number of grammatical patterns. The linguistic features of compliments are easy to acquire. Learning how to use compliments appropriately is not so easy, however. Each speech community has norms of use involving the relative frequency of compliments, the kinds of topics which may be the focus of a compliment and the contexts in which compliments are appropriate, mandatory or perhaps even proscribed. These norms interact with the gender of speakers and addressees, so that knowing who to compliment, how, and when is a sophisticated aspect of sociolinguistic competence. *You look wonderful tonight!* may be a welcome compliment from your partner, but your boss may just find it embarrassing.

References for this reading

Herbert, R.K. (1986) 'Say "thank you" – or something', *American Speech*, vol. 61, pp. 76–88.

Herbert, R.K. (1990) 'Sex-based differences in compliment behaviour', *Language in Society*, vol. 19, pp. 201–24.

Herbert, R.K. and Straight, H.S. (1989) 'Compliment rejection vs compliment avoidance', *Language and Communication*, vol. 9, pp. 35–47.

Holmes, J. (1986) 'Compliments and compliment responses in New Zealand English', *Anthropological Linguistics*, vol. 28, no. 4, pp. 485–508.

Holmes, J. (1988) 'Paying compliments: a sex-preferential positive politeness strategy', *Journal of Pragmatics*, vol. 12, no. 3, pp. 445–65.

Holmes, J. (1990) 'Politeness strategies in New Zealand women's speech' in Bell, A. and Holmes, J. (eds) *New Zealand Ways of Speaking English*, Clevedon, Avon, Multilingual Matters.

Johnson, D.M. and Roen, D.H. (1992) 'Complimenting and involvement in peer reviews: gender variation', *Language in Society*, vol. 21, no. 1, pp. 27–56.

Leech, G. (1983) *Principles of Pragmatics*, London, Longman.

Lewandowska-Tomaszczyk, B. (1989) 'Praising and complimenting' in Olesky, W. (ed.) *Contrastive Pragmatics*, Amsterdam, John Benjamins.

Manes, J. (1983) 'Compliments: a mirror of cultural values' in Wolfson, N. and Judd, E. (eds) *Sociolinguistics and Second Language Acquisition*, Rowley, MA, Newbury House.

Smith, P. (1985) *Language, the Sexes and Society*, Oxford, Blackwell.

Tannen, D. (1991) *You Just Don't Understand*, London, Virago.

Wolfson, N. (1981) 'Compliments in cross-cultural perspective', *TESOL Quarterly*, vol. 15, no. 2, pp. 117–24.

Wolfson, N. (1983) 'An empirically based analysis of complimenting in American English' in Wolfson, N. and Judd, E. (eds) *Sociolinguistics and Second Language Acquisition*, Rowley, MA, Newbury House.

Wolfson, N. (1984) 'Pretty is as pretty does', *Applied Linguistics*, vol. 5, no. 3, pp. 236–44.

2 Using English to persuade

Adrian Beard, based on an original chapter by Robin Wooffitt

2.1 Introduction

In this chapter I focus on texts whose primary purpose is to persuade, convince or elicit support; for example, to convince others of the merit of an argument or an opinion, or to buy, do or believe in something. How this is attempted or achieved is the focus of this chapter. While evaluating the success of a text in convincing someone to do or believe something is problematic, understanding some of the ways in which writers and speakers *try* to influence the reader or listener is possible through analysis of language and other contextual factors. Ways of analysing speech, writing and texts, including pictures, are introduced here, though a short chapter such as this cannot hope to cover all the ways in which people attempt to persuade others.

English is used to persuade in many areas of our lives – both public and private. Two major public areas are politics and advertising, and I examine how these are constructed to fulfil their purpose and how this may be influenced by contextual factors such as mode – speech, writing or pictures – and cultural understandings. I also examine some of the techniques used to influence the reader or listener in different English-using countries. The similarities and differences between persuasive language used in private, and that used in political and public service texts and advertising, will become apparent. (This issue is dealt with more fully in Chapter 6.)

2.2 Contexts of persuasion

By isolating language used to persuade, we are focusing on a particular social purpose. As is always the case when analysing the way language is used for social purposes, the context of a text's production and reception needs to be taken into account. By production here I mean thinking about such questions as:

- Who is writing/speaking the text?
- What is the text about?
- What is its purpose?
- What kind of text is being produced (speech, writing, picture)?

By reception I mean thinking about questions like:

- What audience is the text addressing?
- How is that audience 'constructed' in the text?
- What does the text mean to various possible readers?

Placing texts into categories according to a purpose, such as 'to persuade', can involve some grey areas. It is perfectly possible for the producer of a text to intend it to be persuasive, but for some readers to miss the point entirely. Or we may recognise that a text is meant to persuade us, but that does not mean we accept the message. Most of us, for instance, are quick to sift the junk mail from the real mail, the spam from the genuine emails. Indeed, most texts have more than one purpose. Consider, for example, a familiar text – the ingredients label on foodstuffs: is this informational, telling us what we need to know, or persuasive, telling us the food is good for us and so worth buying? Has the purpose behind food labelling changed over the years?

Personal interactions such as conversation between family, friends and colleagues are also multi-purpose. For example, much of our social conversation contains an element of the persuasive. We may be looking for a friend to agree with our judgement of, say, a work colleague or a film we have both seen, or we may be hoping that the friend will help us in some practical task. Activity 2.1 exemplifies persuasion in the context of a private conversation in order to accomplish a personal objective.

ACTIVITY 2.1

Allow about
15 minutes

The following short extract is taken from a conversation between two young women, Beth and Sue, discussing a possible visit to a nightclub called 'Shindig'. As you read it, consider the following questions:

- What is the purpose of the conversation?
- What is the relationship between the two women?
- What is the influence of the relationship on the conversation?

B   Sue what are you doing Saturday (3) do you want to come to Shindig

S   oh I'm going clubbing on Thursday

B   just crush me why don't you (.) who with (.) WHO with

S   Ben

B   well can't he come to Shindig

S   think he's going away next week (3) I haven't got enough <u>money to</u>

B   <u>god he's never</u>

      <u>here</u>

Transcription conventions

- underlining indicates both speaking at the same time
- (.) means a brief pause

- (3) indicates pauses in seconds
- capital letters indicate words given extra emphasis

Comment

Beth is trying, but failing, to persuade her friend Sue to go clubbing with her. The key point to remember here is that the two women are friends and whatever the result of Beth's attempt at persuasion, they intend to remain so. This means that Beth's attempts at persuasion are going to be carefully managed, and so are Sue's rejections of the request. Beth begins with two approaches to her main task – to persuade Beth to go out with her. The first is indirect, *Sue what are you doing Saturday*, attempting to see if there is room for a more specific request, but the 3-second silence means that Sue is not replying and so Beth has to ask a more direct question. Sue's reply on the surface might seem strange, but in fact it makes perfect sense within the context of their conversation. In saying that she is going out on Thursday she is avoiding a simple *no* to the question, and hoping that Beth will be attuned to the **pragmatics** of the conversation; that is, to both what Sue has said and what meaning was implied. Sue is saying that going out on Thursday is enough for one week. Beth, though, is safe enough in her confidence in the friendship to challenge Sue again, although presumably with a certain irony in her voice. When Sue says she is going to go with Ben, Beth makes another attempt at persuading Sue, by opting for an alternative plan: the three of them can go together. Sue's continuing reasons/excuses for saying *no* mean that Beth gives up and she changes the topic, which is why they both speak at the same time.

It should be clear from the brief example above that the sort of interpersonal negotiations that accompany conversation are informal and unplanned. Beth and Sue are not consciously planning their talk here, but are drawing on their experience of the social talk which has surrounded them since infancy. In particular, they are using social tactics that they have acquired through many similar conversations in all sorts of social contexts. This is very different from more public, multi-purpose communication such as that associated with 'informative' websites – university home pages, for instance, which are the subject of the next activity.

ACTIVITY 2.2

Allow about
30 minutes

Look at the website home pages for three universities, shown in Figures 2.1, 2.2 and 2.3. Do the home pages make you want to look at other pages? How do they achieve this? Would you categorise university home pages as persuasive texts, or do they have some other purpose?

Comment

Your work on the task above should have made it clear that what at first sight may appear to be an informative text can also have persuasive purposes. The home pages are the gateways to further information, but they are also the external face of a university. Universities need students, and increasingly they are in competition to get these students to apply. At the same time, though, they are august institutions of advanced learning, and an over-persuasive, over-commercial approach would be likely to deter readers by looking too cheap and tacky. Instead, a subtle mixture of the academic and the persuasive is required. Consider what image of an institution is conveyed by showing pictures of grand buildings or of an ethnically diverse student body. University website designers are therefore using the resources of a **multimodal** text (a text with both words and images) plus facilities, not apparent in the pictures here, such as moving or flashing images, interactive buttons, and so on to fulfil a number of different purposes.

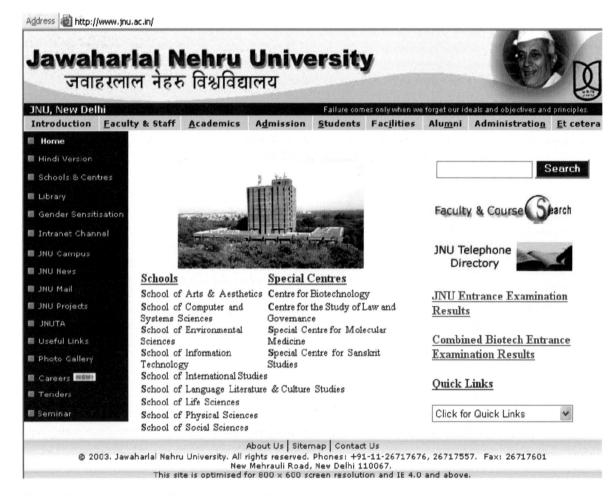

Figure 2.1   Home page of Jawaharlal Nehru University, India

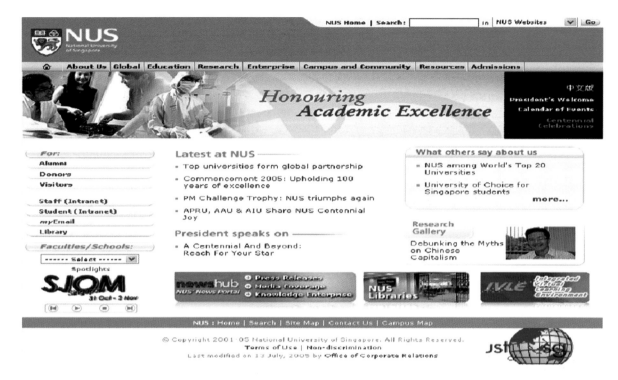

Figure 2.2   Home page of the National University of Singapore

Figure 2.4, which you will find on page 49, shows the home page, as it was in 2004, of The Open University (OU) in the UK, and it contains all sorts of persuasive techniques. Striking yellow and blue colours are used as background, and in the top left-hand corner is the brand image – the OU logo. On the right-hand side is an image which flashes: for half the time it is the globe – a sign which suggests a world of knowledge – and then an injunction to search the OU website. The central band, which is bright blue, contains a backdrop saying *Open University*. In front of this backdrop are photographic images of different people: men, women, black, white, young, old, representing the (ideal) wide range of students studying at the OU. To the right of the images of these prospective students is another flashing button. Four variants were added to the core phrase *Open as to*:

> *Open as to people*
>
> *Open as to methods*
>
> *Open as to ideas*
>
> *Open as to places*

This clearly played with the word 'open', using it both in its naming sense but also suggesting that the organisation is open-minded – receptive to all sorts of influences.

Figure 2.3   Home page of the University of Waikato, New Zealand

In this section you have looked at examples of both private and public contexts of persuasion and seen how it is often embedded within other purposes. In the next two sections, you will be reading about public texts with more overt persuasive purposes: political rhetoric and advertising.

2.3 Political rhetoric

I now move on to political persuasion, the first of my two main topics. Although public speaking is often described as an art (and so presumably a good thing), political public speaking is often labelled as rhetoric, a term with increasingly negative connotations. The idea that rhetoric is dangerous goes as far back as the concept itself.

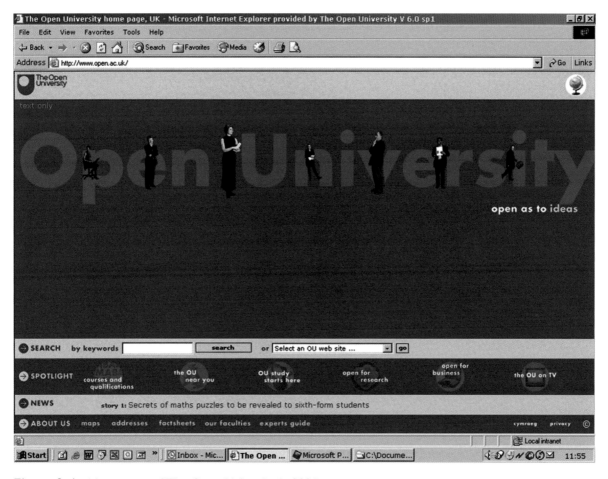

Figure 2.4 Home page of The Open University in 2004

Classical Graeco-Roman oratory

In classical Greece the sophists were a group of paid teachers who travelled round Greece teaching young men how to get on, especially in politics, by using rational arguments. The word 'sophist' is derived from the Greek word *sophia* meaning 'wisdom'. The sophist Protagoras argued that the relativity of truth meant that students needed to be able to see both sides of a question, and so he taught students to praise and blame the same thing – with the idea being that the best course of action would become clear as a result of this debate. It is easy to see, however, how this doctrine could be regarded as encouraging the specious, as deceiving both self and others rather than seeking the truth. In early classical civilisation, therefore, we can already see the dichotomy within political rhetoric which still exists today.

A view of rhetoric as 'mere rhetoric', and therefore as something easily dismissed, is perhaps particularly British, and even in Britain a comparatively recent development. (Rhetoric used to be taught in British universities until the latter part of the nineteenth century.) For nearly 2,000 years, people throughout the world have viewed the study of rhetoric positively. In some parts of the English-speaking world, such as the USA, 'rhetoric' is still an established subject or component of English studies in secondary school and university timetables. It is still associated with the classical civilisations of Greece and Rome and this tradition has strongly influenced how the subject has been taught. Many of the analytical and presentational skills that were part of classical rhetoric are still used today by public speakers. So, before examining modern political speeches and writing, I want to look further at the classical rhetorical tradition of the ancient Greek and Roman civilisations.

Cicero (106–43 BC) was a Roman orator who, drawing on the ideas of the earlier Greek rhetoricians, formulated sets of recommendations for the most effective ways of representing arguments in judicial settings. In ancient Greek society judicial rhetoric was important because it was expected that all citizens would be able to represent themselves in legal debate. Consequently, ordinary citizens needed to be able to develop skills of rhetoric and argument. Let's consider the kind of advice Cicero offered about the most effective way to present a case in a speech in a court of law.

Cicero argued that legal presentations of this type should have six parts: exordium, narration, partition, confirmation, refutation and conclusion. The exordium should prepare the audience and make them receptive and amenable to the speaker (and, if the speaker is representing someone else, the client). The narration should provide a brief, clear account of the case and may include some attacks on an opposing argument. The partition is a description of what is to be proved; this also should be clear and brief. The confirmation is the basic argument for the points that the speaker wishes to prove. The refutation, as the term suggests, involves undermining an opponent's argument. The conclusion should consist of three parts: summing up the speaker's argument, inciting indignation against the opponent, and ensuring that the speaker or the speaker's client is perceived sympathetically. These simple recommendations formed the basis for courses in rhetoric for many centuries.

The main points we can draw from Cicero's analysis are:
- that rhetorical speech designed for use in specific contexts (such as the law courts of ancient Greece) may have some common, distinctive structural features
- that it may be possible to identify some specific, effective techniques for convincing and persuading.

Modern political rhetoric

When analysing examples of rhetoric it is important to put the data into context. One key question involves the extent to which the example being analysed is pre-planned. Another question involves whether or not the data is spoken, or written, or written to be spoken – and many political speeches then also appear in an officially released format which does not necessarily coincide exactly with what was said. Below, you will be reading political rhetoric designed to be read and scripts of speeches that may be tidied up versions of what was actually said, together with short extracts of speeches transcribed from television recordings.

ACTIVITY 2.3

Allow about
5 minutes

As I write, it is the middle of a general election campaign in the UK. Read the extracts below from a Labour Party election leaflet from a candidate who has been the local Member of Parliament for some years. She is a member of the Labour Party which has been the government for the past eight years. The Conservative Party has been the main party of opposition. Underline the pronouns and possessives (e.g. *you/your/we/our/they/them*). Why have these particular words been chosen? What effect do they have?

> The General Election has now been called – and your family's future security is at stake.

> In the last few years, we have seen positive change here in ... Our Health Authority has nearly 5000 more doctors and nurses and we're getting a new hospital. We have record numbers of police and they're being helped by community support officers and street wardens. Crime is down.

> ...

> The Conservatives haven't changed. They've already promised tax cuts. They claim they can make £35 billion savings to pay for them.

Comment

In the first sentence the use of *your* personalises the message. The reader is being directly addressed by the Labour Party candidate. In the next paragraph the use of *we* and *our* seeks to signal inclusiveness between the candidate and the constituents. This is in direct contrast to the use of *they* in the final paragraph which refers to the opposing party, the Conservatives. *They* works to distance the writer and, she hopes, her readers from the Conservatives.

The significance of pronouns

There is obviously much more happening in the text quoted above in terms of its persuasive purpose, but it provides a good introduction to one of the significant features of political rhetoric – choice of pronouns. Personal pronouns are at their most common in talk, helping to provide cohesion to the overall speech and, significantly, giving agency to actions; that is, saying who is doing something. Politicians and their speech writers, then, have some difficult decisions to make when it comes to choosing the pronouns that will keep appearing in their speeches. How much responsibility are they prepared to take on themselves? How much responsibility for success are they willing to share with other colleagues? How confident are they that whole groups of people share their views? How much responsibility for failure are they prepared to accept as their own?

When politicians make speeches, they have two sets of first person pronouns available to them. They can talk in the **first person singular** using *I/me/ myself/mine*, or they can talk in the **first person plural** using *we/us/ ourselves/ours*. With the latter, though, there are several potential meanings. The first person plural forms when used by, for example, a government minister, can have a range of references such as:

> I plus one other (i.e. we = minister + prime minister)
>
> I plus a group (i.e. we = minister + government and/or political party)
>
> I plus the whole country (i.e. we = minister + citizens of the country)
>
> I plus the rest of humanity (i.e. we = minister + people everywhere).

The advantage of the singular forms (*I/me/myself/mine*) is that they show a clear sense of personal involvement on the part of the speaker, which is especially useful when good news is delivered. The disadvantage can be that they show all too clearly where blame lies if something goes wrong. They can also be seen as too self-important, with the individual speakers placing themselves above or outside the collective responsibility of their colleagues. The advantage of the plural pronoun forms (*we/us/ourselves/ours*) is that they help share the responsibility, especially when the decisions are tricky or when the news is uncertain. In their broadest reference they can show the politician in touch with all of the country, even all of the world. The disadvantage is that the individual does not gain so much credit when things go well.

In reality, politicians very often use a mixture of singular and plural pronouns, but analysing just which ones they use, and where, can give considerable insight into what they are saying and how they want to be viewed.

ACTIVITY 2.4

Allow about 15 minutes

The following is an extract from a speech by John Howard, the Australian Prime Minister, given during the 2004 election campaign to members of his own party in the state of Victoria.

- Underline the pronouns throughout the whole speech.
- Who is being addressed here?
- What potential meanings can be derived from Howard's use of pronouns?
- Can you find other persuasive techniques here?

John Howard

I start by thanking the Victorian Division again for the very dedicated way in which it has set about preparing for the upcoming federal election. We face a great challenge. Winning for the fourth time is always hard. There is always temptation to think when things are going well that the nation essentially is on autopilot and it doesn't really matter who is in charge, it will keep going well. Of course nothing could be further from the truth. And we'll face in this state, as we will around the nation, we will face a very big fight when the election is held. But the value of the strength of this division will once again be something that will be important if we are to achieve ultimate victory. I'm impressed with the quality of the candidates chosen and the sense of commitment and zeal of the division at an organisational level.

The stakes are very high. If we lose federally, there won't be a Liberal Government anywhere in Australia for the first time probably since the party was formed in 1944. So we do carry a very heavy responsibility. But more importantly even than the responsibility we carry for the future of our party, will be the implications that that will have for the future of our nation.

And over the past two weeks in federal parliament, we have seen open up a very clear division on something that is very important, not only to the way in which the world responds to the modern and horrible threat of terrorism, but also very important to the reputation and standing of our country around the world. Australians have never cut and run. Australians have always finished the job. Australians have always seen through until their responsibilities have been fully discharged. We may as a nation have differed and quarrelled about whether we should have made the original commitment in Iraq, but I do not believe the great majority of Australians differ and quarrel when it comes to a choice between cutting and running or staying and finishing the job. I believe the great majority of Australians believe that at the present crucial, difficult time in the wake of the bombings in Madrid, in the wake of a resurgent concern about terrorism around the world, I believe that the majority of Australians want us to go the distance and finish the job in Iraq – not separate ourselves from our allies in the United States and elsewhere.

This is not a time to be seen to be dividing the free world. Rather it is the time for nations and countries of goodwill and commitment to stand together in a united fashion. And I say that out of a sense of deep conviction. I say that in the face of an Opposition Leader who out of opportunism and populism invented a policy on a radio programme. You don't make good policy in answer to radio interviewers. You don't make good policy in the full morning flush of having read a couple of good opinion polls in a newspaper. You make policy over the long term out of consideration for what is in the best interests of our country. And it is not in the best interests of our country to cut and run from Iraq. It is in the best interests of our country and in the best traditions of our country to finish the job and to see it through until the circumstances have arisen where out of proper regard for the security of Iraq and proper regard for the interests of our allies and proper regard for sending a united, unambiguous message to terrorists that we will not have our policy dictated by threats of violence and the actuality of violence in other countries. We will make our policy according to what we believe is in the long-term interests of the Australian people.

(Howard, 2004)

Comment

Although the apparent audience is his own party members, Howard is at the same time acutely aware that there is a wider audience for this speech, namely party members throughout Australia, then the whole Australian public and, further beyond that, the international community. Howard had just declared an election, which means this is a campaign speech and a policy speech, as well as a speech to encourage local volunteers.

In terms of pronouns, Howard uses a number of variations. He frequently says *I*, often in combination with the word *believe*. When he says *we* it is possible to see that sometimes this refers to himself and his ministers, sometimes to his party, sometimes to the nation as a whole, and sometimes there is a creative ambiguity which means that both party and nation are in fact the same thing. *So we do carry a very heavy responsibility* would appear to be himself and his ministers. *We will face a very big fight* is probably the party. *[W]e may as a nation* clearly refers to the whole nation. Where there is most ambiguity, though, is in statements such as *I believe that the majority of Australians want us to go the distance* where the reference could be read as being specific to the party, but could also refer to the nation. This ambiguity is not damaging to the persuasive force though – connecting party and state can do the party a lot of good in electoral terms.

A further use of pronouns comes when Howard refers to his opponent (not by name but by title). Having accused the *Opposition Leader* of making up policy as he goes, he says, *You don't make good policy in answer to radio interviewers*. The *you* here is not a reference to his audience but to the all-embracing anyone in general. In other words, his opponent has behaved in a way contrary to all reasonable common behaviour.

Howard's speech uses other persuasive techniques, some of which are:
- the number of references to Australia/Australian(s) (8), the nation (4) and the country (5)

- metaphors and/or euphemisms such as *cut and run, finish the job*
- contrasts
- repetition, including lists of three.

References to country and national characteristics

John Howard's many references to Australia and Australians in the extract above reinforce the view that this speech is not just aimed at the audience present in the hall. It is addressing a wider audience, one that he wants to persuade to vote for him. In the third paragraph he puts forward a strong picture of the Australian character that leaves little space for dissenting views: *Australians have never cut and run. Australians have always finished the job. Australians have always seen through until their responsibilities have been fully discharged.* This is designed to make his audience feel good about their qualities without pausing to think whether it is a justified claim. It taps into the cultural roots of 'mateship' – a true Australian doesn't let his mates down – and is therefore a picture of themselves that Australians would be likely to recognise and support. Politicians try to identify with what they perceive as the positive characteristics which their electorate believe to be typical of themselves and their nation. A UK example could be the idea of the 'indomitable British spirit', where everyone will work together in times of difficulty – typified by Londoners during the blitz bombing of the Second World War. Politicians undermine such cultural stereotypes at their peril.

Metaphor and euphemism

The predominant metaphor of the Howard speech is 'election as war or battle' which has further resonance as he is also referring to Australia's participation in the war in Iraq taking place at that time. It is in the context of this metaphor that the use of euphemisms such as *cut and run* and *finishing the job* need to be evaluated: Howard is 'fighting' an election campaign and Australia is fighting a war. The party workers in Victoria and the electorate in the country are being urged to support Howard's fight. If you reject him and his party, you are also voting for Australia to cut and run from its international responsibilities.

Contrasts

Example

This is not a time to be seen to be dividing the free world. Rather it is the time for nations and countries of goodwill and commitment to stand together in a united fashion.

(Howard, 2004)

One of the strongest ways for a politician to accentuate the value of their own party's approach is by comparing it to that of their opponents. In the example above, Howard implicitly links dividing the free world with the opposition party and contrasts it with the positively evaluated trait of *standing together* that he is advocating. Notice that he also implies that Australia is one of the countries that can be positively evaluated as showing *goodwill and commitment*.

Repetition

Repetition by lists is popular with politicians when they address live audiences, because they send out signals about how the audience should respond. Three-part lists, such as *Australians have never cut and run. Australians have always finished the job. Australians have always seen through until their responsibilities have been fully discharged* from Howard's speech above, can often be used to signal when an audience should clap. Research into political oratory in the 1980s by Max Atkinson, a British sociologist, revealed among other things that speakers prompt their audience about where to applaud or express agreement. There are usually specific intonational shifts. This can be demonstrated by an extract from the transcript of a speech given by the then prime minister, Margaret Thatcher, in 1980, shown in the example below. In the speech itself there was an upward shift in pitch on the first item of the list (*purpose*), and this was maintained on the second item (*strategy*). At the third item, the pitch moved downwards on the second syllable of *resolve*, signalling completion and therefore a suitable place for applause.

Example

THATCHER   This week has demonstrated that we are a party united in purpose, strategy and resolve.

AUDIENCE   Hear hear. *[Applause]*

(adapted from Atkinson, 1984, p. 61)

Repetition can also take other less easily spotted forms, where certain words and phrases are regularly used by a political party. These words and phrases can be used to attach both positive and negative values to what is being discussed. They are most easily identified using computational means. In the late 1990s the applied linguist Norman Fairclough made a study of this use of language as part of his approach to issues of language and power termed '**critical discourse analysis**' (Fairclough, 1995; Chouliaraki and Fairclough, 1999). He compiled a computer **corpus** (a collection of texts) of speeches and other documents issued by the Labour Party in the UK (Fairclough, 2000). At this time the Labour Party was in government after many years in opposition. To disassociate themselves from some of the older, less successful policies of their party, members frequently referred to themselves as 'New Labour'.

Fairclough compared a corpus of New Labour texts from 1997 to 1999 with a smaller corpus of texts from Labour material largely from the period 1973 to 1982 and with more general **corpora** (plural of corpus) of English and identified frequently occurring 'keywords' used by New Labour. These were:

we	Britain
welfare	partnership
new	schools
people	crime
reform	deliver
promote	business
deal	tough
young	

(Fairclough, 2000, pp. 17–18)

ACTIVITY 2.5

Read the extract entitled 'Renewal, modernisation, and reform' (Reading A) from Norman Fairclough's analysis in *New Labour, New Language?*, in which he analyses the uses of the words *new*, *modernise/modernisation* and *reform*. He looks at the **collocates** – which words commonly co-occur with these words – and what message they are signalling. Before reading, try to predict the words that a politician might use in conjunction with *new*, *modernise/modernisation* and *reform*. Do you expect *new*, *modernise/modernisation* and *reform* to convey positive or negative evaluation?

Comment

Fairclough's analysis shows that *new*, *modernise/modernisation* and *reform* were used frequently by Tony Blair. *New* is most often associated with the collocates *Labour* and *deal*. Fairclough argues that this is to focus on a sense of political renewal. *Modernise/modernisation* is not clearly associated with a particular collocate, but is used with institutional entities in the UK such as the health service and education. *Reform*, in contrast, is used with equal frequency to describe European Union entities. By highlighting these tendencies Fairclough is illustrating the way in which politicians use repetition and collocational patterning to insinuate their message. You may have noticed that Fairclough concludes this extract on a negative note, referring to Hall's use of *weasel word* for *reform* in *welfare reform*. This reflects the wider message of his book which takes a critical approach to the discourse of 'New Labour'.

Choice of pronouns, metaphor and repetition are not the only linguistic features through which politicians seek to persuade. Atkinson's research (1984), mentioned above, signalled the importance of intonation, but hand gestures, gaze, body posture and facial expressions also add to the impact of the message.

The two extracts in Activity 2.6 below are the final summing up speeches of the first of three live television debates between presidential candidates George Bush and John Kerry in the USA presidential election of 2004. The rules of this debate were very formal, with time allocated in turn to each speaker. This meant that at least in part they would have had pre-prepared scripts from which to work. Although they spoke in front of a live audience, this audience was not allowed to respond in any way – clearly the real audience who needed to be influenced was the American public who chose to watch the broadcasts.

ACTIVITY 2.6

Allow about
15 minutes

Read the speeches given below and compare the persuasive language used by the two politicians. Look in particular at the following:

- pronouns and what they refer to
- use of repetition and contrast
- use of metaphor.

John Kerry

My fellow Americans, as I've said at the very beginning of this debate, both President Bush and I love this country very much. There's no doubt, I think, about that.

But we have a different set of convictions about how we make our country stronger here at home and respected again in the world.

I know that for many of you sitting at home, parents of kids in Iraq, you want to know who's the person who could be a commander in chief who could get your kids home and get the job done and win the peace.

And for all the rest of the parents in America who are wondering about their kids going to the school or anywhere else in the world, what kind of world they're going to grow up in, let me look you in the eye and say to you: I defended this country as a young man at war, and I will defend it as president of the United States.

But I have a difference with this president. I believe when we're strongest when we reach out and lead the world and build strong alliances.

I have a plan for Iraq. I believe we can be successful. I'm not talking about leaving. I'm talking about winning. And we need a fresh start, a new credibility, a president who can bring allies to our side.

I also have a plan to win the war on terror, funding homeland security, strengthening our military, cutting our finances, reaching out to the world, again building strong alliances.

I believe America's best days are ahead of us because I believe that the future belongs to freedom, not to fear.

That's the country that I'm going to fight for. And I ask you to give me the opportunity to make you proud. I ask you to give me the opportunity to lead this great nation, so that we can be stronger here at home, respected again in the world, and have responsible leadership that we deserve.

Thank you. And God bless America.

(Kerry, 2004)

George Bush

If America shows uncertainty or weakness in this decade, the world will drift toward tragedy. That's not going to happen, so long as I'm your president.

The next four years we will continue to strengthen our homeland defenses. We will strengthen our intelligence-gathering services. We will reform our military. The military will be an all-volunteer army.

We will continue to stay on the offense. We will fight the terrorists around the world so we do not have to face them here at home.

We'll continue to build our alliances. I'll never turn over America's national security needs to leaders of other countries, as we continue to build those alliances.

And we'll continue to spread freedom. I believe in the transformational power of liberty. I believe that the free Iraq is in this nation's interests. I believe a free Afghanistan is in this nation's interest.

And I believe both a free Afghanistan and a free Iraq will serve as a powerful example for millions who plead in silence for liberty in the broader Middle East.

We've done a lot of hard work together over the last three and a half years. We've been challenged, and we've risen to those challenges. We've climbed the mighty mountain. I see the valley below, and it's a valley of peace.

By being steadfast and resolute and strong, by keeping our word, by supporting our troops, we can achieve the peace we all want.

I appreciate your listening tonight. I ask for your vote. And may God continue to bless our great land.

(Bush, 2004)

(Note that this is a transcript taken from the *Washington Post* website, which means that the transcriber has differentiated between *we will* and *we'll*.)

Comment

If we look at Bush's use of pronouns first, we see a pattern emerge, whereby he uses *we will* to talk about policies which will be implemented in the future and *I* when it comes to personal beliefs. Because he is the incumbent president, Bush has a governmental team which the nation would be familiar with – so in that sense he can refer to *we* as the current government and at the same time stress that he is after all the one in power at the moment. After a whole string of references to *we* as the government, there is a possible shift when he says, *We've done a lot of hard work together.* Although this could still be a reference to him and his government, it is also a reference to the whole nation. As Fairclough (2000) points out, the issue with the inclusive *we* is knowing who exactly it includes. The religious metaphors of mountains and valleys carry more weight if they are referring to the whole nation. Interestingly, though, Bush does not actually name the country as often as Kerry does. Other repetitions used by Bush include references to *continuity*, *freedom/liberty* and the three-part list of *steadfast/resolute/strong*.

Kerry is at a relative disadvantage in that, as challenger to the incumbent, he does not yet have a team to work with. This means that he uses the personal pronoun *I* much more frequently than Bush. He aims to turn this to his advantage by referring to his own personal experience as a soldier – *I defended this country as a young man at war* with the implication that Bush did not. Whereas Bush talks of continuing to do things, Kerry, as the challenger, has *plans.* Kerry also talks more directly to his audience, using the pronoun *you* much more frequently than Bush; when he uses *we*, apart from the first time when he is talking about himself and Bush, there is little doubt that he is talking about the nation as a whole. Some of the repetitions and contrasts include *fresh/new, freedom/not ... fear, I ask you,* and the three-part *stronger here/ respected again/responsible leadership.* He also picks up on his literal reference to being a soldier by later metaphorically talking about once again fighting for his country.

It should be clear from the brief analysis above that the challenger and the incumbent inevitably fall into a rhetorical contrast, with the challenger frequently talking of the new, fresh plans, and the incumbent talking of continuity and team work. Analysis of rhetorical techniques can show language at work in one sense, but it cannot in the end say one speech is 'better' than the other; a speech may have more rhetorical intricacy and elegance, for example, but completely fail to engage with what political commentators would call the national mood.

Rhetoric in Indian English

The analysis of political rhetoric so far has depended heavily upon examples from election speeches made by politicians. Reading B, by Julu Sen, Rahul Sharma and Anima Chakraverty, broadens the perspective on English rhetoric in two ways. First, it offers an example of a political speech from another English-speaking country, India, which is also from an earlier historical period (the late 1940s) and which is not an electioneering speech. We can consider how relevant the categories we have discussed so far are for analysing this speech by Jawarharlal Nehru. Second, Sen et al. provide an analysis of a rather different kind, one which shows how some of the principles of an Indian rhetorical tradition are embodied in the speech.

ACTIVITY 2.7

The Indian politician Jawarharlal Nehru was one of the main founders of an independent India in the period after the Second World War. The most famous and influential political figure of the Indian struggle for independence, however, was Mahatma Gandhi. In the appendix to Reading B, you will find a transcript of the speech that Nehru made to the Indian nation on the death of Ghandhi. Read that speech now. As you read it, consider whether or not Nehru uses any of the rhetorical techniques we have been discussing. Consider, too, what the purposes of the speech were. Then read the rest of Reading B by Sen et al. Note the kind of analysis that the authors offer, and their references to Indian rhetorical traditions.

Comment

Sen et al. point to the essentially oral character of Nehru's speech, with its effective use of cohesive devices (such as the use of *and* and 'purposeful repetition', as with the repetition of the phrase *the light has gone out*). They also suggest that Nehru, like other Indian political speakers, drew on established Indian rhetorical practices, such as the 'principles of effective communication' established by Kautiliya. So the reading offers a glimpse of another analytical perspective on the rhetorical use of English, one which might be complementary to those we have presented in this chapter. Although Sen et al. do not draw attention to them, you may have noticed that Nehru's speech contains a three-part list (*We must face this poison ...*, lines 34–6) and a contrast (*But that does not mean that we should be weak ...*, lines 47–9). The movement between the pronouns *I*, *you* and *we* is also significant in illustrating the relationship between Nehru and the Indian public. In terms of purpose, two significant themes emerge — sharing grief and promoting unity and public order. This last theme comes out most clearly from *we must face all the perils that encompass us …* (lines 35–53). Nehru is calling upon the Indian people to unite in peaceful expression of their grief and not to seek to blame the death on any particular community which might then lead to violence. Inter-community violence was a constant threat during this period, so Nehru's rhetoric was necessary to persuade people that this was not what Ghandi would have wanted. The use of inclusive *we* pronouns is therefore prominent in this section, as are the references to *Ghandi/he/him/his*.

2.4 Advertising

I will now move on to look at some of the ways in which persuasive English is used in advertising. There is considerable overlap at this point between the ways in which advertising uses persuasive techniques and the part that language 'play' has in this process. For ways in which advertisements use 'play' you should also read Chapter 3 of this book. This chapter, meanwhile, will look at the ways in which advertising attempts to persuade by acting upon the reader's emotions. In this chapter I will be looking at written texts: when reading this section you should be aware that, although some of the comments will also apply to moving image texts, there are also distinct differences between the way advertising works in different media. In order to make a connection between the two main topics in this chapter, I will begin by looking at a piece of political advertising.

Advertising depends upon the emotional idea that our lives are in some way imperfect; we lack something, we need something, we have the wrong view or belief. If we buy 'x', do 'x', think 'x' then our lives will be better. McNair (2003, p. 98) puts it as follows: 'Advertisements function, therefore, by making commodities *mean* something to their prospective purchasers; by distinguishing one product from another functionally similar one; and by doing this in a manner which connects with the desires of the consumer'. Although the word 'commodities' suggests a physical product, it is equally possible to see the commodities as political ideas and policies. If voters can be persuaded to prefer one policy over another, then they will 'buy' the commodity by 'paying' for it with their vote.

ACTIVITY 2.8

Allow about
20 minutes

Look at the text in Figure 2.5, which was posted to voters in the North-east of England, who were being asked to decide whether or not they wanted an elected regional assembly as part of a process of the devolution of national government. How have the producers of this advertisement attempted to persuade the reader to vote *no*? You could focus in particular on presentational features of the text, the ways in which it is organised, and the emotions which are potentially invoked in the reader.

REGIONAL ASSEMBLY - AN EXPENSIVE TALKING SHOP

- NO POWER to create jobs
- NO POWER to improve healthcare
- NO POWER to improve our schools
- NO POWER to make our streets safer
- NO POWER to upgrade the A1

What an Assembly will do:

- PAY BIG SALARIES TO POLITICIANS. In Scotland each gets £49,315, in Wales each gets £43,283 and in London each gets £45,000 - AND add-on the cost of their pensions and expenses.
- PUT UP COUNCIL TAX.   We will have to pay.
- BUILD ITSELF A NEW PALACE. The new Scottish Parliament cost £431 MILLION (the politicians said it would cost £43 million).

Who benefits?
- Politicians
- Spin doctors
- Cronies

Who loses out?
YOU
THE TAXPAYER

POLITICIANS TALK – WE PAY
YOU HAVE A CHANCE TO SAY "NO"
VOTE NO

For more details call FREEPHONE 0800 107 0304

Promoted by Phillip Cummings on behalf of North East Says No Ltd, both of Owengate House, Owengate, Durham DH1 3HB

Figure 2.5   Regional assembly referendum leaflet

Comment

Although this is a political poster it is a fairly straightforward piece of advertising, and it is possible to find plenty of persuasive techniques. There are presentational features, such as:

- the use of bullet points
- different font sizes
- boxes, etc.

These presentational features not only attempt to catch the eye of the reader, they also allow the producers of the text to organise what they want to say. This involves the following in sequence from top to bottom:

- an introductory statement
- what the assembly will not do (i.e. have an impact on positive things)
- what it will do (i.e. waste money)
- two boxes which rhetorically ask who will gain (politicians or *them*) and who will lose (the taxpayer or *us*)
- two summarising statements.

Narrative voices in advertising

One aspect of literary study which can be useful when looking at written advertisements is the idea of the **narrator** and **narrative point of view** within prose fiction.

(Goddard, 2002, p. 24, original emphasis)

This returns us to the significance of pronouns, which we noted earlier, and the question of who is 'speaking' and who is being addressed in a text. In one sense of course, the 'speaker' is the author who wrote it, and the individual who reads it is the person addressed. But it is not quite as simple as this, because *within* the text there is a created voice which is 'speaking' the text and a created reader who is 'hearing' it. The voice which is speaking the text can be called the **narrator** and the created reader who hears the text can be called the **ideal reader**, a reader who both understands and agrees with the message that is being put forward; so in a sense there are four levels of voice. In the example of the regional assembly text in Figure 2.5, the ideal reader is joined with the narrator in the collective *we – we pay*. The narrator also addresses the ideal reader directly, saying *you have a chance ...* . If you find the notion of ideal reader difficult, then consider that, although the text assumes the reader agrees with everything being said, the actual readers of the text did not necessarily do so – they could always vote *yes* instead.

The way in which advertisements have narrators who speak texts, and ideal readers who agree with what they are being told, makes a significant contribution to the emotional impact of an advertisement. If 'you' are being told that your life is in some way lacking something, that there is a better world possible, then the message has the potential to be seductive even if the real you can always resist the message. In the advertisement in Figure 2.5 the main emotion seems to be a sense of outrage at what is and could be done to us by politicians. The advertisement does not suggest, as such, the possibility of a better world, but it certainly suggests that things could be much worse; in this case the status quo is the best on offer.

ACTIVITY 2.9

Allow about
5 minutes

Look at Figure 2.6 which is part of an advertisement for credit.
- What is the message of the narrator in this text?
- What features within the figure (both words and picture) create that message?
- Who is the ideal reader of a text like this?

The cheque for our new car arrived in a flash.

£10,000 over 60 months for
£294.64 a month 9.9% APR

(This example includes Creditcare Silver)

Ask for the courier service and get your cheque the next day.

When you've set your heart on something, you want it now. So the express courier service will get your cheque to you in a flash.

CALL FREE ON
0800 028 0119
Quoting the response code on your letter.

Lines open weekdays 7am-11pm, Saturday 8.30am-6pm, Sunday 9.30am-5.30pm.

Figure 2.6   An advertisement for a credit company

Comment

Unlike the other texts that we have examined, this advertisement uses both words and a picture – it is a multimodal text, combining different modes of communication. In the original, the picture dominates the advertisement, conveying a very strong image of the ideal readers. These ideal readers are supposed to identify with the couple in the picture and with their lifestyle and desires. The sporty-looking car is particularly significant in giving clues to the successful and fast-paced lives these two people might live – and by implication that the ideal reader either also enjoys or wants to enjoy.

The text uses a number of different fonts to represent different 'voices'. The font on the left looks like handwriting and conveys the voice of the couple confirming and echoing the information given by the text to the right. The first part of the right-hand text is an imperative – telling the reader what to do. The assumption is therefore that the reader wants money quickly. The next paragraph also talks directly to the reader – assuming that they will agree with the proposition *When you've set your heart on something, you want it now.* Notice the use of the contraction *you've* to make the text more like speech, and also the address to *you* making it personal.

It should be clear by now that, although persuasive texts address 'you' directly, they do not as such offer you a chance to respond, at least not in the actual text itself. (You may reply to the advertisement, buy the project, vote or not vote for the party, throw the advertisement away in disgust, but you are doing this outside the text of the advertisement, not inside it.) This means that the voices that speak in texts are engaged in a sort of monologue, albeit a monologue which appears to be part of a dialogue. If this seems complicated, consider the way I am addressing you in this book. Although it seems as though we are having some sort of educational discussion, I am the only one doing the 'talking' in this chapter. I have constructed you as being intelligent, interested in what I have to say and keen to learn – but you remain silent. Advertisements manipulate what can be called this **dialogic**, or dialogue-like, structure of discourse to their advantage. They assume shared opinions which are not necessarily shared and they speak in voices which create an atmosphere of conversation and proximity. (See Chapter 6 for further discussion of informality in marketing language.)

Consider, for example, the type of short personal advertisement, in which a single voice, belonging to a single person, seeks a partner:

> Are you open minded, warm, mature, 25–40. Attentive, loving man, 29, WLTM you. No ravers. Lndn.

(Marley, 2002, p. 81)

The first thing to notice is that there is considerable **ellipsis** – the omission of words which are not required for the meaning to be clear – which is typical of the genre. Although writing *WLTM* instead of *would like to meet* saves money (and of course advertising space does not come cheap), such ellipsis also establishes that the voice here is conversational and informal, and is addressing someone who is also knowledgeable about the conventions of this type of advertisement. The opening of the advertisement, using a question, draws the reader into an engagement with the writer, through responding by checking themselves against the criteria *open minded, warm, mature, 25–40*. The use of *you* and the questioning means that the writer is able to address the reader directly.

Broadly speaking, advertisements, and indeed other types of persuasive texts, can be seen to have four levels of voice. If you look again at the personal advertisement quoted above, we can see the following:

1   The author is the person who wrote it and sent it in to the newspaper.

2   The 'narrator' is the created voice (who is *Attentive* and *loving*).

3   The (imagined) reader addressed is the 'ideal reader' (who is *open minded*, etc.).

4   The advertisement is read by actual people who may or may not reply.

Point 2 above, then, is the narrator of the text, and point 3 the ideal reader. If we now move on to a more substantial text, we will see that narrative voices in advertisements can be both subtle and various.

ACTIVITY 2.10

Allow about
10 minutes

The advertisement shown in Figure 2.7 is one of a series that started to appear on British railway stations during 2005. Its purpose was to highlight the fact that railway staff are subjected to abuse from members of the public. Look carefully at the advertisement and come up with some answers to the following questions:

•   How does the advertisement draw attention to itself?

•   What voices can you detect 'speaking' in the text? What characteristics do these voices have?

•   What ideal readers are being spoken to in the text? What characteristics do they have?

Comment

The advertisement draws attention to itself by its jumbled spelling. As you can imagine, it stopped passers-by who tried to work out just what was being said. The double meaning in the tag line *It doesn't make sense* justifies the strange spelling and at the same time gives out the central message.

"I've been shuoetd at, spat at and had cmomnets mdae aobut the coulor of my sikn... I shuodln't hvae to put up wtih tihs knid of aubse"

It doesn't make sense

Six rail staff are physically assaulted on trains or at stations every day just for doing their job.

We will not tolerate verbal or physical attacks on our staff. They will be given total support in any prosecution.

Help us to ensure a safer environment for everyone.

If you see anyone assaulting staff or passengers, call 0800 40 50 40 making a note of date, time and location.

Figure 2.7 Railway station poster

It seems to me that there are at least three narrative voices here. The first belongs to the abused member of staff (but even here it can be argued that the single *I* is an amalgam of at least three different voices relating three different experiences). Although this voice takes up most space and is the most visual, we know that it is not the dominant narrative voice by the fact that its words are placed in quotation marks. The second voice belongs to an omniscient narrator, who declares the overall moral message. The third voice speaks on behalf of the organisations funding this campaign who will not allow 'their' staff to be abused in this way. It is this final voice which seems to me to be the most powerful and authoritative, even if their text is the least visually prominent.

The answer to the third question above is open to debate. Personally, I feel that the abused staff are speaking out to the public, but it is not absolutely clear. We could be hearing their complaints to their bosses. The issue around to whom the other two voices are speaking is even more complex. It's one thing to raise awareness of a social disorder problem, quite another to accuse everyone of being abusive. The advertisement, therefore, treads a fine line with its readers. I think it is warning us all when it says it will not tolerate attacks on staff. When it moves on to asking for help, though, it is clearly talking to those who would not dream of abusing staff. Yet the phrase *Help us to ensure a safer environment for everyone* might be implying that, given the right circumstances (a delayed train perhaps), we are all potentially abusive.

Clearly, there are no right answers to the questions I posed above, and clearly, too, advertisements are complex texts which, like literary texts, will mean different things to different people. I thought this advertisement was very clever. A colleague, though, pointed out that representing the staff as unable to make sense is hardly flattering to them. What do you think?

ACTIVITY 2.11

Allow about
20 minutes

Figure 2.8 comes from a Malaysian women's magazine. To conclude this chapter, think carefully about, and ideally discuss with others, the following questions, which are designed as discussion topics. The questions are intended to review what has been discussed about advertising in this chapter so far, and to indicate some further lines of enquiry if you wish to take this topic further. They are not, though, exhaustive. Depending upon your own cultural contexts, such as your age, gender, the country you live in, and so on, you may well find other aspects to talk about.

- This text is multimodal, in that it uses visual as well as verbal strategies. What do you notice about the various visual images here, and how do they contribute to the text's overall persuasive design?

- Advertising, by definition, seeks to persuade you that your life could be better if you buy a certain product or service. In what ways does this text suggest that your life is not as good as it could be?
- In this chapter we have looked closely at the use of pronouns in advertisements. Consider the absence of personal pronouns in this text. Can you tell who the ideal reader for the text is? Why doesn't the text address them more personally?
- What cultural ideas about female beauty can be found here? How do you respond to them? What does this tell you about the ideal reader for this text?

2.5 Conclusion

Early in this chapter I pointed out that when analysing the way language is used for social purposes, the context of a text's production and reception needs to be taken into account. In analysing a persuasive text we need to consider its terms of:

- **Production**   Who is writing/speaking the text? What is the text about? What is its purpose? What kind of text is being produced?
- **Reception**   What audience is the text addressing? How is that audience constructed in the text? What does the text mean to various possible readers?

In the case of advertising a product such as the skincare treatment in Figure 2.8/Activity 2.11, three of my questions about production above are easily answered: the topic is, broadly speaking, the product or idea to be sold; the purpose of the text is to persuade the reader to buy; and the type of text produced is a glossy magazine advertisement. Who is producing an advertising text, though, is more complex. Most published advertisements are produced by agencies for clients, so there is multiple authorship at work. In the case of the railway poster in Figure 2.7/Activity 2.10, there are also multiple voices speaking through the text. Similarly, with political speeches, it is often not just the work of the politician speaking the words.

As for reception, this can be the more fluid of the contextual areas outlined above. As I have already noted, in Activity 2.10, different individuals have different responses to advertisements. It also needs to be understood, though, that while advertisements seem to speak to us as individuals, they are, like political speeches, texts aimed at a mass market. (The fact that 'you' in English

The new whitening revolution:
Pure Vitamin C + **Melanin-Block**™
in just one step!

Dark spots and skin pigmentation, a growing concern by many Asian women, are mainly caused by constant exposure to harsh UV rays resulting in overactive melanin production in the epidermis.

With this in mind, L'ORÉAL Skincare Laboratories has successfully formulated the latest breakthrough in whitening skincare treatment. White Perfect Double Action Concentrated Whitening Essence effectively targets pigmentation both on the skin surface and in the epidermis.

THE UNIQUE DOUBLE CHAMBERS

MELANIN-BLOCK™
+ LACTIC ACID
+ DERMOLISS CHAMBER

Melanin-Block™ acts directly on melanogenesis and effectively reduces melanin production by -53%.

Efficient exfoliating agents: Lactic acid and Dermoliss gently exfoliate away melanin-filled dark dead cells to recover skin tone evenness, radiance and greater transparency.

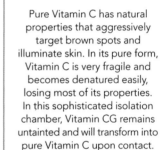

PURE VITAMIN C
CHAMBER

Pure Vitamin C has natural properties that aggressively target brown spots and illuminate skin. In its pure form, Vitamin C is very fragile and becomes denatured easily, losing most of its properties. In this sophisticated isolation chamber, Vitamin CG remains untainted and will transform into pure Vitamin C upon contact.

L'ORÉAL's
Double-Action Solution

ACTION **1**
Soft peeling effect for more transparency

LACTIC ACID + DERMOLISS

ACTION **2**
Regulates melanin production to reduce brown spots

PURE VIT. C + MELANIN-BLOCK™

Proven Efficacy
Against Brown Spots*

After 7 days...
Complexion is visibly brighter
Complexion is more even

After 4 weeks...
Skin is visibly fairer
Complexion is more transparent

Before application   After 8 weeks of application

*Evaluation of the effect of White Perfect Essence on a pigmentation spot.

D E R M O – E X P E R T I S E .   F R O M   R E S E A R C H   T O   B E A U T Y .

Figure 2.8   Advertisement for skin-whitening product in a Malaysian women's magazine

is both singular and plural and 'we' both inclusive and exclusive facilitates this blurring.) This inevitably means that they hit the mark more with some receivers than with others. If we then add a cultural dimension to the context, and understand that persuasive texts represent aspects of the society from which they emerge, then how we 'read' them very much depends upon our own context.

READING A: Renewal, modernisation, and reform

Norman Fairclough
(Norman Fairclough is Emeritus Professorial Fellow, Institute for Advanced Research in Management and Social Sciences, University of Lancaster.)

Source: Fairclough, N. (2000) *New Labour, New Language?* London, Routledge, pp. 18–19.

'New' occurs 609 times in 53 speeches of Tony Blair's between 1997 and 1999 (for comparison, 'modern' occurs 89 times, 'modernise/modernisation' 87 times, and 'reform' 143 times). The most frequent collocations are 'New Labour' (72 instances) and 'New Deal' (70 instances). The sense of political renewal conveyed by 'New Labour' is also evident in references to a 'new politics' (4 instances) and a 'new centre and centre-left' (2 instances). Political renewal is linked to national renewal in the slogan 'New Labour, New Britain', first used in the 1994 Labour Party conference. 'New Britain' is quite frequent (15 examples), and 'new' is also applied (7 times) to other international entities that Britain belongs to (e.g. 'New Europe', 'New Commonwealth'), and even the world (6 instances, e.g. the 'new world we are helping to bring into being'). Political and national renewal are linked to the 'new times' we live in – 34 instances, including also 'new era' and 'new millennium'. And there is a striking number of expressions (41 instances in all) for 'new ways of working' in government (that phrase occurs 8 times, 'new ways' 15 times, and 'new approaches' 11 times) and new relationships associated with them ('new partnership(s)' occurs 13 times). Another prominent set of meanings relates to ideas and attitudes (36 instances in all, including 'new ideas' (7 instances) 'new confidence' (4 instances), 'new sense of hope (or purpose, or urgency)' (5 instances), and there are 20 expressions referring to 'new opportunities' or 'new challenges'). Many 'new' Government initiatives are referred to (57 instances in all), such as the 'new active Community Unit', or a 'new National College for School Leadership', though unlike the 'New Deal' the adjective 'new' is not part of the title.

Despite the impression picked up by satirists that 'new' applies to everything and anything ('New Labour, new underwear'), it is used quite selectively for national, political, and governmental renewal in 'new times' which generate new opportunities and challenges and call for new approaches, ideas, and attitudes. It is perhaps 'modernise' that tends to be used more indiscriminately: 'modernisation' applies to the Labour Party, Britain, the Constitution, the Health Service, education and schools, the welfare state, defence, the Common Agricultural Policy, etc. In 25 cases 'modernisation' (or in a few cases 'modernise') is used in a general way without reference to a specific domain (e.g. 'money for modernisation' (the phrase occurs 3 times), or 'it is modernisation for a purpose' (5 instances)).

A striking contrast between 'modernisation' and 'reform' is that the former is overwhelmingly used with reference to the UK, whereas the latter is roughly equally used with reference to the EU [European Union]. There is also a striking difference in terms of what is 'reformed' as opposed to 'modernised': the collocation 'economic reform' occurs 11 times, and 'reform' occurs 12 times with 'markets' ('labour', 'capital', or 'product') as its object, always with reference to the EU. By contrast, 'modernise' occurs only once with 'markets' as its object (and then the reference is to the EU) and once with 'the economy' as its object. So, economic change is 'reform' not 'modernisation', and it applies only at EU level, not in Britain. The only changes in Britain that are referred to as 'reforms' more frequently than 'modernisations' are 'welfare reform' and 'reform of the House of Lords'. Hall[21] refers to the word 'reform' in the former as a 'weasel word' which effectively masks the 'ambiguity and duplicity' of New Labour around welfare reform – is the welfare state being wound up, or truly transformed?

Reference for this reading

21   Hall, S. (1998) 'The great moving nowhere show', *Marxism Today*, special issue on New Labour, pp. 9–14.

READING B: 'The light has gone out': Indian traditions in English rhetoric

Julu Sen, Rahul Sharma and Anima Chakraverty
(Julu Sen, Central Institute of English and Foreign Languages, Hyderabad, India; Rahul Sharma is a senior lecturer in English in DAV College, Amritsar, India; Anima Chakraverty is a senior lecturer in English at Isabella Thoburn College, Lucknow, India.)

Specially commissioned for Wooffitt (1996, pp. 150–5).

Although English has been used in India since 1600, and we are familiar with Indian writing in English, we have only recently begun to study the speeches in English of well-known Indian orators, such as Gandhi and Nehru. Since India is a multilingual country, most of the broadcasts to the nation are in Hindi as well as in English. Although Gandhi spoke mostly in Hindi or Gujarati, his speeches delivered in south India and in South Africa were generally in English.

While studying these speeches, we have discovered that spontaneous impromptu speeches were very different from prepared addresses. The formal written addresses of both Gandhi and Nehru resemble their writing in English, while in their impromptu speeches we find features of oral speech – additive, aggregative, redundant, conservative, close to human life world, empathetic and participatory. Their transcribed speeches also show evidence of the influence of Indian rhetorical traditions. We will illustrate and discuss some of these features here, with reference to one famous impromptu speech by Jawarharlal Nehru, entitled 'The light has gone out' (as transcribed in Gopal, 1987).

Figure 1   Nehru, Indian prime minister, addressing a public meeting (May 1957)

The assassination of Mahatma Gandhi on 30 January 1948 was a national catastrophe. The brutal murder of the Father of the Nation, barely a few months after independence, sent shock waves throughout the country and plunged millions of Indians into gloom and mourning. In this hour of crisis, Nehru, the then prime minister of India and a trusted lieutenant of Gandhi, addressed the nation on the radio. Widely regarded as one of Nehru's immortal speeches, this spontaneous address to the nation made an indelible impact on the hearts and minds of millions of Indians.

The influence of Indian rhetorical traditions

A salient feature of this speech is that the expression of 'grief' is accomplished without the use of the word 'grief' or any of its synonyms. This is because the feeling is too deep to be directly expressed in conventional words. It can only be evoked or suggested indirectly, and Nehru expresses the inexpressible in the following manner:

> The light has gone out from our lives and there is darkness everywhere.

> (lines 2–3)

This manner of dealing with grief indirectly is in accord with one of the principles of Indian aesthetics, *dhvani*, 'the use of poetic or dramatic words to suggest or evoke a feeling that is too deep, intense and universal to be spoken' (Coward, 1980, p. 148). *Dhvani* forms part of a theory of language propounded by the fifth-century Sanskrit grammarian and philosopher of language, Bhartrahari, and has also been drawn on by other Indian scholars in the analysis of figurative speech.

The speech also embodies several principles of effective communication that can be traced back to the *Artha Sastra*, a series of books dealing with politics, thought to have been written by the scholar Kautiliya in the fourth century BC. Kautiliya advises his readers that:

> Arrangement of subject-matter, connection, completeness, sweetness, exaltedness and lucidity constitute the excellences of communication. Among them, arranging in a proper order, the statement first of the principal matter, is *arrangement of subject-matter*. The statement of a subsequent matter without its being incompatible with the matter in hand, right up to the end, is *connection*. Absence of deficiency or excess of matter, words or letters, description in detail of the matter by means of reasons, citations and illustrations, (and) expressiveness of words, is *completeness*. The use of words with a charming meaning easily conveyed is *sweetness*. The use of words that are not vulgar is *exaltedness*. The employment of words that are well-known is *lucidity*.

> (Kangle, 1988, pp. 92–3; emphasis added)

Later in the same chapter Kautiliya refers to two further principles: *relevance* and *empathy* with the audience. We shall give examples of these principles in Nehru's speech, beginning with *arrangement of subject matter* and *connection*.

In a spontaneous speech like this, unlike in a written/prepared speech, one has to think on one's feet, and the textual order reflects the order in which impressions occur in the mind. Despite the fact that this is a spontaneous speech, it is a good example of arrangement of subject matter and connection, as described by Kautiliya. These can be seen in the sequence of topics in the speech:

> assassination – funeral – homage

Nehru starts with the principal matter of Gandhi's assassination by articulating his deep sense of dismay bordering on helplessness:

> I do not know what to tell you and how to say it.

> (lines 3–4)

This is how he identifies himself with the Indian masses and shares their sorrow. At the same time, however, as their undisputed leader, he is conscious of his responsibility to warn them of the dangers of communalism, and to impress upon them the need to strengthen the bonds of unity to face challenges boldly. With all the force at his command, he reminds his people that the likes of Gandhi never die and that the best homage to Gandhi would be a solemn pledge to work for peace, unity and brotherhood. In the midst of all this, Nehru keeps his cool, pauses, and finds time to give details of the funeral arrangement:

> May I now tell you the programme for tomorrow?

> (line 59)

Finally he advises his listeners on how they can best pay homage to Gandhi.

Nehru is concerned about the welfare of India so he repeats this concern before turning to the funeral arrangements and afterwards at the very end of his speech. Compare these two sentences:

> As in his life, so in his death he has reminded us of the big things of life, the living truth, and if we remember that, then it will be well with us and well with *India*.

> (lines 56–8; emphasis added)

> That is the best prayer that we can offer to *India* and ourselves.

> (lines 96–7; emphasis added)

The speech illustrates other principles suggested by Kautiliya. One of these is *completeness*. Although it is an impromptu speech, Nehru has chosen his words very carefully, whether they concern bringing the first news of the assassination to the nation (lines 1–23), his own reactions (lines 24–58), his plans for the funeral arrangements and advice on paying homage (lines 59–95) or finally the 'prayer' (lines 95–7). We can't strike out any part, claiming it is irrelevant, or deficient. It seems *complete* in all respects.

Sweetness can be found in Nehru's choice of words, word order, sentence construction, elegant variation and purposeful repetition. The first two sentences of the speech comprise a virtual string of 25 monosyllables. This aptly reflects the speaker's deep sense of anguish and helps create an atmosphere of mourning. However, this is soon followed by a little drama and the element of suspense. 'Bapu ... is no more. Perhaps I am wrong to say that ... The light has gone out, I said, and yet I was wrong' (lines 4–13). (*Bapu*, meaning 'Father', is the affectionate name Indians gave Gandhi.)

One of the best examples of Nehru's oratorical skill can be found in:

> The light that has illumined this country for these many, many years will illumine this country for many more years, and a thousand years later that light will still be seen in this country, and the world will see it, and it will give solace to innumerable hearts.

> (lines 15–19)

This rather extraordinary construction effectively illustrates the 'extraordinariness' of Gandhi, and places him far above not only common mortals but also most leaders of men and women. The magnitude of Gandhi's contribution to India's freedom struggle and the eternal relevance of his teachings is communicated most effectively through expressions like 'these many, many years', 'many more years' and 'a thousand years later'.

Nehru concludes the speech with the words:

> That is the best prayer that we can offer him and his memory. That is the best prayer that we can offer to India and ourselves.

> (lines 95–7)

The use of repetition here not only emphasizes the fact that the best prayer would be a life-long commitment to Gandhi's ideals of non-violence and communal harmony but also (by equating 'him' with 'India') acclaims Gandhi as the architect of India's freedom and the Father of this Nation.

The speech also shows great *dignity*: Nehru has not uttered a single word that could be termed socially offensive. That he had suffered a great blow may be gauged from the expression: 'A *madman* has put an end to his life, for I can only call him mad who did it' (lines 30–1; emphasis added). And 'We must face this *poison*, we must root out this *poison*, and we must face all the perils that encompass us, and face them, not *madly* or *badly*, but rather in the way that our beloved teacher taught us to face them' (lines 34–7, emphasis added). Yet he advises his people to be strong and determined. He maintains the dignity of his state and office, as prime minister, and talks about the funeral arrangements in a very calm manner.

The speech is *relevant* to the needs of the moment because in the hour of 'grief', through his 'love for his country', Nehru is making an appeal to his people to remain calm. The style is *lucid*, expressed in simple language so that this request reaches the masses. And finally, anticipating and sharing their love for Bapu, he can *empathize* with the audience. His use of the term *Bapu* itself is an illustration of this.

References for this reading

Coward (1980) *The Sphoth Theory of Language – A Philosophical Analysis,* Delhi, Motilal Banarasidass.

Gopal, S. (ed.) (1987) *Selected Works of Jawaharlal Nehru*, second series, vol. 5, New Delhi, Jawaharlal Nehru Memorial Fund.

Kangle, R.P. (1988) *The Kautiliya Artha Sastra – Parts 1 and 2 – An English Translation with Critical and Explanatory Notes*, trans. from the Malayalam manuscript of the twelfth century AD, Delhi, Motilal Banarasidass.

Appendix to Reading B

On 30 January 1948 at about 5 p.m., Mahatma Gandhi was late by a few minutes for the prayer meeting in the grounds of Birla House, New Delhi, because he had been held up by a meeting with Vallabhbhai Patel. With his forearms on the shoulders of his grandnieces, Abha and Manubehn, he walked briskly to the prayer ground where about 500 persons had gathered. He raised his hands and joined them to greet the congregation who returned the greeting in a similar manner. Just at that moment Nathuram Vinayek Godse pushed his way past Manubehn, whipped out a pistol and fired three shots. Mahatma Gandhi fell instantly with the words *He Ram* (Oh God!) on his lips.

The following speech is Nehru's broadcast to the nation announcing the death of Gandhi (30 January 1948, All India Radio tapes).

The Light Has Gone Out

1   Friends and Comrades,

       The light has gone out from our lives and there is
       darkness everywhere. And I do not know what to tell
       you and how to say it. Our beloved leader, Bapu, as we
5   called him, the Father of the Nation, is no more.
       Perhaps I am wrong to say that. Nevertheless, we will
       not see him again as we have seen him for these many
       years. We will not run to him for advice and seek
       solace from him; and that is a terrible blow, not to me
10   only, but to millions and millions in this country. And
       it is a little difficult to soften the blow by any advice
       that I or anyone else can give you.

The light has gone out, I said, and yet I was wrong. For
the light that shone in this country was no ordinary
15 light. The light that has illumined this country for these
many, many years will illumine this country for many
more years, and a thousand years later that light will
still be seen in this country, and the world will see it,
and it will give solace to innumerable hearts. For that
20 light represented something more than the immediate
present; it represented the living, eternal truths
reminding us of the right path, drawing us from error,
taking this ancient country to freedom.

All this has happened when there was so much more
25 for him to do. We could never, of course, do away with
him, we could never think that he was unnecessary, or
that he had done his task. But now, particularly, when
we are faced with so many difficulties, his not being
with us is a blow most terrible to bear.

30 A madman has put an end to his life, for I can only call
him mad who did it. And yet there has been enough
of poison spread in this country during the past years and
months, and this poison has had effect on people's
minds. We must face this poison, we must root out this
35 poison, and we must face all the perils that encompass
us, and face them, not madly or badly, but rather in the
way that our beloved teacher taught us to face them.
The first thing to remember now is that none of us dare
misbehave because we are angry. We have to behave
40 like strong, determined people, determined to face
all the perils that surround us, determined to carry out
the mandate that our great teacher and our great leader
has given us, remembering always that if, as I believe,
his spirit looks upon us and sees us, nothing would
45 displease his soul so much as to see that we have
indulged in unseemly behaviour or in violence. So we
must not do that. But that does not mean that we
should be weak, but rather that we should, in strength
and in unity, face all the troubles that are in front of us.
50 We must hold together, and all our petty troubles and
difficulties and conflicts must be ended in the face of
this great disaster. A great disaster is a symbol to us to
remember all the big things of life and forget the small
55 things of which we have thought too much. Now the time
has come again. As in his life, so in his death he has reminded
us of the big things of life, the living truth, and if we remember
that, then it will be well with us and well with India.

May I now tell you the programme for tomorrow? It
60   was proposed by some friends that Mahatmaji's body
should be embalmed for a few days to enable millions
of people to pay their last homage to him. But it was
his wish, repeatedly expressed, that no such thing
should happen, that this should not be done, that he
65   was entirely opposed to any embalming of his body,
and so we decided that we must follow his wishes in
this matter, however much others might have wished
otherwise.

And so the cremation will take place tomorrow in
70   Delhi city by the side of the Jumna river. Tomorrow
morning, or rather forenoon, about 11.30, the bier will
be taken out from Birla House and it will follow the
prescribed route and go to the Jumna river. The
cremation will take place there at about 4.00 p.m. The
75   exact place and route will be announced by radio and
the press.

People in Delhi who wish to pay their last homage
should gather along this route. I would not advise too
many of them to come to Birla House, but rather to
gather on both sides of this long route, from Birla
80   House to the Jumna river. And I trust that they will
remain there in silence without any demonstrations.
That is the best way and the most fitting way to pay
homage to the great soul. Also, tomorrow should be a
day of fasting and prayer for all of us.

85   Those who live elsewhere, out of Delhi and in other
parts of India, will no doubt also take such part as they
can in this last homage. For them also let this be a day
of fasting and prayer. And at the appointed time for
cremation, that is 4.00 p.m. tomorrow afternoon,
90   people should go to the river or to the sea and offer
prayers there. And while we pray, the greatest prayer
that we can offer is to take a pledge to dedicate
ourselves to the truth and to the cause for which this
great countryman of ours lived and for which he has
95   died. That is the best prayer that we can offer him and
his memory. That is the best prayer that we can offer to
India and ourselves. *Jai Hind.*

(Cited in Gopal, 1987, pp. 35–6)

(Note: *Jai Hind* roughly translated means 'Long live India'.)

3 Language play in English

Adrian Beard, based on the original chapter by Guy Cook

3.1 Introduction

In Chapter 2, I introduced ways of looking at language that uncovered its persuasive function. I noted there that one of the means by which advertisements often achieve their purpose is through playing with language. In this chapter I focus on the creative use of language, particularly on ways in which we play with aspects of the language in English.

Language play is a feature of many types of discourse, both spoken and written. It often occurs in casual conversation where it may serve practical purposes or seem to be more talking for talking's sake. It is also found in literature, one of the most highly valued of all discourse types, the paradigm case of language art.

Literary language is often described as creative. It generates imaginative fictional worlds, expresses original insights into the real world, and skilfully manipulates language to create patterns and new usages. Apparently, it is this creativity which earns it such high social status as a form of 'art'. Yet English and other languages are also used creatively or playfully in other, less exalted, more everyday discourses. For instance, the fact that the majority of graffiti (an interesting form of language art, which is discussed later) are linguistically unoriginal expressions of banal or narrow-minded ideas does not exclude the possibility that there are also linguistically skilful graffiti reflecting mental agility and imagination. It is important to keep in mind that any evaluation of language is ultimately subjective and often influenced by the context in which it is read.

3.2 The value of play

Play in child language learning is recognised as important because it allows children to learn the cultural ways and values of the society in which they live. Play with language is also a common feature of adult discourse and we come across it regularly in unremarkable settings. There is no reason to believe that adult language play is not also important. Play and creativity with language is not an additional extra to our relationships with the world and with other people – it is *part* of those relationships. I am not saying here that play must always have a serious purpose, because sometimes it does not, but it does seem that playing with language is an essential part of being human. As David Crystal (1998, p. 1) says, 'We play with language when we manipulate it as a source of enjoyment ... And if someone were to ask why we do it, the answer is simply: for fun'. Having fun, then, is integral to our daily lives and sense of well-being, and playing with language is an intrinsic part of that.

Guy Cook, in a book entitled *Language Play, Language Learning*, notes that humour can perform the social functions of 'aggression, rebellion, reconciliation, or solidarity' (Cook, 2000, p. 73). In addition to these he adds that psychoanalysis sees humour as 'the outcome of release', that a cognitive explanation sees humour as resulting from 'the perception of incongruity' and that a growing view of medical science is that humour can have beneficial effects on health (Cook, 2000, p. 73).

At first glance this may seem to contradict what Crystal says above. While Crystal is saying that we have fun when we play, Cook is saying that this fun serves social purposes. The list of purposes which Cook gives, though, suggests an extensive network of effects, and that not all of them are necessarily fun for all those concerned. We all know what it feels like to be the butt of someone else's joke, and the more others laugh, the more it hurts. This is taken a step further by satire, which is often aimed at politicians and well-known figures and has wide appeal. It is sometimes forgotten, though, that satirists are ridiculing real people whose feelings can also be hurt.

Different values placed on play can be observed in how the word is used in conjunction with others. While playing the violin, playing chess and playing Hamlet, for example, traditionally carry greater social prestige than playing in a rock band, playing snooker or playing in a soap, it is the latter activities which will deliver the greater potential financial rewards.

ACTIVITY 3.1

Allow about
10 minutes

Make a list of the activities you engage in which you might consider to be play. Is it possible for you to say what purpose these activities serve?

From your list, which of your activities have high social prestige in your society?

Look at the following list of activities, all of which involve aspects of language play. Try to rank them in terms of the prestige each activity carries.

- doing a wordsearch
- playing the game of Scrabble
- doing *The Times* crossword
- going to watch a Shakespeare play
- watching a television soap
- telling a joke at someone's expense at a party
- telling a joke at someone's expense in parliament
- reading a comic
- reading a Dickens novel
- writing graffiti in a public space
- writing advertising copy.

Comment

In the third part of Activity 3.1 it is likely that you have placed certain activities above others in terms of how they are viewed in your cultural and social context. You may yourself have ranked activities out of personal preference, but at the same time it is hard to deny the fact that some forms of play carry high prestige, some rather less prestige, some very little prestige, and some a rather ambiguous social position. So, for example, attempting *The Times* crossword, and other 'cryptic' crosswords in 'quality' newspapers, carries more prestige than finishing a wordsearch. Comics count less than novels, a television soap less than Shakespeare. Ridicule in parliament is almost certainly seen as clever by parliamentarians but may be viewed with more of a jaundiced eye by the general public. And although graffiti are seen by most as a public nuisance, some graffiti are enjoyed, providing they are not on our own property. Advertising holds a somewhat ambiguous position also – it can make us smile, but we tend not to value it culturally. What criteria are at work here in influencing how we perceive these activities? They are all based on using language creatively or playfully and yet some are considered literature or art and are socially sanctioned, while others are not. In the following sections, keep in mind this ambivalent relationship between creativity and playfulness, and literature and art.

3.3 Playing around us

Having given some background to the topic of language and play, I am now going to move on to look in more detail at some aspects of language play in everyday life, and at some of the ways in which it can be seen to work.

Cook (2000) separates the features of language play into three broad areas which are useful to the analysis of language and play in the sections below.

1   **Linguistic form**   This focuses on the look or sound (phonology) of words and includes, for example, patterning, repetition and emphasis.

2   **Semantics**   This focuses on meaning in language and includes, for instance, ambiguity and the inversion of language/reality.

3   **Pragmatics**   This focuses on the factors affecting language choices, such as the creation of solidarity, enjoyment and/or value.

Shop names

Take a walk down any high street and you will see commercial premises whose names involve a form of language play. This at once suggests that playing with language has a commercial aspect as well as a recreational one – in drawing attention to itself the business is also hoping to sell its products or services.

Not all categories of business, though, deem it suitable to give themselves a title which is playful. Lawyers and doctors, for example, see themselves as professionally above such practice – and indeed we would be unlikely to go to a medical practice called 'You've Got a Nerve', or a lawyer's called 'Arguments R Us'. This suggests that where playful naming does take place, there is a certain element of risk. Do we see the business as serious enough to warrant our trade?

There are certain types of business, therefore, that are more likely to have playful names than others. One such is florists: in London there is the wonderfully named florist 'Flowerstalk', for example. Here the linguistic form has been manipulated to create a word with semantic ambiguity, and with the consequent pragmatic effect of making us stop, consider and probably smile. The Yell.com website (2006), meanwhile, offers the following on its pages for florists in Yorkshire and Humberside:

> Double Dutch
>
> Daisy Chain
>
> Fleur de Lys
>
> Floraganza
>
> Forever Green
>
> Forget-Me-Not
>
> Garden of Eden
>
> Just to Say
>
> Secret Garden
>
> White Rose Florists

The semantics of these names is the most significant factor in making them playful and memorable. Four of the names involve the actual name of a flower: 'Daisy Chain', 'Fleur de Lys', 'Forget-Me-Not' and 'White Rose', yet each works in a slightly different way. 'Daisy Chain' involves reference to a childhood practice of making a chain out of small wild daisies, certainly not the sort sold in the shop. 'Fleur de Lys' uses the exotic (to the British) sound of the French word for the stylised flower used in heraldic designs, thought to be either a lily or an iris. 'White Rose' has a cultural meaning that will be recognised in Yorkshire, but not necessarily elsewhere, as the white rose is the emblem of the county of Yorkshire. 'Forget-Me-Not' both names a flower and the reason for buying flowers – it conveys the meaning that the giver wants the recipient of the flowers to remember them.

'Garden of Eden' and 'Secret Garden' can be placed together, not only because of their use of the word 'garden', but for their literary associations (The Bible and the novel by Frances Hodgson Burnett). 'Floraganza' is an example of word creation, a portmanteau word formed from flora and extravaganza. 'Double Dutch' is perhaps the hardest to explain satisfactorily. To talk double Dutch is not to make sense, but here the fact that there is a well-known expression, and that it is memorably alliterative, is enough to build upon the association of The Netherlands and flower growing.

Headline news

News-stands provide another place in the public arena where language play is on clear display. Headlines clamour with each other for prominence, and although it is not just linguistic play which attempts to capture attention, it is frequently one aspect of the process. Indeed, there seem to be times when the front page story, traditionally the story which carries most significance on any given day, is chosen because it allows prominent word play, rather than because it is of importance as such. So, for example, the *Sun*, on 28 August 2003, reporting an art theft, came up with the headline LEONARDO DA PINCHI which plays with linguistic form and semantics. This joke, based upon a sound similarity between the name of the painter, Leonardo da Vinci, and 'pinch', a slang expression meaning steal, proved enough for an otherwise unspectacular story to make the front page. The sound similarity echoed in the repetition of the (inch) sound, is not a perfect sound match, but paradoxically this imperfection, this sense of it being a bad joke, seems to make the headline more memorable. It draws attention to itself through making us want to groan, through the play being self-conscious.

There are some legendary headlines which may be apocryphal, such as SITE FOR SORE EYES, referring to a new eye hospital building which was branded as ugly; and THE SHAMING OF THE SCREW, based on the Shakespeare play entitled *The Taming of the Shrew*. The headline refers to a *screw* (a slang word for a prison officer) being arrested for fraud.

It is worth stressing that playing with language can be as much a feature of so-called quality papers, as it is for their racier rivals. The following headlines appeared in *The Times* on 21 February 2005:

> CASINO BILL OPPONENTS CANNOT CALL OUR BLUFF, SAY MINISTERS
>
> COE HAS SECRET PLAN TO WIN RACE WITH LAST-MINUTE BURST OF SPEED (reference to the London Olympic bid and the Olympic gold medal winner Sebastian Coe)
>
> AROUND THE WORLD IN 80 HOURS (a solo flying record attempt)
>
> BELL MAY APPEAL TO ENGLAND (reference to a rugby player being picked to play for England)
>
> BOLTON STILL ALIVE BUT FULHAM'S CUP RUN HAS CEASED TO BE (Bolton 1, Fulham 0, in the FA Cup)

On the same day, meanwhile, the *Daily Mirror* had the following:

> HOUND THEM (anti-hunt protesters called for stricter laws against hunting)
>
> FOURGONE CONCLUSION (Chelsea football club were beaten and so missed the chance to win four trophies)

WATCH OUT (story suggesting that bombs could be hidden in expensive watches)

GREGORY'S GOAL (Gregory Vignal scored for Rangers football club against Celtic in the Glasgow derby match)

BUYS V GIRLS (story suggesting that men and women shop in different ways)

The traditional view of newspapers has been that the so-called quality papers, as represented by *The Times* here, provide a more complex and sophisticated form of reading than the popular papers. While this may well be true in many ways, these headlines, admittedly selected at random, indicate that the *Mirror*'s headlines have an economy of language which is in its way more subtle. They are ironically reminiscent of a *Times* crossword clue. So, for example, FOURGONE CONCLUSION works in a number of ways:

1   It echoes the well-known saying 'foregone conclusion'.

2   *Fourgone* means that the chance to win *four* trophies is now *gone*.

3   The word *conclusion* means that it is the end of Chelsea's participation in the cup.

In other words, the headline, in just two words, combines phonological and semantic play, while at the same time drawing upon the reader's knowledge of the well-known saying. This partial dependence upon prior knowledge can be described as being part of an intertextual process – by relying on readers' prior knowledge there can be no guarantee that the *full* meaning is going to be accessed by all readers. This is even more the case when the references are cultural rather than merely linguistic, as in the headline GREGORY'S GOAL. This is a reference to a film (*Gregory's Girl*) about football, set in Glasgow. The headline is therefore especially apt and clever as it is referring to a real player in a Glasgow football match.

The Times' headline BOLTON STILL ALIVE BUT FULHAM'S CUP RUN HAS CEASED TO BE takes this notion of shared references between text and reader to a real extreme – so much so that the opening of the article had to make it clear just what was being referred to. The source of the headline is a comedy sketch about a dead parrot which appeared in the BBC television comedy series *Monty Python's Flying Circus*. The sketch notionally takes place in Bolton, and in it a customer claims that the parrot he has been sold is dead, a fact which he repeats using numerous synonyms such as *ceased to be*. The game being played in Bolton, and Fulham losing the game, is enough to provide ammunition for the headline, but arguably it is all rather laboured. How many people would get the joke, and to what extent can losing a game be compared to dying?

A much more succinct headline appeared in the *Sun* on 23 February 2005 with reference to the Queen's decision not to attend the wedding of Prince Charles and Camilla Parker-Bowles. THE LADY IS NOT FOR TURNING UP gives a clear meaning while playing with the title of Christopher Fry's play *The Lady's not for Burning*. This reference may have been arcane on its own, but the fact that former British Prime Minister, Margaret Thatcher, had famously described herself as 'not for turning' means that the phrase is likely to be known by many. The shift from 'turning' to the colloquial *turning up* is especially pointed, saying something about the royal family as well as being humorous.

On the same day the *Sun* also carried a story about a vacuum cleaner with the headline WINDBAG. The cleaner was to be fitted with a microchip which would allow it to 'talk' to its owner when it needed emptying. The headline is playful in a number of ways. A windbag is someone who talks too much, and there is the implication here, as there often is with technology stories, that technology is going too far. At the same time the vacuum cleaner in question made its name by not having a bag which needed emptying – and most readers would know this. This headline, given no particular prominence in the paper, seems to sum up the creative play that can be seen in the popular press. There are, no doubt, many reasons why one can be critical of the press, but we also need to acknowledge that they bring to their readers a sense of fun. It is likely too that readers are sophisticated enough to know this; part of the fun of reading popular newspapers is the way they play with words and ideas. However, the majority of such journalistic play is ephemeral and quickly forgotten, unless researchers happen to see such headlines and keep a copy.

ACTIVITY 3.2

Allow about
1 hour

This section has looked at some public and frequently encountered examples of language play. Now collect examples of your own, from such areas as shop names, business names, newspaper headlines and advertisements, and, ideally, share them with others. Try to explain the nature of the play being used for each example and consider the cultural knowledge that is required for the play to work.

3.4 Song

As a form of language art, song falls somewhere between poetry, with its fixed written texts, and an oral performance art such as stand-up comedy with its variable routines. A song may come into existence through performance and never be written down by its author. The representation of the text of a song may also be modified by the way the words are sung, or by the way they are musically accompanied. A song may be sung for generations and considered a work of art or soon forgotten and considered of little consequence.

As an introduction to this section on song, I will look in detail at a comic song. Many songs show aspects of play in the way in which they are constructed, often using linguistic patterning such as repetition or rhyme. Comic songs also draw on semantics, particularly ambiguity in language, and pragmatics with elements that are designed to shock, amuse or intrigue the listener. As with all comedy, the meanings intended by a comic song rely on shared understandings – listeners will need to recognise allusions if they are to get the joke.

ACTIVITY 3.3

Allow about
30 minutes

The following song appeared in an episode of the BBC comic sketch show *Monty Python's Flying Circus* (1970). Written by Eric Idle, himself an Australian, the song was 'performed' by members of an imaginary Australian university philosophy department. Broadly speaking, the song is an ironic take on various aspects of Australian culture, or at least how that culture is often represented.

First, make notes on the patternings of language use that are evident here. Then try to explain how inversions of expected meanings, and the representation of national stereotypes, contribute to the humour. In both cases it will help if you can discuss your findings with someone else. (If you want to hear the song, it is available on a number of websites. Try http://www.library.adelaide.edu.au/guide/hum/philosophy/philos_song.html [accessed 11 November 2005].)

The Philosophers' Drinking Song

Immanuel Kant was a real pissant
Who was very rarely stable.

Heidegger, Heidegger was a boozy beggar
Who could think you under the table.

David Hume could out-consume
Wilhelm Friedrich Hegel,

And Wittgenstein was a beery swine
Who was just as schloshed as Schlegel.

There's nothing Nietzsche couldn't teach ya
'Bout the raising of the wrist.
Socrates, himself, was permanently pissed.

John Stuart Mill, of his own free will,
On half a pint of shandy was particularly ill.

Plato, they say, could stick it away –
Half a crate of whisky every day.

Aristotle, Aristotle was a bugger for the bottle.
Hobbes was fond of his dram,

And René Descartes was a drunken fart.
'I drink, therefore I am.'

Yes, Socrates, himself, is particularly missed,
A lovely little thinker,
But a bugger when he's pissed.

(Eric Idle)

Comment

One obvious set of patternings is phonological – as you would expect when words are allied to music for the overall effect. There are rhymes at the end of lines (usually lines 2 and 4) and there are rhymes within the lines (lines 1 and 3). The three-line verses act as a sort of chorus, with the same sound (*wrist*, *pissed*, *missed*) being repeated. In most cases the internal rhymes are a philosopher's name being rhymed with another word (*Kant*, *pissant*), but a variation on this comes with Plato. Here, inclusion of the otherwise unnecessary *they say* is used to create the possibility of the rhyme. Note also that Eric Idle sometimes uses the philosophers' full names to exploit the rhythmic possibilities, and sometimes does not.

In terms of semantic fields (patternings involving meaning), the most obvious patterning involves the endless repetition of references to alcoholic drinks and their effects. These range from *boozy*, *beery*, *dram* to the more unusual *raising of the wrist*. It can clearly be seen, though, that the need to maintain the song's structure is partly determining which expressions will be used.

If we now look at the inversions of cultural norms, perhaps the most obvious is that a university philosophy department should sing a song together, let alone a song about drinking. (This incongruity seems to be recognised by philosophy departments themselves. Search the World Wide Web and you find that a number of sites about this song are from philosophy departments.) You might have noticed, too, although you need to know about philosophy to get the joke, that at some points in the song, it is not just the philosopher's name that is referred to, but also his ideas – Mill and his free will is one example, and the changing of Descartes' famous *I think, therefore I am* to *I drink, therefore I am* is another.

The national stereotype of the Australian presented here is of a man (they are all men who sing the song, and all are named Bruce) who has little grasp of the finer points of culture, who makes free with conventional English usage, and whose main interest is in drinking. The fact that many promoters of this stereotype are themselves Australian suggests that, unlike some stereotyping, it is managed with a knowing sense of irony.

What we have seen, then, in this comic song, is a number of contributory and interlocking elements. Some of these are compositional: the effects of rhythm and rhymes which give the song its generic identity; the comic effects produced by the juxtaposition of sounds and stresses. These effects, though, depend upon the subject matter, and the way the normal seriousness of philosophy is inverted by its key players being represented as drinkers. And then there are the cultural references to Australians which add a further layer of meaning – provided the reader/listener understands them, of course.

ACTIVITY 3.4

Read 'Songs in Singlish' by Marie Tan (Reading A), which is a linguistic analysis of the songs of Dick Lee, a Singaporean songwriter and performer who uses the varieties of English heard in Singapore to comic and satirical effect. The 'Singlish' referred to in the reading is a vernacular form of English which includes elements of other languages used in Singapore (particularly Mandarin Chinese), and SSE (Standard Singaporean English) is the variety normally used in print and formal speech in Singapore.

As you read through it, bear in mind the following questions:
- Lee's songs are in English; but does it seem that his intended audience is English speakers everywhere?
- How does Lee ensure that the Singlish elements of his lyrics are represented not only on record, but also on the printed page?

Comment

Tan notes that Lee uses features of Singlish (pronunciation and vocabulary) to represent aspects of Singapore's culture. Much of the humour of his songs appears to depend on 'insider knowledge' – not only of linguistic variation, but also of the cultural practices, images and stereotypes which are a familiar part of life in Singapore. As playful uses of English, then, Lee's songs appear to be relatively inaccessible in their full intended meaning to English speakers outside Singapore. As I mentioned earlier, language play often depends upon the reader's prior knowledge and for this reason comic songs such as those discussed by Tan do not always travel well.

You will also have seen that Lee is able to represent his Singlish lyrics through modified spellings – a technique used by many other writers with an interest in oral vernacular tradition.

As words can be written and music scored, a song can be abstracted from both singer and situation. It may even begin life on paper and generate many performances in many places, none more authoritative than another. Or it may fall somewhere between the two extremes. There are songs which are valued independently of singer and singing, although good performance may be needed too. These are more like poetry: texts with potential for performance. On the other hand, there are songs where singer and performance seem essential to their value (some of the songs of Elvis Presley or of the French singer Edith Piaf, for example), and the words alone can seem quite lame.

The advent of rock and roll in the mid 1950s initiated a major new departure for popular music, one whose influence continues worldwide to this day. The growing international appeal and influence of rock and roll (and its progeny) have a close relationship with the spread of English as a world language; one of the common vehicles for carrying English (mainly US English) into the lives of young people the world over has been the popular song.

In the 1950s limited technology and restricted media access made early rock music intimately tied to live performance. The record was still a relatively new phenomenon and in many ways was regarded as a substitute for presence at a live performance in which the audience would be actively involved, dancing, clapping and applauding: a relationship captured in Chuck Berry's song 'Round and Round' from the late 1950s.

Round and Round

Oh it sounds so sweet
Got to take me a chance,
Rose out of my seat
Just had to dance,
Started moving my feet
Well and clapping my hands.
Well the joint started rocking,
Going round and round,
Yeah reeling and a rocking,
What a crazy sound.
Well they never stopped rocking
Till the moon went down.

(Chuck Berry)

With this emphasis on song as sound, text could often seem unimportant, at times even dispensing with conventional language and meaning altogether, creating or stringing words together just to keep singing, as in the Little Richard song 'Tutti Frutti' which begins:

Wo bop a loo bam a lop bam bam

From the 1970s onwards, changes and advances in technology brought performance to the fore, with an emphasis upon the visual, and less interest in lyrics. The growing importance of the 'pop video', often employing elaborate computerised images, and the immense investment of money and technology in ever more dazzling stage shows (also recorded and distributed on video), encouraged the presentation of songs as multifaceted mixtures of dance, film, drama, music and singing that were quite different from the raw rock and roll of the 1950s. Despite their considerable differences, both the early rock bands and many contemporary performers share an emphasis on song as performance in which words are only part of a larger whole.

Let us consider in some detail '(What A) Wonderful World', as recorded by Sam Cooke in the late 1950s. The apparently simple words and melody, and the repetitive structure of the verses, ensure that the song is both memorable and hummable.

(What A) Wonderful World

Don't know much about history,
Don't know much biology,
Don't know much about a science book,
Don't know much about the French 'I took';

But I do know that I love you,
And I know that if you love me too,
What a wonderful world this would be.

Don't know much about geography,
Don't know much trigonometry,
Don't know much about algebra,
Don't know what a slide rule is for;

But I do know one and one is two,
And if this one could be with you,
What a wonderful world this would be.

Now I don't claim to be an A student,
But I'm trying to be;
For maybe by being an A student baby,
I can win your love for me.

Don't know much about history,
Don't know much biology,
Don't know much about a science book,
Don't know much about the French 'I took';

But I do know that I love you,
And I know that if you love me too,
What a wonderful world this would be.

La ta ta ta ta ta history,
Mmm mm mm mm biology,
Wa wa cha cha cha cha cha science book,
Mm mm mmm mmm mmm mm French 'I took' yeah,

But I do know that I love you,
And I know that if you love me too,
What a wonderful world this would be.

(Sam Cooke, Lou Adler and Herb Alpert)

This is a recording where words and music seem largely a vehicle for a gifted individual rendering. Released in the sound-oriented 1950s and re-released (with powerful advertising images superimposed, see Figure 3.1) in the vision-oriented 1980s, this song seems the epitome of the performance-oriented recording. In such circumstances it might seem appropriate for words to be subordinated to music and performance, and not to interfere with the overall effect by being too striking. Semantically, the words of this song, because they plead sincerity over cleverness, seem ideally suited to this role. They assert the simplicity of the singer and, iconically, they seem to be simple themselves. The song is endearing precisely because it eschews the threat inherent in assertions of cleverness. The repeated structures of the verses, the clichéd declaration of love, seem to bear this out.

Figure 3.1 Advertisement for Levi jeans

And yet these words, without foregrounding the fact, are far more accomplished and complex than at first appears. The lyrics depict and alternate between two different value systems: the public world of the school,

where personal worth is measured by knowledge and assessed by grades
(A, B, C, etc.); and the private world of love, where worth is measured by
sincerity and depth of feeling. The two worlds are incompatible and in
conflict. The sweetheart addressee is faced with a simple plea: I'm not
successful in the world of school, but I love you, so please love me. Right
at the heart of the song, however, are two devices, one metaphorical and
one phonological, which bring the two separate worlds together through
language play:

> Don't know much about algebra,
> Don't know what a slide rule is for;

> But I do know one and one is two,
> And if this one could be with you,
> What a wonderful world this would be.

Here, something from the world of school (1 + 1 = 2) becomes a metaphor for
the world of love (lonely individual + lonely individual = happy couple), as
though the singer sees images of his passion even when looking at the most
passionless schoolbooks which are the cause of his failure. The equation
1 + 1 = 2 is also a common-sense fact, reliable and constant like the singer,
contrasting with the dangerous sophistries of education. All in all, it is an
ingenious and striking metaphorical conceit (a poetic figure of speech, often
associated with metaphysical poetry, that establishes an elaborate parallel),
which makes a play to win over by the very intellectual ingenuity that the
singer explicitly denies he possesses. It offers a bridge between the two
separate worlds, creating a harmony represented in the alliteration and
consonance of the line:

> *Wh*at a *wonderful world* this *would* be

This harmony through sound patterning continues in the four lines following
the second refrain. If the singer is not an A student, perhaps he is a B student,
and the sounds of these letters (/eɪ/ and /biː/) occur in stressed syllables
throughout the lines:

>   /eɪ/   /biː/ /eɪ/
> Now I don't cl<u>ai</u>m to <u>be</u> an <u>A</u> student

>   /biː/
> But I'm trying to <u>be</u>

>   /eɪ//biː/   /biː/   /eɪ/   /eɪ//biː/
> For m<u>ay</u><u>be</u> by <u>being</u> an <u>A</u> student <u>ba</u> <u>by</u>

creating an alternating pattern of these sounds:

> abab ab baab

as harmonious as the metaphorical *one and one* or the alliterative *wonderful world*, or the melody, rhyme scheme and balanced structure of the song itself.

Such analyses of pop lyrics as this are often perceived as pretentious, overdone or simply 'reading too much into it', and it may be argued (with some justification) that millions of people have listened to and enjoyed this song on many occasions without subjecting it to any structural analysis of the patterns and parallels described above. It may also be argued (though without any hard evidence) that the three songwriters (Cooke, Adler and Alpert) are unlikely to have been conscious of, or to have deliberately deployed, the symmetrical and punning sound alterations or the complex and disarming *one and one* metaphor. If this lack of awareness by both the senders and the receivers of the song is actually the case, then it seems to follow that the structures had no existence before being described and were not therefore part of the song. This reasoning has some force, but it also has two important implications which cannot be avoided if it is adopted. First, if it is applied to the interpretation of songs, there is no reason why it should not also apply to the interpretation of high literature such as poetry, where stylisticians often point out intricate linguistic features of which appreciative readers, and very probably the poet too, had no conscious awareness. Second, if we begin with the premise that the words of this song give pleasure, and investigate why this may be, the argument against analyses has to insist that the causes of pleasure must always be conscious and that the mind can neither produce nor perceive patterns subconsciously. In the case of language this seems to be manifestly untrue, as we are all constantly producing and receiving phonologically and grammatically structured utterances without any conscious access to the rules which govern them, and it may well be that the pleasure listeners feel when hearing the words of this song – like the sense of 'rightness' that the composers may well have felt when they put words and music together – derives from the subconscious perception of exactly the kind of patterns described above.

You must reach your own conclusions, but the problem is a useful one for helping us to focus on what exactly we do believe about how language works, and why certain uses of it are experienced as beautiful and enjoyable.

Meaning in '(What A) Wonderful World' is achieved through a combination of words, music and performance. Words are less readily detached from the music than they are in the case of some 1960s songs or, more recently, in the 1990s and beyond in rap. It is not that the words lack complexity – far from it – but they are not foregrounded: they work in conjunction with, rather than independently of, their nonverbal context, and their meanings are enriched by it.

In the next section I look at another discourse type that is highly dependent on its context – graffiti.

3.5 Graffiti

Allow about
10 minutes

Which of the following do you think are graffiti? What factors influence your judgement? If they are not graffiti, what kind of writing are they?

1   Who's afraid of Virginia Woolf?
2   Glory to God in the High St.
3   When a man has married a wife, he finds out whether
    Her knees and elbows are only glued together.
4   Even such is Time, which takes in trust
    Our youth, our joys, and all we have,
    And pays us but with age and dust;
    Who in the dark and silent grave,
    When we have wandered all our ways,
    Shuts up the story of our days;
    And from which earth and grave and dust,
    The Lord shall raise me up I trust.
5   Letting rip a fart –
    It doesn't make you laugh
    When you live alone.

Comment

If by graffiti we mean any illicit writing in public places on surfaces such as walls, (1) and (2) are graffiti. Item (3) is a poem by William Blake. There is a tradition (not, unfortunately, supported by historical evidence) that (4) was carved with a diamond ring by Sir Walter Raleigh on the window of his cell the night before his execution; if this were true, though undoubtedly a poem, the piece would also, technically speaking, be graffiti. Item 5 is the translation of an eighteenth-century Japanese *senryu* – a kind of poem similar to the better known seventeen-syllable *haiku* (Bowans, 1964).

If you were misled, this exercise illustrated two very important points. The first is that graffiti are not reliably identified as such by their language or subject matter, but rather by their physical situation and realisation. The second is that their low status in part derives from the authors we assume to have written them. A knighted Renaissance explorer-scholar such as Sir Walter Raleigh is not a prototypical graffiti writer.

Because they can damage and disfigure, graffiti are regarded as antisocial and illegal. Many are objectionable in subject matter, banal and clumsily expressed. Yet there is no discourse type which offers such an opportunity for the disinterested, individual voice. Here is language anonymous, unsolicited, unrewarded and uninfluenced by reactions, repercussions or payment. It is significant that Sir Walter Raleigh is supposed to have turned to this genre when he was deprived of power and privilege.

Etymologically, the word 'graffiti' (from the Italian *graffiare*, to scratch), like the word 'literature' (from the Latin *littera*, a letter), is intimately connected to the act of writing. Yet whereas, in general, writing allows the abstraction of a message from a particular situation or realisation, for graffiti the place and circumstances of production are definitive. Graffiti are necessarily written illicitly on a surface in a communal or public place (bridge, bus shelter, wall, cell, school desk, toilet door).

Many of the effects in graffiti are only evident in writing, creating puns by using phrases that are **homophones** (words that sound alike), but not **homographs** (words that look alike). This technique seems to play off the tensions between orality and literacy, and although graffiti are by definition written rather than spoken, they often seem to use writing in a way which perpetuates a rebellious oral tradition, challenging the authority of the establishment by humorously and deliberately abusing the rules of writing. Whereas the writing system tends to reduce all dialects to one standard written form, graffiti often orthologically represent non-standard forms. Taken away from their situation and reproduced legitimately in a book like this, therefore, although the linguistic form and the meaning remain the same, they lose their edge and, in a sense, cease to be graffiti. This situation-bound nature explains the futility of attempts to divert graffiti away from the valued surfaces that they disfigure, to specially provided ones where they do no harm.

From data collected in Germany and Britain, Blume (1985) concluded that the degree to which the chosen surface is enclosed or open correlates with subject matter. She observed that the most enclosed spaces (toilet cubicles) yield the highest numbers of graffiti concerning sex, and are addressed by a single individual either to no one in particular or to another single interlocutor, while the most public places (such as bridges) yield graffiti about politics or religion addressed to society in general by the (self-appointed) representative of an interest group within it. But is this always the case?

ACTIVITY 3.6

Read the extract from 'Social issues on walls: graffiti in university lavatories' by O.G. Nwoye (Reading B). This reading looks at political and more personal graffiti dialogues written in the 1980s in Nigeria. This, as Nwoye points out, was a turbulent time in Nigeria, but also in South Africa where the apartheid regime was still in place and Nelson Mandela was still in jail. You will see that Nwoye observes that, in situations where expression of political opinion is banned or may lead to persecution, it is often political graffiti which are written in the safety of enclosed spaces.

Many graffiti are particular in that they express a single wish, opinion or thought by a single individual, sometimes quite specific in reference. In *Tracey go out with me* (written on a house wall in Leeds in England), both *Tracey* and *me* presumably refer to individuals.

Nigel Rees is well known in the UK as an author and broadcaster on the topic of quotations and graffiti. An analysis of his early collections of graffiti (Rees, 1980; 1981) shows that the average length of each item is between seven and eight words. None is less than two words, but few are more than eighteen words long.

It might be argued that it is *only* simplistic ideas that can be expressed in so few words. Yet, surprisingly, some of the best graffiti achieve their impact not by intensifying or enriching an individual voice, but by deploying two contradictory voices at once. *Glory to God in the High St* (see Activity 3.5) is a case in point. Here, through the inspired deletion of a single letter from the Christmas angels' message to the shepherds ('Glory to God in the highest', Matthew, 2:14), the writer invokes simultaneously, and thus juxtaposes, both this original text and the new one derived from it, thus satirising the distortion of the original Christmas angels' message by the commercialism of its contemporary celebration, for *the High St* is a current metonym for the buying and selling of goods. This effect depends upon the message being written down, as the two texts that are simultaneously suggested in the graffiti are closer graphologically than phonologically.

Graphology	Phonology
High St	/haɪ striːt/
Highest	/haɪəst/

(Note here how explaining the message takes much more space than the message itself.)

Such extraordinary compression of meaning is rare but not unique. The generation of multiple meanings, rich connotations and associative resonances through very few words is implicitly applauded as a virtue in academic criticisms of literature by such critical movements as New Criticism. Yet because we are encouraged and trained to perceive multiple meanings in poetry, we can often overlook them in 'lower' discourse types such as graffiti.

ACTIVITY 3.7

Allow about
I hour

Over the next couple of weeks, note down any graffiti which you encounter, in both open and enclosed places. Classify them by topic, place, probable sender, implied receiver, and any notable linguistic features such as dialect, misspelling, unusual grammar, etc. How many different types can you identify?

The most common evocation of two contradictory voices is created through a particular sub-genre of graffiti: additions to public notices and to other graffiti. Here the authority, sentimentality, prejudice or pomposity of a message is subverted by being incorporated as a part of a longer one, the whole of which contradicts the original. Consider the following examples (from Rees, 1980 and 1981).

Addition to a notice:

> Warning. Passengers are requested not to cross the lines
> *It takes hours to untangle them afterwards*

Addition to a book:

> To my father and mother (dedication in law book)
> *Thanks Son, it's just what we wanted*

Additions to graffiti:

> Are you a man?
> *No I'm a frayed knot*

> Ave Maria
> *Don't mind if I do*

> Women like simple things
> *Like men*

The wit, inventiveness and effectiveness of such criticism through calm and controlled irony are striking.

ACTIVITY 3.8

Allow about
30 minutes

The discussion of graffiti so far has focused on the verbal elements of such texts. In fact, though, much graffiti is multimodal, relying on a combination of the visual and the verbal for the full effect. Look at Figures 3.2 and 3.3 and write notes on how these texts combine the visual and verbal to make potentially interesting meanings. What does the reader of these texts need to know for the meanings to 'work'?

Figure 3.2
Multimodal
graffiti 1

Figure 3.3
Multimodal
graffiti 2

3.6 The slip of the pun

In the last section and in the subsection on newspaper headlines in Section 3.3, I looked at language play which relies to a large extent on the use of puns – meaningless coincidences of form (Brown, 1991, p. 133). Puns can involve playing with meaning, playing with sound and playing with appearance. Here are three examples of crossword clues, all with the solution 'open'.

> The university which never shuts (meaning)
>
> O! write to this university (sound)
>
> Nope. Confused? A university here (appearance – an anagram of 'nope')

These demonstrate the exploitation of language form over language meaning, which is a common feature of newspaper cryptic crossword clues. Solving crosswords is a playful activity, but solving cryptic crosswords, in particular, can also be viewed as a proof of one's intelligence and skill with language.

All languages contain coincidences of form, and the punning which is enabled by this is probably a feature of all cultures. Up to now, the examples I have looked at have all been monolingual, based on English alone, but there are also cross-linguistic puns. Below are a couple of examples of these that play on the fact that Nair is a typical surname for the Malayalees (the people of Kerala in India):

> What do you call a rich Malayalee?
> Milaya Nair (millionaire)
>
> What do you call a handsome Malayalee?
> Debu Nair (debonair)

Bilingual speakers can play on the fact that a word in English has a similar form to (but different meaning from) a word in another language. Because there is no meaning in such coincidences, punning focuses attention away from meaning and on to form, but quite why it is so popular and so widespread deserves some investigation.

In contemporary Western society, punning is kept at arms' length; people frequently apologise for punning (by saying 'no pun intended') and the ritual response to puns is a groan, even when their wit is also simultaneously enjoyed or admired. Puns are regarded as childish trivia, unsuitable for serious subjects or discourses, and in a sense all puns, even good ones, are bad puns. While other forms of word play that force incongruous juxtapositions of semantically separate concepts (rhyme, alliteration, metaphor, irony) receive serious and respectful attention in literary criticism, punning is largely ignored or scathingly dismissed.

Opposition to, if not fear of, puns has a long and respectable history. Aristotle saw them as a danger to philosophy (Ulmer, 1988); Dr Johnson regarded them as 'the fatal Cleopatra' which spoiled Shakespeare's plays (Redfern, 1984); the literary critic William Empson described them as not 'manly' (Ahl, 1988). Yet this rationalist disquiet and disapproval, the downgrading of puns to the realm of childish play, is in no way a universal or historically consistent phenomenon. The oracles of ancient Greece used puns as prophecy, and classical Roman poetry is often structurally dependent upon puns. In the Bible, the verse which provides the authority for the Roman Catholic belief in the apostolic succession, Christ's charge to Peter:

> Thou art Peter, and upon this rock I shall build my church.

> (Matthew 16:18)

is a pun in the original Greek, where the Greek name 'Petra' also means 'rock' (the pun survives in French, where both Peter and rock are *pierre*). Yet it is hardly a light or culturally unimportant utterance. Shakespeare was a dedicated punster, not only for comic but also for tragic purpose, though this is often obscured by etymological change and needs explication by glossaries and notes. An example is Hamlet's cry:

> Is thy union here?

> (*Hamlet*, V. iii. 340)

when he realises that his mother has drunk wine laced with a poisoned pearl (a *union*) by the man she has joined in *union* or marriage, thus bringing about her *union* with death. Here a pun compresses meanings and emotions in a powerful and poignant manner. The pearl was an established symbol for the soul, and Gertrude's life is slipping away as the pearl dissolves in the wine, just as her virtue (in Hamlet's view) was destroyed by her intoxication with her brother-in-law Claudius. Although, since the eighteenth century, puns have often been treated by critics as slips of taste (or even of the pen), there has never been a time when the 'best' writers have avoided them. In modern(ist) times they have resurfaced with a vengeance in high literature and art, visually as well as verbally in surrealist poetry and painting, most notably in James Joyce's *Finnegan's Wake*. In the twentieth century, puns also gained respectability from their importance in psychoanalysis. Freud (1952 [1905]) saw unintentional puns as reflections of people's covert thoughts and motivations. In some cultures, puns have traditionally been given higher status (they are regarded, for example, as a navigator of thought in Zen Buddhism – see Redfern, 1984, p. 146).

ACTIVITY 3.9

Allow about
10 minutes

The pun features in many advertisements. Below, the text of the advertisement from Figure 2.7 in Chapter 2 is reproduced. How is a pun central to the point being made?

"I've been
shuoetd at,
spat at and had
cmomnets mdae
aobut the coulor
of my sikn …
I shuodln't hvae
to put up wtih
tihs knid of
aubse"

It doesn't make sense

Six rail staff are physically assaulted on trains or at stations every day just for doing their job.

We will not tolerate verbal or physical attacks on our staff.

They will be given total support in any prosecution.

Help us to ensure a safer environment for everyone.

If you see anyone assaulting staff or passengers, call 0800 40 50 40 making a note of date, time and location.

Comment

The main pun here is *It doesn't make sense* which involves noting the double meaning in the phrase. In one way the words do not make sense because the letters are not in the right order (although of course they do make sense, in that on seeing the advertisement we rearrange them in our heads). In another, and more important, way, though, we are meant to consider the colloquial meaning of the phrase – if an action does not make sense, this is because it is without any rational explanation, which is the only way to explain the appalling treatment of the railway staff.

Why are puns so controversial and why do they arouse such widely differing responses: of pleasure and a sense of profundity on the one hand, and of contempt and derision on the other? Why do they figure so prominently in the popular press and in the other discourse types I have been examining? Perhaps some insight may be gained by examining particular instances more thoroughly and contrasting a modern light-hearted use of a pun with more serious uses in the past. In his excellent book *Puns*, Walter Redfern gives (without further comment) the following example of a modern punning joke:

> A man always bought his wife her favourite flowers, anemones, for her birthday. One year, he arrived at the flower shop late, and, as they had run out of anemones, he bought her some greenery. When she received the bouquet she commented: 'With fronds like these, who needs anemones?'

(Redfern, 1984)

This is a classic punning joke, using the slightest phonemic substitution and addition to yield virtual homophony. It is also a story in which the pun is the point itself, rather than some additional embellishment or decoration. If, therefore, the reader does not like puns, or does not like this particular pun, then they will not like the whole story, for there is nothing else there: the pun does not emerge from a fictional world; the fictional world is constructed in order to create the pun. If we reconstruct the creation of this story, it is very likely to have proceeded backwards, beginning with the set utterance 'With friends like these, who needs enemies', proceeding to the spoof substitutions, and then creating the man, his wife and her birthday in order to lead to the conclusion. Why are her favourite flowers anemones rather than tulips? Why had the flower shop run out of them? Why did it have only greenery instead of, say, daffodils? The answer to all these questions is clear: to enable the punch line to take the form it does. This illustrates both the nature of the pun and its disruptive anarchic power. For not only does the composition of the story run backwards, but the whole functioning of language is thrown into reverse. Meanings are there to create forms rather than forms to create meanings. The orthodox view in linguistics, reflecting both popular wisdom and the standard outlook of a rationalist scientistic world view, is that language serves to represent the world. Within a language, signifiers ('anemones', 'friends') have an arbitrary but socially conventional and shared relationship to concepts (Saussure, 1960 [1916], p. 16), which in turn represent both the external and internal world. This enables language to perform, in a fairly orderly way, its main functions of conveying information – the **ideational function** – and the establishing of social relationships – the **interpersonal function** (Halliday, 1973, pp. 22–46).

The code is there to serve a purpose, not to take on a life of its own. There are, however, confusions, crossovers and coincidences within the code. **Homonyms** (both homographs, words which look the same and homophones, words which sound the same) – the stuff of puns – are obvious instances of such crossovers, though the sense intended is usually clear from the context. If it is not, clarification is made by the sender or sought by the receiver of the message, all in an orderly manner. In the story above, however, this is overturned. Confusion and meaningless coincidence are not only *not* avoided, but deliberately sought out and created. Signifiers do not *represent* events and people but, through a chance association, *create* them. Rather than conveying any information about the world, language says something useless about itself. Although the story may be used interpersonally to maintain social relations rather than to communicate ideas or facts when there is nothing else to say, this does not explain why a punning story should be used to do this rather than something else.

In the case of the fronds and anemones, all this may seem rather trivial. This story can be taken or left as we please; punning uses of language and more rational ones can be kept apart. Though punning may have the *potential* to overturn the rational empiricist view of language, it is not through stories such as this one. When we turn to other examples, however – Christ's words to Peter, or Hamlet's to his mother – the issue is less easily dismissed. If both the choice and the qualities of the apostle seem to emerge from a chance and apparently meaningless coincidence, and if the themes and images of what is considered to be one of the greatest works of English literature can be so focused in four words, then puns seem to be of quite a different order: the most extreme instance (and therefore the least tolerated) of language which creates reality rather than only reflecting it. In punning, we allow language itself to take charge and to guide our thoughts.

These considerations may help us to reach conclusions about the function of language play. The situation is by no means as clear as it may seem at first, and there may be no simple conclusion to be reached. A number of points, however, can be made. They lead in two opposite directions, and whether one or both may be true is for each reader to decide. The potential of puns to derail the socially sanctioned uses and nature of language may account for the atmosphere of unruliness, disrespect and boisterous insolence which they seem to create. In most contemporary English-speaking societies, puns are more often the expression of insubordination by the less powerful (naughty children, football fans, graffiti writers) than a feature of the declarations of oracles, gods, God or dying princes.

3.7 Interpersonal play

So far in this chapter I have focused on texts which are essentially public in their contexts, even if understanding the playful meanings can depend upon whether the individual reader/listener understands the specific cultural references. I will now turn finally to a brief look at the way in which play operates in more private contexts. Because the contexts are private, they are of course much less accessible to an audience in an academic textbook. This should not diminish, though, the significance of the way we play with language and ideas when we interact with our family, lovers, friends, work colleagues and others who are close to us.

The nature of electronic communication media make these media a fruitful area to explore for interpersonal play. The fact that such texts are often multimodal, showing a mixture of written text features with features more akin to speech, means that they tend to be less formal than earlier forms of communication: so even when the email is about serious business, it can still exhibit features of playfulness. And this very playfulness, it can be argued, helps to oil the wheels of successful working practice by introducing a more personal element to the otherwise more alienating material of working life.

The box below contains a short exchange between two colleagues who work for the same organisation, but live in different parts of the country. Most of the rest of the context can be worked out, although clearly for the participants, who were meant to be the only parties to this exchange, they knew that they would be understood. Note that the opening message of the exchange is at the bottom, the reply at the top.

I run courses on (a) patronising and insincere flattery and (b) navigation for beginners – want to join?

Mark

Hi Mark

Thanks for the email and feedback. When we went to Amsterdam our luggage had its own special little minibreak in belfast
It would have been nice to talk to you on the train last Friday – pick up all those names you've dropped Tony – there's a good bloke
I've finished the review so am sending last feedbacks etc plus my stroppy and spiteful report which have just reread – and must have been utterly mardy cow when I wrote it but what can you do?
See you on Tues – how do you get there from KX? Its in the middle of nowhere acc to map and I failed geog you know

N

If you look at N's email first, you see that she mixes necessary work details such as *Thanks for the email and feedback*; *I've finished the review*; and *how do you get there* with other material which is not so strictly business, but may nonetheless act as a bond between the two. So, her reference to her luggage's holiday will refer to Mark having lost his, while her hostile take on Tony, presumably another colleague whom they'd rather not have met, and who kept mentioning people he knew, is permissible because she trusts Mark to agree with her. Note, incidentally, how the less strict rules of writing in emails (punctuation omitted, irregular use of capitals, dashes and abbreviations, etc.) 'support' this mixture of the serious and the playful in a way that an official letter in the post would not. Note too how the nature of the email allows N to move rapidly through a range of different 'voices' and to create a range of identities for herself. At various times she is the efficient worker, the friend, the 'mardy cow' ('mardy' is a dialect term for 'grumpy'), the hopeless navigator.

Mark's brief reply doesn't mention the work at all – he assumes it is all in hand. Instead he responds to two areas where N has playfully implied she needs help: with her inability to cope with people she does not really like, and with her inability to get to places. In effect, then, Mark acknowledges receipt of the email by acknowledging that he has understood and approved of N's outlook on the problems of daily life.

ACTIVITY 3.10

Allow about
30 minutes

If you use email, look at your own inbox and sent mail and explore how far you and your various correspondents engage in communication that can be deemed playful. Can you describe your play in terms of its linguistic form, semantic and/or pragmatic features? Can you find different methods of play with different people? The same investigation could then be undertaken on other modes of communication such as SMS texting, answerphone messages, and so on. To what extent are the methods of play a product of the communication channel that is being used?

The second set of data to be looked at in this section involves students communicating with each other in a chat room, established for them by their tutor as a forum for sharing ideas about their course. Many of the students were new to this type of communication, and as can be seen from the brief extracts below, soon realised its potential for creative play. Even more than email, this electronic mode of communication blurs many of the traditional distinctions between speaking and writing.

If you look at the text below, RyanS is in the virtual chat room looking for someone to play with. Note that the 'room' and the 'looking' are metaphorical here – but that Ryan creatively plays with that interesting gap between the reality of the technology and the represented familiar world of rooms and chatting.

RYANS>>	pooo
RYANS>>	helo
RYANS>>	hello?
RYANS>>	ooooooiiiiiiiiiii!!!!!
RYANS>>	oi oi oi oi oi oi oi oi oi ioi ioi iooi ioio ioio ioioi
RYANS>>	excuse me
RYANS>>	are you there
RYANS>>	fine
RYANS>>	be like that
RYANS>>	by then
RYANS>>	seeya

> RYANS>>   oi
>
> RYANS>>   hello
>
> RYANS>>   youre no fun

(Goddard, 2004, p. 44)

Angela Goddard says of this text that it is 'essentially dramatic ... where a one-sided conversation constructs an identity for two participants, [it] has obvious similarities with literary soliloquy, particularly in the realization of strong attitudes by the participants: Ryan is aggressively pursuing his recalcitrant and stubbornly silent interlocutor, with little success' (Goddard 2004, p. 44). While Ryan would no doubt have liked to have found someone to talk to, he has at the same time clearly had fun on his own – and he perhaps knows his efforts are not wasted, because unlike 'real' talk, this talk is recorded and can be read later by the friends who have temporarily deserted him.

The second extract from Goddard's data shows the students, including RyanS, in full flow.

ACTIVITY 3.11

Allow about
10 minutes

Comment on the features of language and communicative play in the short extract below.

> NADIA>>   Andie can you stop your twitching please
>
> GLYN>>   thanks
>
> ANDREW>>   ~I don't
>
> RYANS>>   simon?
>
> GLYN>>   your name has been added to the list you will not see another sunrise andrew
>
> RYANS>>   the blair twitch project
>
> ALEXANDRA>>   So your a twitcher then Andy
>
> RYANS>>   smack my twitch up
>
> RYANW>>   the wicked twitch of the west
>
> RYANW>>   or wirral
>
> NADIA>>   Whos going to America next season in our course
>
> RYANS>>   i might pop in
>
> ANDREW>>   I would but if your going.....................
> ....Perhaps not

(Goddard, 2004, p. 42)

Comment

What is especially noteworthy here is how the participants pick up on a reference, in this case to Andie *twitching*, and then pursue it with an ever increasing pleasure in the pursuit itself. Semantically, much of their communication has little 'meaning' in the traditional sense, but, pragmatically, the shared enterprise shows the students bonding together through their mutual play. Indeed, the apparent threats (*your name has been added to the list*) and the apparent antagonism (*I would but if your going*) are just that – apparent. Imagine how different the text would be if these comments really were hostile.

As with types of play we have seen earlier in this chapter, there is semantic play – *twitiching/twicher* – and various intertextual references, references which spin off the original idea of 'twitching': that is, moving about. There are references to films (*The Blair Witch Project* and *The Wizard of Oz*), music ('Smack My Bitch Up') and bird watching (a twitcher is a birdwatcher who compiles lists of all the species spotted). Meanwhile, RyanS uses incongruity for effect, suggesting that he might *pop in* to America, and Andrew uses the visual possibilities of the medium by using lines of dots to suggest delayed thought. Elsewhere, Goddard also notes that:

> ... the play on twitch-bitch-witch certainly involves sound patterning, as does the use of /w/; but there is also a cumulative force in the frequent appearance of the letter sequences 'i-t-c-h' and 'w' within a short space of time (consecutive lines of play in a multi-party context suggests a fast response time). ... the media texts invoked all have a menacing theme, as if to perform Glyn's original threat; then Ryan's 'or wirral' executes a nice piece of comic bathos.

(Goddard, 2006, pp. 44, 45)

One feature of the play that we cannot see here is the use of colour and icons common in chat room discourse. These help to distinguish the turns and to act as identity markers for those taking part. If you have taken part in chat room conversations or even 'lurked' without contributing to see what is going on, you will be aware that it is not only the text that creates the playful nature of the communication, but also the way in which the features of the electronic context are exploited. Like graffiti, chat room conversations exploit their medium as an integral part of their message.

3.8 Conclusion

In this chapter I have looked at some aspects of language play in English, from punning headlines, to comic songs, to politically motivated graffiti. It has been argued that play is everywhere around us, in both our public and our private worlds, and that such play is an important element in the way we communicate, rather than a luxury extra. I have argued that the forms play can take are mediated by the channel of communication being used at any given time. I have also shown that, for language play to work, there has to be an interplay of understanding between the producer of the language and the receiver – contexts of understanding, in other words. Play only works fully when the producer's intention to play is detected and when the full range of cultural references invoked by the producer are understood by the receiver. Moreover, the techniques employed in language play have much in common with other kinds of more prestigious and valued forms of language 'art' and, as such, have their own intrinsic value, both as sources of humour and as a means of challenging a view of language which focuses on it only as a means of conveying information.

READING A: Songs in Singlish

Marie Tan
(Marie Tan is a graduate in English Language and Literature at the National Institute of Singapore.)

Source: Tan, M. (1992/3) Revised and abridged version of 'Language play in Dick Lee's songs – the Singapore element', BA (Hons) thesis, Department of English Language and Literature, National University of Singapore.

Introduction

Dick Lee is one of Singapore's best-known singer-songwriters. As the 'creator of Singlish pop' he started the trend of writing and singing songs with a distinctive Singaporean flavour [see Figure 1]. Dick Lee claims that his music is unique because he has injected the Singapore element into his songs. This injection, I suggest, is achieved by:

1   references to Singaporean life – the national symbols, the places, the historical figures, the food, etc. which reveal what it means to be a Singaporean;

2   the use of Singlish, with its own syntax and lexicon – reflecting how English in Singapore has developed into a unique variety;

3   the use of several languages (Chinese dialects, Malay, Tamil, etc.) – which reflects the multilingual nature of Singapore and also the way Singaporeans codeswitch.

I will briefly describe some linguistic features of Lee's songs, with reference to three aspects of Singapore's cultural life – Indian movies, eating and shopping – and to the way in which the phonology of Singapore English is used.

Indian movies

References to Indian movies in relation to the Singapore element may seem an oddity. On the contrary, they bring back memories of a favourite pastime of many Singaporeans – watching Indian films and laughing at the exaggerated love scenes, in which the male and female leads sing love songs to each other while chasing each other around trees. These memories are evoked in two songs, 'Mustapha' and 'Chin Chin Choo', in which Indian love scenes are 'acted' out by Dick Lee and Jacintha, another Singaporean singer. The chasing scenes are alluded to in the following verses:

J   But to take a sip,
     you have to catch me first.

D   I am going to be catching you,
     you little curry puff.

THE DING DONG SONG

Here's an old Chinese number that was popular in the fifties, dedicated to my dear mother, who, incidentally, kindly consented to sing on the track. Thanks to her, I was introduced to Rebecca Pan, Asia's songbird This song is a bit of a family affair, with my brother Wah going, "What is this thing called love?"

I hear that bell go ding dong
Deep down inside my heart.

Each time you say, "Kiss me"
Then I know it's time for Ding Dong to start
Each time you say, "Hug me", Ding Dong,
Ding Dong.
Each time you say, "Love me", Ding Dong,
Ding Dong
I hope I won't wait too long
You hear my bell go Ding Dong
You hear my bell go Ding Dong

MUSTAPHA

This song figures vaguely somewhere in my childhood. I've ressurrected it — with new lyrics — as a tribute to my favourite Saturday afternoon pastime — Tamil movies! (P.S. This also features my fave Tamil Actress — Jacintha!)

CHORUS:

Cherie je t'aime, cherie jet t'adore
My darling I love you a lot more than you know
Cherie je t'aime, cherie je t'adore,
My darling I love you a lot more than you know.
Oh Mustapha, Oh mustapha
Yen Kathalan my Mr. mustapha
Sayang, sayang, na chew sher wo ai ni
Will you, will you fall in love with me.

Oh your lovely eyes, I feel I know them well
Let me look into them and fall right under their spell.
Oh, my sweetness what a beauty
You are such a pretty cutie
I can't tell you, tutti frutti,
All the things you're doing to me

(Repeat chorus)

Honey, honey, sugar's not as sweet
Oh, my papadam, you're good enough to eat.
Mama, mama, you are such a tease,
Oh, my harm cheen pang, can
I give you a squeeze?

(Repeat chorus)

Putumayam, I am asking, please
Won't you come and give your Mustapha a kiss?
Onde-onde, can I quench your thirst?
But to take a sip, you have to catch me first!

LITTLE WHITE BOAT

A Chinese nursery rhyme with an endearing melody. Something I've always wanted to redo.

Sailing in my little white boat
Far as I can be
Drifting in my little white boat
Set my spirit free.
Take me deep inside my dream
over seas of blue
To your magic place
Where I can be with you

I AM BABA

A "soundtrack" based on my recollections of Peranakan songs, sung to me by my granny when I was a child. Folksongs featured. Lenggang kangkong, Chan Mali Chan, Trek Tek Tek, Suah Suih Kemuning. As a true Singaporean, you ought to know the words!

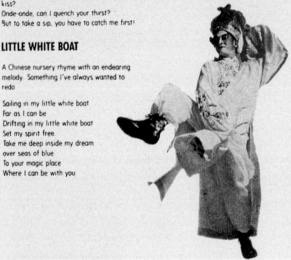

Figure 1   The Singapore songwriter and performer Dick Lee, with lyrics in Singlish

Both singers even sing in a strong Indian-accented English, emphasizing especially the Indian English stereotype of realizing /w/ as [v] – for example, in the line 'what's the time, what's up, what's news?' Like many kinds of language play, this humour depends heavily on shared experience. The references to Indian movies are only hilarious if listeners have shared in the experience which Dick Lee wants to evoke.

Singaporean likes: eating and shopping

Eating – the pastime Singaporeans indulge in with consummate passion – has a special place in Dick Lee's songs, appearing in at least three songs, including 'Fried Rice Paradise ', 'Rasa Sayang' and 'Mustapha' ... Another favourite Singaporean pastime, shopping, is also mentioned. The two main passions of Singaporeans are captured most succinctly in these two lines from 'Rasa Sayang':

> We can eat, eat, eat till we nearly drop
> Then we all get up and we shop, shop, shop.

A number of lexical items have developed new meanings in Singapore English. Occurrences of such lexical items include 'hawker centre'. As used in Singaporean Standard English (SSE), this means 'an area set aside for cooked food stalls'. Its meaning has developed from the general English meaning of 'hawker' as 'an itinerant salesman' (Platt and Weber, 1980, p. 88).

Use of nonstandard spelling

Another interesting feature of Lee's songs is the (nonstandard) pronunciation of Singapore English speakers in the spelling of words, as represented in the lyrics printed on the covers of his recordings. Features such as consonant cluster simplification, palatalization and the realization of /θ/ as [t] are exemplified below. (SSE translations of Singlish are given in square brackets, and the particular songs referred to in round brackets.)

Palatalization

> For example: 'Can I *hepchew* ?' [Can I help you?]
> ('Say Lah!')

[t] substituted for /θ/

> For example: '*Tingwat?*' [What do you think?]
> ('Say Lah!')

Consonant cluster simplification

> For example: 'Oi, why you all *dowan* to say?'
> [*dowan* = don't want]
> ('Rasa Sayang')

> For example: '*Wen*, lah – must let off steam, what!' [*wen* = won't]
> ('Rasa Sayang')

These spellings thus represent stereotypical features of pronunciations commonly heard in Singapore. They are considered by Lee to be part of Singlish (he refers to them as Singlish features in 'Say Lah!').

The examples I have presented show how, in what seems to be a self-conscious, playful use of features of Singaporean English that have strong cultural connotations, Dick Lee is successfully able to represent aspects of Singaporean life in ways that are – to his intended audience – both immediately recognizable and hilarious.

Reference for this reading

Platt, J.T. and Weber, H. (1980) *English in Singapore and Malaysia: Status, Features, Functions*, Kuala Lumpur, Oxford University Press.

READING B: Extract from 'Social issues on walls: graffiti in university lavatories'

O.G. Nwoye
(O.G. Nwoye is Professor in the Faculty of Humanities, English Language & Literature, University of Swaziland.)

Source: Nwoye, O.G. (1993) 'Social issues on walls: graffiti in university lavatories', *Discourse and Society*, vol. 4, no. 4, pp. 419–42.

Wall writings were used early in human history to record and preserve the activities of humankind. The invention of writing, and later printing, led to more permanent methods of such record-keeping. Apart from advertising and other such purposes, wall writing is no longer a recognized method of preserving records by mainstream society. Nevertheless, groups prohibited from, or denied, avenues of public expression seek other outlets, with graffiti on walls of public places as a favoured option. One such group is the student population in most parts of the world. In particular, Nigerian university students have been seen as agents of destabilization by successive governments in Nigeria. Within the individual universities, they are not involved in decision-making in matters that affect their academic and social life as students. Nationally, they are not allowed to contribute to discussions of socio-economic and political issues. Even where campus newspapers exist, they are often subject to censorship by university authorities. A few daring publications run by individual students and organizations are proscribed as soon as they run foul of the authorities by publishing what are considered to be inciting or inflammatory articles. The young, in their impatient idealism, see most leaders as inept, uncaring and therefore unconcerned with their well-being. In Third World countries in particular, students can constitute the most articulate opposition to bad governments and oppressive regimes. They are often, if not always, on collision courses with established authorities both within and outside their campuses. Denied the means of expressing their views on matters they feel they should be involved in, they resort to graffiti, and on college campuses all over the world, lavatory walls and other public places are used extensively for this purpose ...

At the University of Benin, the walls of the lavatories in the faculty buildings, as well as other semi-public places like walls of stairways, are covered with graffiti. Chalkboards are also used for this purpose, but these lack the relative permanence of the lavatory walls. Graffiti thrive in lavatories because they afford the 'authors' relative privacy in which to express their views without fear. Second, the lavatory walls have not been painted over since 1980 when the faculty building was erected. It is therefore possible, given limitations of space, to record 'dialogues' that run for a long time. 'Authors' do compete for the available space, and often wipe out previous 'dialogues' to create space for new ones.

The materials for this paper were collected and transcribed between July and September 1991 from men's lavatories in faculty buildings at the main campus of the University of Benin, Benin City, Nigeria ...

Analysis

The subject matter of the graffiti can be divided into the following broad topics: politics, socio-economic issues and others. Politics (national and international) accounts for 113 graffiti or 48.09 percent and socio-economic issues for 81 or 34.47 percent. National political issues are those directly related to the internal affairs of the country and its governance, while international political issues deal with global matters in which Nigeria may or may not be directly involved. Of the political issues, some of the graffiti show evidence of being out-dated, since their topics were no longer relevant, or had been overtaken by events. One such topic is 'Free Mandela' (Mandela was released from prison in 1989).

The following extract was obtained from the walls of a lavatory in the Social Sciences building:

(1) (a) – Free Mandela

     (b) – Jail De Klerk

     (c) – and Buthelezi, his stooge.

These graffiti must have been written some time before Mandela was released from prison, but since the lavatory walls have not been painted since the building was completed in 1980, this text remained *in situ*. It is interesting to note that this piece has survived frequent erasures by other writers seeking space for initiating new topics ...

The above graffiti (1) are representative of the many others on the same topics and are characterized by the terse nature of the contributions. The style of these graffiti is that of the 'banner-headline' as used in newspapers. Coherence is achieved by linkages. The 'jail' in 'Jail De Klerk' thus makes for cohesion between the first 'turn' and the subsequent ones, particularly when it is appropriated and used in the third 'turn' (c), thus dispensing with its repetition. The *and* in (c) functions as an additive marker of cohesive relationship (Halliday and Hasan, 1976, p. 234) between (c) and the two previous moves. Such a rhetorical device contributes to the terseness and brevity of the graffiti ... Contributors seem to take a cue from what they are responding or contributing to ...

In (3) below, a long initiating contribution elicits long responses.

(3) (a) OAU [Organization of African Unity] should form an African High Command for the liberation of South Africa.

(b) – Fool, that country is called AZANIA.

(c) – Who will lead the High Command, IBB?

(d) – No, he can't even shoot.

(e) – Does he fire blanks?

(f) – Be serious! Let's chase all whites out of Azania.

(g) – I suggest all students from next semester should volunteer to fight the Apartheid regime in SA.

(h) – Good suggestion, but I suggest it should take effect after I have graduated.

(i) – Not me o, SA has atomic bomb!

(j) – Coward.

(k) – No, he is a traitor.

(l) – He should be shipped to SA, where he will use Blacks only loo.

(m) – Not funny.

The above graffiti covered a large space on the wall of a lavatory. Unlike (1) ... above, the structure is characterized by a long initiating contribution and fairly long responses. The structure of the initiating contribution which invited a 'dialogue' was responsible for eliciting the type of contributions that followed ... By opening the extract with a proposition (a), the writer has invited a discussion of that proposition. The rhetorical device used in turns (c) and (e) is a question–answer format. The play on the words 'shoot' and 'fire' moves the discussion from serious and formal to non-serious and informal and therefore merited the call for a return to the seriousness which the subject matter demanded. The call for a return to seriousness after the comic relief introduced by the sexual allusions (d) and (e) serves as an overt indicator of 'return-to-topic' (Yule and Mathis, 1992, p. 208) and resembles such spoken, face-to-face discourse strategies as, 'seriously speaking', 'and so, anyway'. There is, however, no shift from standard English to non-standard to correspond with the shift in seriousness as one would expect. Supportive discourse strategy is present in 'turn' (h) (Good suggestion), even though the contributor made a suggestion that differed slightly from that of the previous contributor. A style shift, from standard to non-standard Nigerian English, occurred in 'turn' (i) (Not me o, ...), marking the first of such style shifts. Repetition as 'a strategy toward the pragmatic goal of persuasion' (Johnstone, 1983, cited in Rains, 1992, p. 253) is employed here to give support to a proposition. Thus a suggestion (g) that students volunteer to fight in South Africa is taken up (h) and the words 'suggest' and 'suggestion' used twice in one move. This creates the effect of reinforcing the suggestion and advancing the proposal in (a).

Apart from the first response, which sought to correct the first contributor's use of the name South Africa instead of the unofficial Azania, all other contributions advanced the discussion in some way. There was, therefore, a steady progression in the development of the argument. Both the scepticism about the OAU chairman's ability to lead the High Command (c) and the sexual response (e) are evidence of the type of regard in which he is held by the students, and evidence of the not too cordial relationship between the two. The use of the word 'loo' [in (l)] for lavatory or toilet is strange and unusual, since the word is rare in students' repertoire. Abbreviations (SA for South Africa) are common. Their frequency in graffiti may be explained by the need to economize space and because they are a response to previous usages. It seems to be the case that if an item has been referred to in an abbreviated form by a previous contributor, subsequent contributors tend to adopt and use that form. The use of 'coward' (j) which a later contributor changed to 'traitor' (k) is significant in the context of students' politics. Those two lexical items are synonymous for many students in a restricted area of usage. During student demonstrations and strikes, lecture boycotts are frequent, and those students who do not take active part are labelled cowards because they are afraid of the results of physical confrontations with the police and the Army, who are invariably brought in to quell the 'riots', as these demonstrations are labelled by university authorities and government. The students who fail to take part in these activities are also perceived as traitors to the cause of student unionism and the fight against social injustice. ...

Not all the graffiti on these walls deal with political and socio-economic matters. We expected to find, and found, those that were concerned with the more mundane issues of student interpersonal relationships, comments on academic courses and professors. The graffiti on students' interpersonal relationships were romantic in nature, most of them sexual in tone. Some were declarations of love for some female, most probably a student, as in the following:

(12) (a) Uche loves Ngozi

(b) – Does she love you?

(c) – Love is dead.

The initiating contribution has a heart drawn around each of the names. The use of this additional pictorial device is aimed at enhancing the romantic nature of the message, hearts being icons universally recognized and associated with love. In some other graffiti of the same subject matter, two hearts with names written inside them sufficed as the entire communication. Such personal declarations of love were not expected to attract rejoinders, but many of them did, as the extract above indicates. The rejoinders were often found to be contradictions of the stated propositions or some other propositions denying the content of the first, such as the declaration that love is dead. If love is dead, then nobody can claim to be in love.

Very uncomplimentary remarks on courses and their teachers were also made, and opposing viewpoints expressed.

(13) (a) SAA 324 is a joke, the guy has no stuff.

(b) – A hint for an A – memorize his notes.

(c) – You are the problem, not the Prof.

(d) – If you don't buy his handouts, you qualify for an F.

(e) – He just copies textbooks.

(f) – Where do you want him to get it from, from his garden?

(g) – From his empty head [followed by a drawing of an oversized head].

In the extract above we find a discourse feature, mutual support and encouragement, in the hint given by a contributor on how to make an A in the course ... Cole (1991, p. 405) found such mutual support devices in her study of women's graffiti in an American university campus. She attributes them to politeness features said to characterize women's discourse. It might be that mutual support is a feature of all groups which perceive themselves as minorities and which are in need of mutual bonding for protection from perceived oppressive groups. The student body fits into such a group, bound in solidarity against an 'oppressive' group (university administration, lecturers), who, they argue, have forgotten all they ever learnt, and are busy producing handouts for sale to their students, who are bound to buy them to prevent getting failing grades. Such a view of lectures is very widespread and, given the relative lack of freedom to articulate them openly, graffiti become a ready avenue for so doing. ...

The use of graphics (drawing), for emphasis and effect is another rhetorical device employed here. The picture of an oversized head said to be empty does much to reinforce the intended message that the lecturer under reference has nothing in his head. ...

Conclusion

The samples of graffiti analysed show that graffiti, far from being mere vandalism, as many people like to regard them, are, in fact, expressive modes adopted by subgroups that have been denied other avenues of self-expression.

References for this reading

Cole, C.M. (1991) 'Oh wise women of the stalls ...' *Discourse and Society*, vol. 2, no. 4, pp. 401–10.

Halliday, M.A.K. and Hasan, R. (1976) *Cohesion in English*, Harlow, Longman.

Johnstone, B. (1983) 'Presentation as proof: the language of Arabic rhetoric', *Anthropological Linguistics*, 25, pp. 47–60.

Rains, C. (1992) '"You die for life": on the use of poetic devices in argumentation', *Language in Society*, 21, pp. 253–76.

Yule, G. and Mathis, T. (1992) 'The role of staging and constructed dialogue in establishing a speaker's topic', *Linguistics*, 30, pp. 199–215.

Literacy practices in English

Mike Baynham and Janet Maybin

4.1 Introduction

In this chapter we focus on written English and its use across different social and cultural contexts in a variety of modes, electronic and print-based. Written English of course includes a wide range of texts, from the literature canon and the laws of the land, down to street signs, emails, text messages and scribbled notes to friends. We start by looking at the linguistic differences between written and spoken English and examine some ways in which electronic means of communication seem to have shifted the relationship between speech and writing. We then go on to show that the ways in which English is used in different kinds of text, and how we read these texts, are strongly influenced by social factors. The writer's purposes, the relationship between writer and reader, and the social conventions and practices surrounding the text all shape our use and interpretation of language. In this chapter we use examples of different kinds of reading and writing from monolingual and multilingual settings to show what people do with literacy in English, and also what they make of what they do.

4.2 Speech and writing

There are certain immediately obvious differences between speech and writing. Spoken language often includes hesitations, self-corrections and interruptions, and part of the meaning is conveyed through intonation and gestures. Written English is organised by standard conventions concerning spelling, punctuation and the organisation of the text into sentences and paragraphs. But apart from these features, is there also something about our use of English vocabulary and grammar in writing which is somehow different from the way we use these in speech?

ACTIVITY 4.1

Allow about 5 minutes

Which of the two extracts below would you say was more likely originally to have been spoken, and which written? Why?

Extract 1

It probably means if you invest in something to do with trains, it means that you'll have to leave your money there and you probably won't be able to get your money back for quite a long time.

Extract 2

Investment placed in a rail facility implies a long-term commitment.

Comment

Some features of spoken English, such as intonation, emphatic stress and gesture, are usually lost in transcription. Nevertheless, although it is possible to imagine some contexts where (1) is written and (2) spoken, it is much more likely that you decided the longer, more informal sounding first extract was originally spoken and the more concise, formal second extract was written. We go on below to discuss some of the precise linguistic differences between the two pieces of language given in this activity, which make them so obviously 'speech' and 'writing'.

Vocabulary

Because of the different ways in which spoken and written language is produced (we can take hours to compose a formal piece of writing: drafting and redrafting, finding the most concise terms and editing out repetitions), it has been suggested that written texts contain a wider vocabulary than spoken language and more polysyllabic words – such as *investment*, *facility* and *commitment* in Extract 2. All three of these words come from Latin and do not belong to the basic Anglo-Saxon word stock. Spoken English, on the other hand, has a higher proportion of Anglo-Saxon words, and more repetition of individual words (notice the repetition of *you, probably* and *money* in Extract 1).

Lexical density

Linguists have found that spoken English tends to have many more words which knit the text together (called **grammatical items**) in proportion to words which carry content (**lexical items**).

Because words change their meaning and function in different contexts, the distinction between grammatical and lexical items is not always clear-cut. Generally speaking, however, grammatical items in English maintain the relationships between the lexical items and keep the text together. They include:

- articles – *a, an, the*
- pronouns – *he, she, you, them*
- most prepositions – *in, beside*

- conjunctions – *and*, *because*, *while*
- some classes of adverbs – *usually*, *often*
- certain auxiliary verbs – *have*, *was* (as in *have left*, *was going*, etc.).

Grammatical items belong to a closed system in the language in the sense that we do not invent new prepositions or conjunctions. They are part of the grammatical system we use to make meaning. Lexical items, on the other hand, are an open system of nouns, verbs, adjectives, and so on, which can be added to in response to new ideas and new technology (Halliday, 1985). In Extract 1 the lexical terms are *means*, *invest*, *trains*, *leave*, *money*, *get*, *long*, *time* (eight items), and there are 30 grammatical items. In Extract 2, however, there are seven lexical items (*investment*, *placed*, *rail*, *facility*, *implies*, *long-term*, *commitment*) and only three grammatical ones (*in*, *a* and *a*). Because the proportion of lexical to grammatical items is usually higher in written texts, they are said to have a higher **lexical density**.

Nominalisation

If you compare Extracts 1 and 2, you will see that the verb *invest* in Extract 1 has been replaced by a related noun *investment* in Extract 2. This business of replacing one syntactic form, in this case a verb, by another syntactic form, in this case a noun, has been termed **nominalisation**, and is said to be particularly characteristic of formal written texts. Halliday (1987) comments that spoken language tells a story in verbs, while written language tells it in nouns. Nominalisations make a text more lexically dense.

Written texts may be more precise in terms of choice of vocabulary, but the use of nominalisations often means that information about processes, about who did what to whom, is lost. For example, in a clause from a formal written text such as 'The reinstatement of the chairman was not well received' we do not know who reinstated the chairman or why, or how he came to lose his chair in the first place. The passive tense, in this case *was not well received*, is also used much more commonly in written than in spoken English, and similarly omits to mention who is the agent (in this case the person or people who are unhappy about the reinstatement).

Grammatical intricacy

Written English is often thought of as more complex than the spoken language; for instance, writing frequently contains (embedded) subordinate clauses (e.g. 'The work on this project, which we had hoped would have been completed by now, has not even started'). However, Halliday (1987) points out that, although spoken language may appear simpler, in fact there are often complex grammatical relationships between clauses. Compare Extract 2, which consists of a single main clause, with the string of short clauses in Extract 1:

(a) It probably means

(b) if you invest in something to do with trains

(c) it means

(d) that you'll have to leave your money there

(e) and you probably won't be able to get your money back for quite a long time

The spoken extract seems to show the effects of planning 'on the hoof'. The speaker begins *It probably means*, then inserts a conditional clause *if you invest* ... From here to the end of the utterance there is a reformulation of the main clause *it means,* followed by two dependent clauses (d and e) functioning as a direct object of *it means.*

Modality

One final contrast you may have noticed between the two texts is that, even though they are dealing with the same topic, the first seems more personal, informal and subjective. For instance, the speaker's relationship to the listener is expressed more explicitly (through the use of *you*), and there are expressions of vagueness (*probably means, something to do with*), and modal auxiliary verbs (*have to, won't be able to*). **Modal forms** express the speaker's attitudes, towards him- or herself, listeners or subject matter and are much more common in spoken English, with its direct, face-to-face interactional purposes, than in the more 'distant' medium of formal writing.

ACTIVITY 4.2

Allow about
15 minutes

The following sentence comes from an article by a student in his school magazine, reviewing the activities of the student dance company over the previous year. What features of the text make it much more likely to have been written than spoken?

> The Dance Company's performances showed a deep understanding and respect for their work which was executed with the utmost professionalism and focus.

> (*Stantonbury Campus News*, issue 12, summer 1995)

(To answer this activity you might like to consider lexical density. We analysed the lexical items in this text as *Dance, Company, performances, showed, deep, understanding, respect, work, executed, utmost, professionalism, focus.*)

4.3 Text and context

As we explained at the beginning of the last section, there is an enormous range of different ways in which English is used in writing, and the linguistic differences discussed above come from contrasting somewhat idealised, 'typical' examples of informal speech with formal writing. In fact, distinctions between the two kinds of language use are not always so clear. When we start to look at a range of texts we find that many examples of writing contain a mix of 'oral' and 'literate' features, depending on the formality of the writing, the relationship between the writer and reader, and how ephemeral or permanent the text is intended to be. The growth of electronic communication in recent years appears to be reworking the distinctions between speech and writing in a particularly interesting way.

ACTIVITY 4.3

Allow about
20 minutes

Look at the following data from a study by Merchant (2001) of teenage girls' use of chat rooms. Extract A is from a taped interview with two of the girls in the study. In Extract B one of them is interacting with a friend in a chat room. It has a very spoken-like feel, as if the two girls are engaged in a written conversation. What are the features of the text that make it seem more like speech? How are the participants using the resources of written language?

Consider the following questions:
- How many characteristics of spoken language can you find in the chat room interaction?
- How do the participants use the resources of the written medium to compensate for the lack of face-to-face interaction in this mode?

Extract A

(In this extract 'I' is the interviewer.)

R	Sometimes ... people suddenly send you a message and you say 'Oh, I think I know you'.
I	Mm
S	... or you can say: meet me on-line at 6 o'clock.
R	Yeah.
I	OK – do you ever do that?
R	Yes
S	Yeah
I	... and they are there in the chatroom?

R   Yeah ... or you can look for them because I get messages from people on my pager thing.

I   ... so you know they're in there.

(Merchant, 2001, p. 298)

Extract B

ADZ46   hows you

PINTSIZE   fine thanx u?

ADZ46   great

PINTSIZE   cool wot u up2?

ADZ46   not A LOT

PINTSIZE   wot av u bin up2?

ADZ46   Writeing a Macbeth Essay

PINTSIZE   o gr8 fun!

ADZ46   mmmmmmm

ADZ46   :-(

PINTSIZE   :)

ADZ46   :-(

PINTSIZE   cheer up!

ADZ46   :-

PINTSIZE   Stop it!

(Merchant, 2001, p. 301)

Comment

Features of spoken language which the participants use include non-standard grammar (*hows you*) and pronunciation (indicated by non-standard spelling *wot av u bin up2?*), ellipsis and one-word utterances, all typical of casual conversation. Non-verbal responses are conveyed through emoticons – for example, :-(and :).

Notice how the participants use CAPITALS to signal emphasis and emoticons to signal mood. Something distinctive to the chat room and texting medium are spellings which incorporate numerals (*gr8*).

In order to understand the meaning and significance of any text in English we need to look beyond the words on the page or screen, to consider the purposes of the readers and writers involved, and the social and cultural aspects of their literacy activity.

Let's look now at a multilingual text which raises these issues directly.

ACTIVITY 4.4

Allow about 20 minutes

Figure 4.1 is an extract from a letter written by an Indian father to his daughter in England. In what ways does it conform to the features of written English discussed above? What additional kinds of information might you need in order to understand the full meaning of the letter?

For information, in Figure 4.1 the underlined item in Sanskrit in the middle of the top of the page is *Om Sri Ram*, which means 'In God's name'. Blessings in Kannada (the state language of the south Indian state of Karnataka) for each member of the family then follow: 'May you live long, may you live like a king' for males, and 'May you live long, may you be prosperous' for females. The last two lines in Kannada read: 'To all of you, abundant good wishes. We expect by the grace of God that both you and we are well, and now let me commence the letter.'

Comment

The English part of the letter uses fairly simple repeated verbal structures with a lexical density somewhere between that of Extracts 1 and 2 in Activity 4.1 (38 lexical items and 47 grammatical ones). The phrases *erect posture*, *eagerly awaiting* and *latest photos* all suggest the formality of writing, but the numerous references to people and feelings are closer to the subjective involvement of oral communication. The blessings at the beginning seem much more formal, and this reflects the generally more formal style in which letters in Kannada are written. Notice how the *Well* at the beginning of the English section signals not just a switch in language, but also a switch to the chattier, more informal conversational style of personal letters in English.

Apart from the additional family information we need to have in order to understand the references to particular individuals in this letter, we also need to know something about letter-writing conventions in Kannada in order to understand the significance of the phrases written in this language. For instance, someone receiving a letter in Kannada always looks first at the top left-hand corner to check for the word 'safe' in Sanskrit, which indicates that the letter does not contain news of a death. If the corner is empty, then the reader knows to expect bad news. The blessings and greetings at the beginning of Jaya's father's letter are those usually given by a higher status person to a

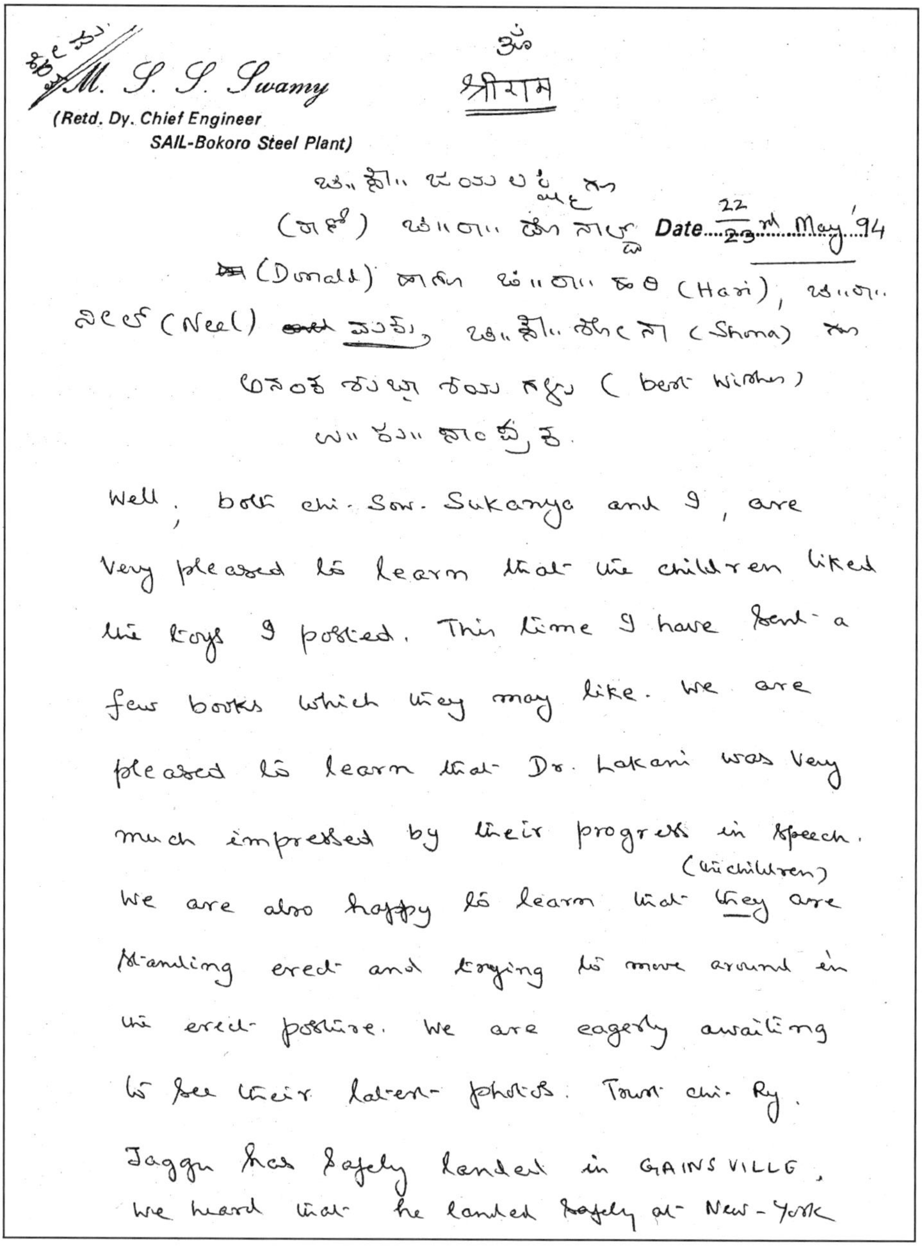
M. S. S. Swamy
(Retd. Dy. Chief Engineer
SAIL-Bokoro Steel Plant)

श्रीराम

Date 22nd May '94

(Donald) (Hari), (Neel) (Shona) (best wishes)

Well, both chi. Sow. Sukanya and I, are
very pleased to learn that the children liked
the toys I posted. This time I have sent a
few books which they may like. We are
pleased to learn that Dr. Lakani was very
much impressed by their progress in speech.
(the children)
We are also happy to learn that they are
standing erect and trying to move around in
the erect posture. We are eagerly awaiting
to see their latest photos. Tour chi. Ry.
Jaggu has safely landed in GAINSVILLE,
We heard that he landed safely at New-York

Figure 4.1 First page of a letter from M.S.S. Swamy to his daughter Jayalakshmi (Jaya)
(We are grateful to G.D. Jayalakshmi for permission to reproduce this letter.)

lower status one (e.g. a father to a daughter), and are set out appropriately for everyone in the family depending on whether they are male (in this case, Donald and his sons Neel and Hari) or female (Jaya and her daughter Shona). This is a standard formula for the openings of letters in Kannada, but it has a special significance in Jaya's case.

Jaya is a fluent Kannada speaker, but because her family moved to northern India when she was still a child, she was taught to read and write Hindi and English, rather than Kannada, at school. When she left home to go to university in Hyderabad, Jaya was keen to strengthen her original language roots and asked her father to teach her some written Kannada through the letters he wrote to her. He decided that the opening formulaic phrases might be a useful place to start. Although Jaya has never become fully literate in Kannada, her father has continued to write to her in this way. Some years after leaving university, Jaya married a Scotsman and settled in England. Her father's use of the Kannada phrases now has an added importance in reminding his daughter of their shared cultural background and of her own efforts while at university to reaffirm both this background and her relationship with her father through letter writing.

Here we have a fairly informal personal letter (with some formal features) passing between close family members with much shared knowledge and history. In order to read and understand the letter we do not just need to be literate in English and Kannada, we also need to know about the social conventions of letter writing in these two languages, and how Jaya and her father use and adapt these conventions to pursue individual purposes to do with their own identity and relationships.

To understand any text in English we need to know something about its context (for instance, whether it is a personal letter received in the post, part of a business correspondence, a newspaper article, a work from a literature syllabus) and about the conventional practices which people usually follow in engaging with such texts. Some texts, particularly those from a genre with which we are not familiar, may require a conscious struggle not just to decode the words, but also to try to understand unfamiliar ground rules. When presented with a clause in a legal agreement, for example, or a complex assignment set by a tutor, our response needs to be conventionally presented to comply with legal or educational ground rules respectively. At the other extreme, we read and interact with numerous texts as part of our daily life without being particularly conscious of all the knowledge about social and cultural practices which we are using in the process. Think, for instance, about the different texts you encounter in a typical day.

In Jaya's father's letter we see examples of switching between Sanskrit, Kannada and English. This can also be true of an electronic medium such as email and online chat. Warschauer (2002) shows how Egyptian Arabic speakers in the early part of this decade developed a Latin alphabet-based transcription for colloquial Arabic, which they use for email, texting and chat room communication, often mixing and switching between English and Arabic. In this example, Laila, emailing Dalia, shifts between Arabic and English. A translation is given below in square brackets.

ACTIVITY 4.5

Allow about
20 minutes

Do you see any similarities between the chat room interaction in Activity 4.3 and Laila's email below? Drawing on the discussion of language choice from Activity 4.4, what do you notice about her choice of language in the email?

> Hello Dalia
>
> 7amdellah. 3ala el-salama ya Gameel.we alf mabrouk 3alal el-shahada el-kebeera …
>
> Keep in touch … I really hope to see you all Soooooooooooooon (Maybe in Ramadan).
>
> Kol Sana Wentom Tayyebeen.
>
> Waiting to hear from you …
>
> Laila
>
>
> [Hello Dalia,
>
> Thank God for the safe return, my sweet. Congratulations for the big certificate. Keep in touch. I really hope to see you all Soooooooooooooon (Maybe in Ramadan).
>
> Happy Ramadan.
>
> Waiting to hear from you …
>
> Laila]

(Warschauer, 2002, p. 68)

Comment

Laila uses the expressive stretching of the word 'Soooooooooooooon' to express the emotion of longing. The length of the stretched word seems to indicate the stretching of time till the two meet. She also uses a numeral, to represent a sound not available in the English alphabet. Laila uses the transcribed Arabic primarily for religious expressions and culturally charged formulae at the beginning and towards the end of the email. Compare this with Jaya's father's use of Sanskrit and Kannada in his letter (Activity 4.4). Warschauer points to a current use of English on the internet in Egypt, due to a variety of factors and corresponding to the dominance of English in other technological and business domains. He identifies a pattern in online communication with English-only emails typical of formal business communication, and switching between English and colloquial Arabic in less formal contexts. However, he points out that this may be a transitional state of affairs and that changes in the technology and, indeed, in the social world could alter this: 'As Arabic operating systems continue to improve and expand, it can be expected that more websites will be created in modern standard Arabic and people may begin to write e-mail messages in Arabic script' (Warschauer, 2002, p. 68).

It is important to be aware that literacy practices shift and change as part of technological advances and changes in the social world. We seem to be in a period of particularly rapid change in means of communication. Below, Cruickshank (2001) describes some of the changes that took place over a three-year fieldwork period in an ethnographic study of the literacy practices of Arabic-speaking teenage boys in Sydney, Australia:

> In the three years of interviews and visits the most dramatic change was in the use of computers, since, by 1996, many of the families had computers. These were often placed in the living room or an area of general access. ... From 1997 to 1999 there was a dramatic increase in the number of computers and the new computers tended to be placed in bedrooms. ... In 1997 the most common use was computer games and PlayStation and Nintendo. By 1998 and 1999 students were using mostly the Internet and Chatrooms. Computer games were seen as being for younger children. The teenagers would use the computers on week nights in their bedrooms and also on weekends. Often on weekends they would visit relatives or friends' places to use the computers.
>
> ...
>
> Two of the teachers in the local schools commented on the students' use of chat rooms and how it had effected an improvement in their writing in English.
>
> (Cruickshank, 2001, p. 192)

We have looked at some examples of how changes in literacy practices, technological development and social organisation are all closely interconnected. Cruickshank (2001) points out, for example, how locating new computers in bedrooms brought about a reorganisation of social space in the households he visited. In the next activity it becomes clear that literacy is not something that exists in and is confined to pages and screens. We live in a print-saturated world where even streetscapes have words and images which can be read like texts.

ACTIVITY 4.6

Allow about
10 minutes

The photographs in Figure 4.2 were taken in streets in Singapore, India and Britain. What are the main purposes of each photographed text (e.g. to persuade, to entertain, to inform)? Which texts carry the greatest authority? How far do the writing medium and the context of each text influence your answers?

In order to investigate further the idea of the street as a textscape, you might like to extend this activity: note down the written texts that are found in the public space of your local shopping area. What media are they written in (typeset/neon/handwritten)? What languages and language varieties do they represent? Do some texts have greater authority? What is the source of this authority? Are there examples of slogans and graffiti and other 'illegitimate' texts? How do the words in the texts relate to images?

Activity 4.6 showed you how words interact with images in the everyday texts we encounter in the street. This interaction of words and images highlights the multimodality of many texts around us (a feature first noted in the home pages you looked at in Chapter 2). Just as some of the texts we have examined – Jaya's father's letter, Laila's email – are multilingual texts composed of more than one language, so a multimodal text is composed of more than one mode such as writing and still or moving pictures and images. The idea of reading, then, broadens from interaction with words on a page or screen to interaction with texts and images and, indeed, reading other sign systems in the world around us.

'Reading the street' in Activity 4.6 involved interpreting multimodal signs designed to convey certain messages. In the case study in the box overleaf we extend the notion of semiotic systems to encompass signals from the natural world. This case study introduces Jonathan, a boy in his mid teens living with his family on a small farm in New South Wales, Australia. Jonathan's passion is rainfall and the weather more generally, a crucial issue in a drought-stricken rural area. His environment provides him with opportunities to read not only written text but other sign systems in the world around him.

Singapore

Lancaster

Singapore

Singapore (English, Tamil and Chinese)

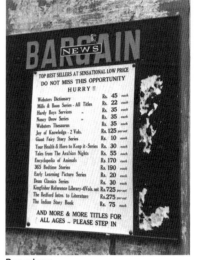

Bangalore

Bangalore (English and Kannada). The Kannada phrases translate (top to bottom) as: 'with love', 'we will build' and 'this world'.

Lancaster

Figure 4.2 Street texts from Singapore, Bangalore (India) and Lancaster (Britain)

Reading the weather: towards a social semiotic perspective on reading

In a memorable formulation, Paolo Freire talked of both 'reading the word' and 'reading the world' (Freire and Macedo, 1987). Recent developments in social semiotics (Kress and van Leeuwen, 2001) have given an additional force to the notion of 'reading the world' by enabling us to extend the notion of reading beyond print literacy to multimodal texts, for example media texts, and indeed to reading the environment. (Anything that can be construed as a semiotic system can be *read* in this sense.) In this case study I (Mike Baynham) develop this broader social semiotic notion of reading to examine the different ways that Jonathan reads the weather. In his round of daily activities he reads the signs of impending weather changes in the sky around his home. Another kind of reading is of the multimodal media text of the nightly weather report, complete with maps, charts and diagrams. A third kind of reading involves the reading of rainfall counts off a scientific instrument.

Jonathan's media-derived knowledge from TV weather charts intersects with highly localised knowledge, as can be seen in the following interview extract (in which 'M' = Mike Baynham):

M   Do you watch the weather on the television?

J   Yes, I do yeah.

M   Do you understand all the charts and the diagrams?

J   Yes, the high and lows and – and troughs and yeah, cyclones and all that, I know them ... like one [storm] we had a couple of months ago ... it could have been the start of a small tornado ... it started off a little pimple in the sky ... miles and miles away, then it got up closer to a pretty big storm front and then right out of the middle, I don't know why, it took about five minutes for it to happen and then there's just this big swirl of cloud just went straight up in the sky ... it took about five minutes to reach as high as it could and then it was like that for the rest of the day ... at night I was still studying it ... I think the storm front came up and we had a low draught coming along the ground and it must have hit ... mountain and went straight up.

We see here the interaction between the technical language of *troughs and cyclone, storm front* and the everyday language of his first hand observations with vivid uses of metaphor *it started off a little pimple in the sky.*

Another form of reading is evidenced in one of Jonathan's household chores, which is to measure and record the rainfall. Gathering and recording the rainfall involves him in complex mathematical activities and associated writing practices:

M   How do they measure the rainfall?

J   We measure that in inches.

M   So, who measures the rainfall?

J   Um usually I do.

M   Do you keep a record of it?

J   Yeah, yeah, we have a [recording sheet] like a you get one from the Land newspaper. We usually buy one off them. I just get up and always write down ...

M   Tell me how you record on the chart?

J   The rainfall.

M   What's it – is it like a calendar or what?

J   Yeah, it's like a calendar. Okay this is 97 okay and you got all your line there and days and whatever. Um now you add up – say that's your first one you write all your numbers down, how much rainfall you had. So say on the 5th of April from 9.00 o'clock on the 5th of April you had rain up until um 9.00 o'clock the 6th of April.

M   24 hours, in effect?

J   Yeah, right 24 hours, you don't write it for the 6th of April you write it for the 5th. So, say all together in this month you had say 6 and blah, blah, blah, all the way through and what you say is a grand total of say 71 inches, all right, okay.

(based on Baynham, 2001, pp. 308–11)

Figure 4.3 A rain gauge

Jonathan is involved in three kinds of reading, each rather divergent from the traditional print-based conception of literacy, but each is an instance of a broader semiotic notion of reading. These different kinds of reading involve at least three different sign systems. First, Jonathan reads and interprets the natural signs from his local environment, watching the cloud formations and movements around his home for signs of the weather to come. Second, he reads and adds up the rainfall count on the rainfall gauge. Third, he also reads the weather charts and maps on the nightly television weather report, interpreting the arrangement of the isobars to identify highs, lows, troughs and cyclones. Jonathan's reading of instruments and charts also involves interpreting and computing numbers. Street (2005) argues that numeracy, like literacy, should be conceptualised not as an abstract set of skills and competencies, but as embedded within social practice in everyday life. In addition to knowledge about mathematical procedures such as addition and multiplication (which may be carried out using a variety of local methods), numeracy events often have a literacy dimension. For instance, reading the rainfall gauge and the weather chart involves reading both words and

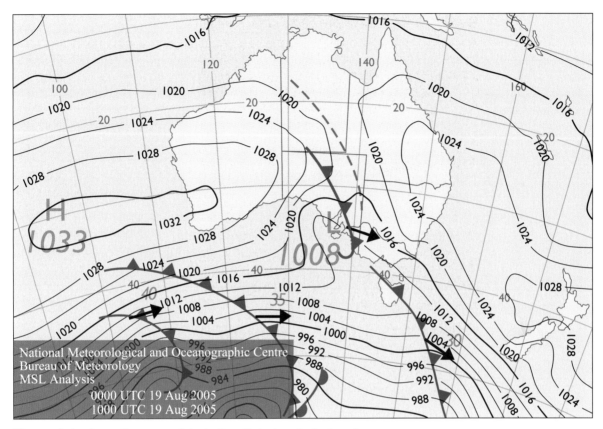

Figure 4.4   A weather map of Australia with isobars indicating air pressure

numbers (literacy) and computing (numeracy). Finally, Jonathan interprets the implications of his readings of words, numbers and images in these three different semiotic systems, for life in his small rural Australian farming community.

This case study illustrates what multimodal reading looks like: reading that routinely draws on both verbal and visual modalities and on literacy and numeracy practices, and incorporates how we read the world around us. What is important here is to understand how the activities, and their associated literacy and numeracy practices, in which Jonathan engages are highly situated in different ways. He draws on his local knowledge as he stands on the porch or looks out of the window and reads the weather signs; nightly he reads the media text of the weather report to access the scientific media-derived knowledge of the weather; and he reads the instrument for recording rainfall in his own scientific, but also highly localised, measuring and recording of the rainfall. Jonathan's ruling passion is driven in part by a very material interest:

the significance of rainfall for farming communities in rural Australia generally. On the coast a good shower of rain may mean a day you can't go to the beach. In the country it could mean the difference between crop failure and harvest.

ACTIVITY 4.7

In this activity, we return to examples of reading the urban landscape of street signs. Read Ron and Suzie Wong Scollon's analysis of the significance of how English and Chinese were used together in street notices in Hong Kong and China during the time approaching the handover of Hong Kong from Britain to China, in 'Place semiotics: code preference' (Reading A). Notice the distinction they draw between **indexical signs** in the notices (i.e. pointing to some aspect of where and when they are located in the world) and **symbolic signs** (arbitrary representations of something in the world). What kind of additional information is needed in order to understand the reasons behind the positioning of the different languages in the notices?

Comment

Scollon and Scollon suggest that uses of English or Chinese in street signs in Hong Kong and China may index the language community they address, or may symbolise 'something about the product or business which has nothing to do with the place in which it is placed'. This is also the case where two languages occur together in a sign, and the dominant code is signalled by its placement above, to the left of, or in the centre, in relation to the secondary code. Where this is not in line with an official policy, the Scollons found that they needed to conduct ethnographic research to find out the reason for a code preference which might, for instance, index Hong Kong's colonial past, or symbolise the global status of Hong Kong commerce. The system of values underlying the preference system, which might be related to 'geopolitical ideology', pragmatic convenience or current fashion, could not simply be read off the text, but required ethnographic and historical analysis.

4.4 Reading and writing practices in English

We have extended the notion of 'reading' to include a variety of sign systems; now we want to turn to the practice of reading and writing. Think about your own uses of reading and writing in English and other languages. You are reading now. Are you sitting comfortably? Where are you reading? Are you reading a page from a book, newspaper or magazine, or are you reading a screen? Are you perhaps reading while sitting at or near a screen? Are you alone in a room, in a library, on a bus, in a doctor's waiting room? How are you reading? Are you reading for study, marking the margin of the page, underlining with highlighter, writing notes as you read? Are you searching websites and bookmarking likely sources to read later? What other kinds of reading have you done during the day? Have they been print based or online? Think also of your own various different uses of writing, at home and at work. Is there a division of labour within your family in terms of the different writing tasks which need to be done? Do you ever write collaboratively with others, or on their behalf?

ACTIVITY 4.8

Allow about
15 minutes

In the Mass Observation Archive extract below a correspondent for the Archive is talking about writing. Look through the extract and note the different uses of writing described by the speaker. How do these compare with your own?

The Mass Observation Archive at the University of Sussex runs a research project in Britain which asks numbers of 'ordinary' people to write in regularly about their everyday activities and about their thoughts concerning key national issues and events of the day. The aim is to document unofficial everyday experience, which is not necessarily recorded in history books. Mass Observation began to collect information during the 1930s and the archive has been sending out regular 'directives' (giving topics for writing) to people all over Britain since 1981. In the extract the researcher (D) is interviewing a regular current correspondent (W).

D   How do you find the time to write for the Mass Ob[servation] project?

W   *[Laughs]* Well at the moment I do it – when it [the directive] arrives I read through it and I think about it at odd moments you know like waiting for the train or on the train going up to work and sort of scribble bits down on bits of paper here there and everywhere and then when I've got the time, which might not be for – nearly 'til the next directive is due, I sit down and write it all out. So – one day, yeah.

[Laughs]

D   And do you write it in this room, or in another room in the house?

W   No I'm usually sitting in the chair and there's probably football or something on the telly that I don't want to watch so I write it then.

[Laughs]

D   Do people mind you sitting there writing away –

W   Oh no they're quite used to it now – I usually do my books [household accounts] in the chair, the finances and a crossword or something, you know – I'm not usually sitting watching television, I'm usually doing something else as well ...

D   Do you – do most of the kind of writing and things in the house, I mean like the books that you talked about, or correspondences and –

W   Yeah, writing letters, everything, yeah ... I don't very often now but I used to write letters to the newspaper and belong to other groups, or – and – yes I read all the mail that comes in and answer the letters and everything ... other people are just not comfortable with writing – I know my dad never was – my mum always wrote the letters. If he did sit down to write a letter he was asking how to spell every other word, and she said to him 'It's laziness with you.' And he said, 'I can't write and think at the same time.' *[Laughter]* And my husband leaves it to me to write all the letters – he'll sign them but he leaves it to me to write the letters. And again it's laziness because he can do it ...

D   – And I also remember from reading your literacy diary that at work you seem to do a lot of reading and writing with other people.

W   Yes, formulating training notes – so with each group, with each – might only be one person – but with each section I would be writing and writing and writing – is this what we want, is this what you're saying we're getting, to make sure ... if I have a meeting like I'm having a meeting with you now, then I would go and write it up afterwards and say do you agree this is what the meeting was about, before I then started to incorporate it into testing or procedures or so on. And then they could come back and say, well no I didn't quite agree to that point, or they come back and say yes, but you missed out that I agreed to more than that, and you've left out this – so that it's to-ing and fro-ing the whole time.

(Interview transcript 2 November 1992, Mass Observation Archive
Project (W632))

Was it clear to you even before she mentioned her husband that the correspondent in the extract was a woman? If so, why? Are there gender differences in the literary practices within your own household?

It is common practice in many British households for the women to do most of the letter writing to relatives, remembering birthdays within the family network, and so on. People also have distinctive patterns for organising communication between members of the household and for organising the many texts which come into the house. For example: both of us, in addition to using a diary to communicate with ourselves and organise our work life, use a family calendar on the wall at home to note down important family appointments and dates.

The kinds of text and the various different reading and writing activities you are regularly involved in, reflect the different '**literacy domains**' within your life – for example, home, workplace, school, shops, bureaucracies, the street. These different domains are associated with different kinds of text and practices, and sometimes, in multilingual communities, with different languages. Domains are of course not totally discrete and in fact literacy activities in English and other languages may cross the boundaries: a child brings her English-language schoolwork home to a house where Panjabi is the primary means of communication; a letter from a government department in Standard English is read at the kitchen table and discussed in a non-standard variety; a personal letter is written in a mix of Kannada and English during a tea break at work.

People's literacy practices are tied up with social and work activities, and are used in maintaining and developing their social networks. Family and social networks can also provide support for people who have particular difficulties with literacy, as was found in a study of people's writing practices in Lancaster, in the north of England:

> Sometimes there was support for people who identified problems. Often it was within the family. Neil, Paul, and Bob all mentioned getting help from their partners. Mark took writing problems to his sister, while Duncan relied on his parents. Liz got help from her husband and her daughter as well as from a friend who worked 40 miles away. Sometimes particular people were chosen for help; Julie's mother would approach an uncle 'because he worked in an office' – one of several examples where work skills extend into the home. When Sally got married, she found that there were many everyday tasks she could not deal with, and she turned to her mother to help her learn the new writing tasks.

> (Barton and Padmore, 1991, p. 69)

In multilingual communities, relatives or friends may perform a particularly important role in helping people to deal with bureaucratic literacy in English. In a study of the communicative practices of urban adolescents in Philadelphia, Amy Shuman describes the ways in which Puerto Rican teenagers, bilingual in English and Spanish, are drawn upon to accomplish literacy purposes within their families. The teenagers act as '**literacy mediators**':

> Many of the Puerto Rican girls took responsibility in their families and community for reading English and translating texts into spoken Spanish. They filled in forms for medical or governmental offices ...

Particularly in their roles as interpreters, the Puerto Rican adolescents performed specialised tasks that were not duplicated by other members of the family. Ordinarily, teenage girls would not be involved in family business of this kind, and their participation as translators sometimes disrupted the social conventions for appropriate age behaviour. All of the teenage girls, black, white, and Puerto Rican, had responsibilities at home, but such assignments did not conflict, as did Puerto Rican translating tasks, with either one's social role in the family or attendance at school. Girls who stayed home to help when a parent was sick tended to be those who preferred not to go to school. The Puerto Rican girls whose skills were needed as translators were most often the best students who otherwise did not miss school and who saw their assistance with translation as a necessary choice between family and school responsibilities.

(Shuman, 1993, p. 259)

ACTIVITY 4.9

Allow about
15 minutes

Can you think of any occasions when you have made use of someone else as a mediator to accomplish a literacy purpose, in English or another language? Conversely, have there been occasions when you have been enlisted by someone else to accomplish a literacy purpose for them?

Comment

When I (Mike Baynham) worked as an adult education worker in London in the 1970s and 1980s, I frequently needed to have publicity information about courses translated into different community languages. My friend Mohammed F., who had been educated in Qur'ānic school, wrote a beautiful Maghribi Arabic script and I would occasionally visit him to ask him to translate a publicity leaflet into Arabic. Conversely, I would often receive a message at work asking me to drop round to see Mohammed as he had a form that needed filling in in English. Both Mohammed and I were serving as mediators of literacy for each other in different languages and for different purposes.

Street typist, Bangalore, India

When asked about his work, the street typist says that he types for 'all sorts of people', including those who are quite well off but might not have a typewriter at home. Almost all the typing he does is for communication with government departments or the courts, including legal documents such as contracts. Some people may bring a handwritten document that he retypes; others may speak English but are not literate in English and will dictate a letter; others may be literate, but not in English, so he will translate from Kannada; he may also compose a letter for those who aren't sure how to do this. He charges 4–5 rupees per page, irrespective of the nature of the task: those who need most help are also the poorest. He makes 100 rupees a day (a modest but sufficient daily wage). He also has a photocopier and employs a man to operate it. He says that many street typists are graduates and some have higher degrees. They need to be fairly well educated as they give advice; they don't just type.

(We are grateful to Donald Mackinnon for this photograph and information.)

Literacy mediation can include help with writing technologies, language and generic conventions. The kind of help people need, and their power to use literacy in the various domains of their lives, is related to socio-economic, political and technological change. Reading B focuses on a community that was experiencing particularly dramatic changes. It examines how the associated changes in literacy practices were having an impact on people's lives.

ACTIVITY 4.10

Read 'Changing literacy practices in a South African informal settlement' by Catherine Kell (Reading B). In what ways were the changes in literacy practices in Site 5 affecting Winnie's role within the community?

Comment

The subject of this case study, Winnie, was living through the period of rapid change brought about by the ending of apartheid in South Africa. At the beginning of the case study we see the powerful role that she played within her community as a problem solver, a political activist, working in three languages – Xhosa, English and Afrikaans – within the horizontal communication networks (i.e. between people and groups of equal status) in the local struggle against apartheid. At the end of the case study, it seems that the pace of political and social change has shifted the communication practices to such an extent that Winnie and other women like her have become disempowered within the fast-developing new networks of bureaucratic communication, and the new discourse of reconstruction.

4.5 Diversity and change

We have seen how reading and writing in English are not just abstract language skills, but are always an intrinsic part of particular social activities and practices. **Literacy practices** (the ways in which people interact with texts and the meanings these hold for them) are tied up with individual identity, personal relationships, community membership, religious practices and political manoeuvring. They also, as we have seen, reflect sociohistorical changes.

We will take an example from the British legal profession to look more closely at the evidence in texts of changes in literacy practices, which are related to broader social and technological change.

ACTIVITY 4.11

Allow about 15 minutes

Look at the two letters in Figures 4.5 and 4.6, each written from one solicitor to another about the sale and purchase of property, one written in 1803, the other in 1995. What differences are there in the two texts and what clues do they give us about changes in literacy practices?

Comment

You were probably immediately struck by the different overall appearances of the two letters. The long hand-written 1803 letter, with only the seal imprint to identify the solicitor's office, looks very different from the short 1995 version, printed on paper letterheaded with all kinds of information, from lists of the firm's members and of the locations of its various branches, to the authorisations from the Law Society and the Legal Aid Board. In addition, the initials and figures used for 'Our ref' at the top right-hand side of the 1995 version not only identify the individual solicitor and secretary who produced the letter, but also give the client number, which can be used by members of that law firm to access a whole range of information held on the firm's computer.

At a more detailed level, there are differences between the two versions in orthography, letter-writing conventions and grammatical style.

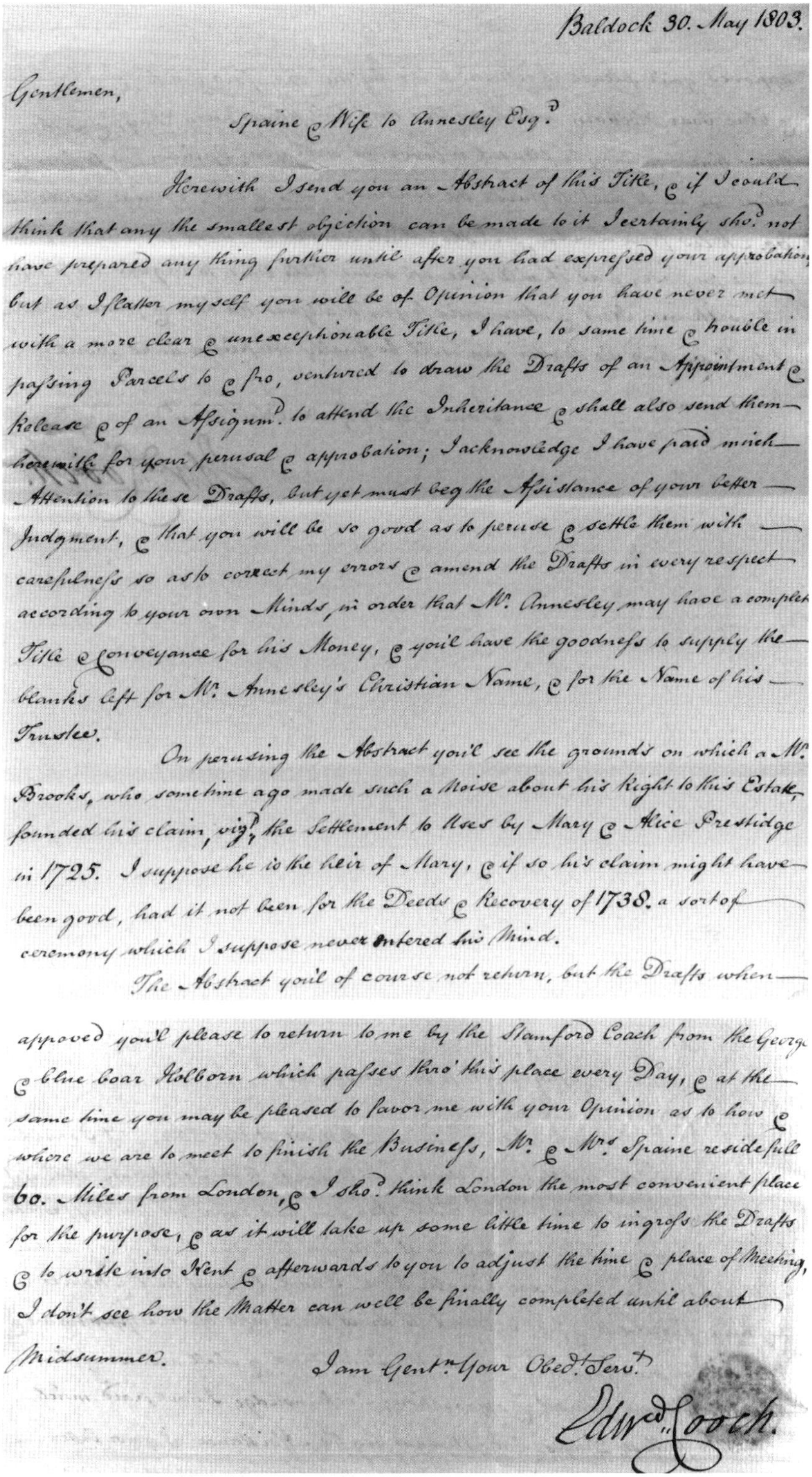

Baldock 30. May 1803.

Gentlemen,

Spaine & Wife to Annesley Esq.r

Herewith I send you an Abstract of this Title, & if I could
think that any the smallest objection can be made to it I certainly sho.d not
have prepared any thing further until after you had expreſsed your approbation;
but as I flatter myself you will be of Opinion that you have never met
with a more clear & unexceptionable Title, I have, to save time & trouble in
paſsing Parcels to & fro, ventured to draw the Drafts of an Appointment &
Release & of an Aſsignm.t to attend the Inheritance & shall also send them
herewith for your perusal & approbation; I acknowledge I have paid much
Attention to these Drafts, but yet must beg the Aſsistance of your better
Judgment, & that you will be so good as to peruse & settle them with
carefulneſs so as to correct my errors & amend the Drafts in every respect
according to your own Minds, in order that Mr. Annesley may have a complete
Title & Conveyance for his Money, & you'l have the goodneſs to supply the
blanks left for Mr. Annesley's Christian Name, & for the Name of his
Trustee.

On perusing the Abstract you'l see the grounds on which a Mr.
Brooks, who sometime ago made such a Noise about his Right to this Estate,
founded his claim, viz.t, the Settlement to Uses by Mary & Alice Prestidge
in 1725. I suppose he is the heir of Mary, & if so his claim might have
been good, had it not been for the Deeds & Recovery of 1738. a sort of
ceremony which I suppose never entered his Mind.

The Abstract you'l of course not return, but the Drafts when
approved you'l please to return to me by the Stamford Coach from the George
& blue boar Holborn which paſses thro' this place every Day, & at the
same time you may be pleased to favor me with your Opinion as to how &
where we are to meet to finish the Busineſs, Mr. & Mrs. Spaine reside full
60. Miles from London, & I sho.d think London the most convenient place
for the purpose, & as it will take up some little time to ingroſs the Drafts
& to write into Kent & afterwards to you to adjust the time & place of Meeting,
I don't see how the Matter can well be finally completed until about
Midsummer.

I am Gent.n Your Obed.t Serv.t

Edw.d Cooch.

Figure 4.5 Letter written on 30 May 1803 from Edward Cooch, Baldock, concerning the conveyance of property from Spaine to Annesley. (This letter has been reduced to approximately half its original size.) [Key: & = ampersand; ſ = long s]

PARTNERS   M.A. Hughes*   J. Lloyd-Jones LL.B   J.E. Clarke BA
M.J. Linnell*   J.P. Sutton BA   C.P.G. Gregan LL.B   C.A. Plews BA
A.E.R. Beesley MA*   A.M. Cowell LL.B   A.G. Hopgood BA   S. Jackson LL.B
M.N.E. Ess LL.B*   S.N. Potter MA   C. Oster MA   E.M.F. Temple MA
J.C.W. Burrough   P.F. Quigley LL.B   ASSOCIATES   CONSULTANT
J.S. Deech MA D.PHIL   J.P.T. Irwin-Singer MA   J.M. Stansfield LL.B   Peter Butler MP

Linnells
SOLICITORS

60 High Street, Newport Pagnell,
Milton Keynes, Bucks MK16 8AQ

Telephone (01908) 613545

Fax (01908) 210654 DX 90905 Newport Pagnell

Messrs. Wenfields
DX 41090 Milton Keynes

OUR REF: NH.AT.RK.30751-1-4
YOUR REF: 09.SP.

21st May 1995

Dear Sirs,

Re:

We enclose herewith Epitome of Title, draft Contract in duplicate, fixtures and fittings form and Replies to Pre-Contract Enquiries. Kindly supply details of your client's full name and address to be inserted into the Contract.

We look forward to receiving one part of the Contract as soon as possible together with an indication of when your client would be ready to exchange. We wish to complete by 24th June 1995 at the latest as our clients have a dependent purchase which is part of a chain.

Yours faithfully,

Linnells

Linnells

BICESTER   HEADINGTON   KIDLINGTON   CENTRAL MILTON KEYNES   NEWPORT PAGNELL   OXFORD   WALLINGFORD

* Notary Public   This firm is regulated by the Law Society in the conduct of investment business.

A QUALITY SERVICE
Approved by The Legal Aid Board

Figure 4.6 Letter written on 21 May 1995 from Linnells, Newport Pagnell, concerning the conveyance of property from one client to another. (This letter has been reduced to approximately half its original size.)

Orthography

- In the 1803 letter capital letters are used for most nouns.
- Different forms of abbreviation (e.g. *you'l*, *sho.d*) were used in 1803.
- The form of the ampersand *℮* and the long s where a word contains two consecutive s's (e.g. *exprefsed*) are no longer used in contemporary English.

Letter-writing conventions

- Abbreviations and ampersands were acceptable and are used in the 1803 version.
- There are different ways of opening and closing the letters.
- The 1803 letter has a more personal tone and uses *I* as opposed to the more impersonal *we* of the 1995 letter.

Grammatical style

- The more tentative, negotiating tone of the 1803 letter comes from its greater use of modal verbs; for example *could* and *should*, and hedging expressions such as *you will be so good*, *you'l have the goodnefs*.
- Although the earlier letter does include nominalisations (e.g. *perusal*, *approbation*, *assistance*), it is less lexically dense than the 1995 version, with its high concentration of legal vocabulary and phrases (*Epitome of Title*, *draft Contract*, *fixtures and fittings form*, *Replies to Pre-Contract Enquiries*, *exchange*, *complete*, *dependent purchase which is part of a chain*).

The differences we have identified between the two letters in Activity 4.11 show how a particular **genre** of text, in this case solicitors' letters, develops and changes over time. The genre of a text is determined by its medium (e.g. spoken, written, visual), the way it uses English (e.g. vocabulary and grammatical forms, text presentation), type of content, and the relationship between writer and reader. Particular genres emerge as the result of institutional needs and practices, and they change alongside them. The first letter comes from a small family law firm which has long-standing personal relationships with its clients, and the second is part of a much faster moving, streamlined transaction by a company dealing at a distance with large numbers of clients every day. The telephone, fax and email, together with more rapid mail services, have largely replaced face-to-face meetings such as the one being arranged in the 1803 letter, and business can now be conducted in a much swifter and more impersonal manner.

The 1803 letter is longer because of its more personal, long-winded tone, but it also has to be longer because the business of proving ownership of a property was more complex and more open to dispute in the nineteenth century. Since the 1925 Land Registration Act, British documentation is more exhaustive and easily obtainable; in the few instances where properties have not yet been registered, photocopies of all existing deeds are supplied to the buyer (the 'Epitome of Title'), replacing the abstracted and hand-copied summaries necessary in the 1800s (the 'Abstract of this Title').

Thus, although these letters both come from a series of correspondence between solicitors about buying and selling property, the contrasts between them reflect changing practices in business and law, and changes in technology, between the early nineteenth and the late twentieth centuries. There are therefore both technological and social reasons behind the changes in genre between the first and second solicitors' letters.

Genres encode social relations (compare, for instance, the way English is used in the personal letter written by Jaya's father with the business letter from Linnells – see Figures 4.1 and 4.6), and they also position the writer and the reader as, for instance, friend, colleague, client, supplicant (think of the different kinds of positioning of people in the texts produced in Site 5 in Reading B; for example, the memo asking for permanent homes and the Development Forum minute).

4.6 Literacy as a loaded term

In this chapter we have discussed a wide range of texts, from street hoardings to legal documents, and a wide range of literacy practices, from committee minute taking to email and participation in chat room discussions. Literacy practices are the observable activities in which reading and writing play a part, but they also depend on the meanings people attach to what they do: the values, attitudes and ideologies that are interwoven with literacy activities.

One of us (Mike Baynham) remembers several years ago noticing the following graffiti on the climbing frame of a north London playground:

> SHARON IS ILLITERATE

What do those three words tell us about the social values connected with literacy in a society like that of Britain? Perhaps the first thing is that 'illiterate' counts as a term of abuse. The kind of social knowledge that the reader brings to the message draws on the emotive force of powerful values, attitudes and ideologies ('literacy good, illiteracy bad') which shape what we read in the newspapers and debates about educational standards. Literacy itself as a social construct is a powerful sorter and categoriser of persons into those who can and those who can't. We saw in the South African case study (Reading B) how Winnie's son taunts her for her inability to read and write, mimicking the discourse of school with its levels and categories of achievement:

> He [the younger son] laugh now, he say 'Mama, are you Sub A?'

These powerful values, attitudes and ideologies attached to literacy, often expressed as moral imperatives, are clearly a significant feature in the social landscape of most countries in the contemporary world. The linkage between literacy/illiteracy is one we ignore at our peril, since it makes up part of the discursive framework within which literacy is conceptualised and discussed.

ACTIVITY 4.12

Allow about
10 minutes

What metaphors and models of literacy do you find in the following quotations from the media in various different English-speaking countries?

1   Like a germ that learns to enjoy penicillin, illiteracy consumes all the armies sent to fight it. No matter what we do about it – and we do a good deal, contrary to complaints from the literacy lobby – the condition persists. Depending on how you count them, adult illiterates make up anywhere from a tenth to a fifth of the Canadian population.

(*Financial Times of Canada*, 4 July 1988, quoted in Barton, 1994, p. 10)

2   Literacy: A Shameful Problem for Every Seventh Australian? Illiteracy is a bigger problem in Australia than most of us probably realise. Some say up to two million people – 14 percent of our population – are afflicted ...

(Australian *Women's Weekly*, 24 September 1977, pp. 16–17, quoted in Hodgens, 1994, p. 17)

3   NSW [New South Wales] schools are turning out a growing number of irresponsible and often illiterate citizens. But the students are not to blame, according to Professor Harry Messel ... 'Changes' had wrecked the system and students were encouraged to do whatever they liked, Prof Messel said.

(*Daily Telegraph* (Australia), 22 May 1978, p. 5, quoted in Hodgens, 1994, p. 22)

4.7 Conclusion

In this chapter we started out by looking at differences between speech and writing in English at the level of text, but moved on to show that engaging with any kind of text involves far more than decoding the symbols on the page (or screen, or wall). Texts are written and read in particular contexts and this influences both their form and their meaning. Because texts are used to achieve social purposes they are written with particular aims in mind, and these also shape their generic form and structure.

We have looked at how literacy practices in English vary across different social and cultural contexts, across monolingual and multilingual settings and across modes. We have also looked at how the characteristics of specific genres of texts change over time, alongside changes in social organisation and technology. Literacy practices in English are always imbued with social values, linked to ideological discourses and are an important aspect of the development and expression of people's personal and social identity.

READING A: Place semiotics: code preference

Ron Scollon and Suzie Wong Scollon
(Ron Scollon and Suzie Wong Scollon are consultants in geosemiotics in
Haines, Alaska.)

Source: Scollon, R. and Scollon, S.W. (2003) *Discourses in Place: Language in the Material World*, London, Routledge, pp. 116–24.

Indexing the geopolitical world

One of the surest ways we locate ourselves in the geopolitical world is through the signs we see here and there about us in city streets, marking road regulations alongside the highway, and labelling consumer products. The snapshot of a city street in [Figure 1] may not tell us exactly which city we are in but we are likely to make an immediate assumption that we are somewhere in an English-speaking community.

Similarly, the sign prohibiting smoking on the construction site shown in [Figure 2] signals presence in a Chinese community. Actually for those with the knowledge to see it, this sign is written using the simplified Chinese characters used in Mainland China (and in Singapore), not the traditional characters which are used in Hong Kong or Taiwan. In this way it indexes not only 'Chinese-speaking community' but 'Mainland China'. The sign further places this photograph in time as these simplified characters were introduced in several waves of language reform which occurred sometime after the 1949 Revolution. Thus it indexes a period of time somewhere between about 1960 and the present.

Here it is worth a momentary return to the signs in [Figure 1]. We see the brand name Casablanca® written in a font which is not much used in our contemporary period but which was widely used at the turn of the nineteenth to the twentieth century. Was this photo taken then? Obviously it was not because we also see signs with much more recent lettering styles on the same store, not to mention a glance at the windshield of a very recent model car. Furthermore, the image is taken in color photography which was not available at the time that 'Casablanca' font might have been used as a straightforward advertising sign. In other words the font choice in this brand name is symbolic rather than indexical. It symbolizes the period of time in which ceiling fans were once popular and with which they are associated in the modern public mind. It does not index that time in the way that the contemporary fonts and signs as well as the color photography index our own period.

Figure 1

Figure 2

It is possible that we could be deceived, however, in going by the language used in and of itself. The sign for a beauty parlor shown in [Figure 3] is in English. It says, 'Beauty Island'. Of course it is possible that this would index an English-speaking community as did the signs in [Figure 1].

This sign was seen in Nanjing, China. Here we think that the use of English is much like the use of the 'Casablanca' font in [Figure 1]. It is to symbolize rather than index. English is used to symbolize foreign taste and manners; it does not index an English-speaking community.

Figure 3

We believe that there are at least two clues to this in this sign. One is the name itself which, at least to our ears, is rather non-native-like in its style. 'Beauty Island' seems a bit odd as the name for a beauty salon. In fact, by the same principle that this Chinese beauty parlor has an English name, in the US one might find a European name – most likely French – to symbolize this same placement of the business within a class social structure.

The second clue is in the elaboration of the final 'y' of the word 'beauty' as the visual centrepiece of this image. The image is constructed within a circular center-and-periphery design which, as Kress and van Leeuwen have pointed out, is often used in Chinese and other Asian picture constructions. What makes this stand out as quite likely *not* a native use of the language is the emphasis that this design principle gives to the 'y'. We would not want to say that such a thing would be impossible for an English-speaking designer, but it does seem to us that other semiotic conventions such as the capitalization of only word-initial consonants works very strongly against the choice of this design principle.

From these examples we can see that the actual language used – English, Chinese, French, etc. – can either **index** the community within which it is being used or it can **symbolize** something about the product or business which has nothing to do with the place in which it is located. These same distinctions can be made through the choice of fonts or indeed preferred visual semiotic systems of construction. ...

... Whether our concern is with code preference based on geopolitical indexing or with symbolization based on sociocultural associations, we must have some evidence from *outside* the signs themselves to make this determination.

...

As we shall see below, the main semiotic resource by which code preference is produced when more than a single code is used is placement within the picture or in physical space.

A point on methodology

When a text is in multiple codes (two or three or more languages such as English and Chinese) or multiple orthographies there is a system of preference. ... The preferred code is on top, on the left, or in the center and the marginalized code is on the bottom, on the right, or on the margins.

...

Of course we will need to clarify more carefully that we do not really have any solid evidence about languages that have a normal text vector (direction of writing) from right to left such as Arabic, nor about how Arabic and English are displayed to show code preference where both of those languages are used. Much research remains to be done in this area. ... [I]n places such as Hong Kong and Quebec the relative position of the two official codes is governed by law and is in agreement; that is the upper position in signs is the preferred position, the lower position is secondary as shown in [Figure 4]. Also the preferred code in Quebec, French, must be presented as more salient than any secondary or peripheral code.

Figure 4

Naturally, these legal policies are frequently violated, particularly in domains at some distance from legal concern. For example, in Hong Kong street signs and governmental offices fall within these strictures, but commercial signs and private notices are not regulated by these policies. The methodological problem arises when there is no legal or policy requirement to guide the analysis. ...

[In such a context] we need to have independent evidence either for the semiotic system or for the preference of the code. This is an empirical question that can be settled largely through ethnographic means. In our research in Hong Kong and China, for example, we found there was almost a continuum of domains from tightly controlled ones to extremely loose and occasional ones. Government regulations control the code in street signs, for example, and throughout Hong Kong English is placed on top and Chinese is placed below that, this despite the fact that Hong Kong is overwhelmingly a Chinese speaking and reading speech community. This code preference rather transparently represents a carryover from some century and a half of colonial rule.

In commercial domains it is somewhat more complex an issue. If we take large shopping malls as an example, there is a continuum from those in which there is a uniform design principle which is carried throughout the mall and all official signs, that is all signs that are prepared by the owners of the mall, fit within a single design principle. One mall, Festival Walk, maintains a rigorous pattern of English on top or on the left, Chinese below or on the right as exemplified in [Figure 5].

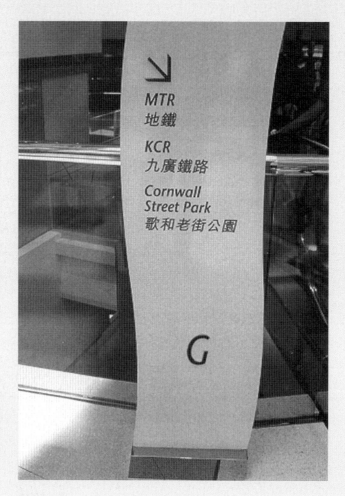

Figure 5

In this case one might say that the principle invoked was that this is one of the newest malls in Hong Kong – it just opened as we were doing this research – and it is firmly positioned within the broadly international sphere of globalizing commerce. Characteristically the mall has many upper-end fashion shops as well as restaurants providing offerings from the major world cuisines. It might be going a bit too far to argue that this mall was firmly asserting the global status of Hong Kong and its commerce just at the historical moment when sovereignty over Hong Kong was returning to China, but there is some feeling in this mall that goes much beyond just the positioning of words in signs that the same code positioning is here indicating a global (English) vs local (Chinese) pattern of choice rather than the colonial (English) vs colonized (Chinese) pattern we see in the street signs.

Our point is that the same binary choice of English and Chinese is a semiotic code system which may be used in the service of quite different ideological positions – colonialization on the one hand and globalization in the twenty-first century on the other.

In Hong Kong the Mass Transit Railway (MTR) is another unified complex which carries throughout its entities a single semiotic system. Throughout the territory color schemes, train, station, and platform designs, colors, and materials are uniform. Likewise, the code preference system is uniform, but in the case of the MTR it is Chinese which is placed in the upper position, English in the lower (or left and right and center and periphery).

This flip-flop is perfectly consistent through these two coherently designed systems operating within the same speech community. We believe this tells us two things: first, there *is* a coherent code preference system which privileges the top, the left, and the center, and second, the code preference should not be assumed to reflect any particular community or ideology in some *a priori* way. That must be determined through further ethnographic research.

In this case of the MTR system we believe that the selection of Chinese as the preferred code does not reflect a resistance to or inversion of the British colonial history – the company is, after all, a Hong Kong government company – nor does it reflect a resistance to the forces of globalization – it is one of the sleekest and most efficient of the world's high technology metropolitan transport systems. We believe the code preference for Chinese in the MTR represents a pragmatic decision to maximize indexability for the vastly dominant Chinese-reading population of Hong Kong (about 98 per cent). Chinese is where it is because that is the code being indexed by the predominant users of the system. All the more then does the 'preference' for English in street signs reflect the colonial ideology and the English in the shopping mall reflect the globalizing economy because this flies in the face of the pragmatics of simply reading the signs.

We believe such comparative broad systems as those of a shopping mall or of the MTR (and there are many others which we have considered as well) indicate a clear code preference semiotic system, upper–lower, left–right, center–periphery. What is much more difficult to 'read' is what system of values is selecting this preference system. It might be geopolitical ideology, it might be pragmatic convenience, it might be current fashion. This aspect of the analysis cannot be 'read off' simply from seeing the code choice which has been made but must be subjected to historical and ethnographic analysis.

References for this reading

Kress, G. and van Leeuwen, T. (1996) *Reading Images: The Grammar of Visual Design,* London, Routledge.

Kress, G. and van Leeuwen, T. (2001) *Multimodal Discourse: The Modes and Media of Contemporary Communication*, London, Arnold.

READING B: Changing literacy practices in a South African informal settlement

Catherine Kell
(Catherine Kell is a learning designer at the Centre for Flexible and Distance Learning, University of Auckland, New Zealand. She was previously a lecturer and researcher in the Department of Adult Education, University of Cape Town, South Africa.)

Specially commissioned for Baynham and Maybin (1996, pp. 67–76). (Revised by the current chapter authors.)

(Catherine Kell's research in Site 5 is more fully documented in her thesis: see Kell, 1994.)

This reading draws on my literacy research near Cape Town, just before the first national democratic elections in South Africa in April 1994. 'Winnie' is the real name of Winnie Tsotso. All other names are pseudonyms.

I am sitting in Winnie's wood and iron shack in Site 5. The relentless wind is blowing, whipping up the sand and sending it back inside the houses through holes in the iron and plastic roofs. In the darkened room, I am talking with Winnie, and while we talk, a stream of people come in and out of the house, asking for things. It is difficult for me to understand what they say as all the conversation is in Xhosa, but Winnie goes to the cupboard and takes out a tin, riffling through some papers in it, while the person watches. I notice that the tin contains numerous documents. 'No,' she says, 'your identity document has not yet arrived' ... 'Is this your clinic card?' ... 'Here is your ANC [African National Congress] membership card.' Winnie, who speaks fluent English, Xhosa and Afrikaans (and knows a little Sotho, Tswana and Zulu), plays the role of unappointed and unpaid community advice worker. Yet she does this largely without literate skills, and is in the local night school class for those who cannot read and write, classified as a 'beginner'.

The establishment of Site 5

Site 5 was an informal settlement of about 3,500 mainly black, Xhosa speaking people, which was established outside Cape Town in 1993 after decades of struggle by its residents for land in an area previously designated for whites. Winnie, a 48-year-old black woman, was one of the local women leaders who were thrown up during the years of struggle when former farm labourers who found work as domestic workers or gardeners in the surrounding white homes started to live in the bush, but were repeatedly harassed by the authorities. These women leaders, with assistance from anti-apartheid

Figure 1   Winnie

organisations, took the residents' case to the South African Supreme Court in 1988 and won the right to stay in the area.

The anti-apartheid organisations had brought the squatters together with other groupings facing similar problems. At these meetings and workshops there was no reliance on text: problems were talked out, expressed through narrative, drama and song, and collective action such as marches or sit-ins planned. Sometimes memoranda were drawn up together. At times the squatters' own voices were represented, but these were mediated by the anti-apartheid activists, as in this extract from a memorandum written by the squatters with activists' help, and sent to the Cape Provincial Administration in 1988. The memo asks for the right to permanent homes and freedom from harassment:

> We write to you as elected representatives of the above communities. All of us are people who have moved from bush to bush for many years searching for a permanent place to stay ... What we want are houses we can afford, near our places of work. We see houses being built around us, but they are for people who already have houses. They are not for people like ourselves. Although some of us are grey we have never had a key to our own home ...

In the late 1980s and early 1990s, horizontal communication between the squatters remained oral, in Xhosa and face to face. Vertical communication, however, between the squatters and more dominant groups with power and resources, was increasingly taking written form, in English, through the mediation of staff in the anti-apartheid organisations. Throughout their history of resistance, the squatters never gained access to the means of delivering their words themselves beyond their community. For this, English schooled literacy and the means of distributing it were becoming increasingly necessary.

Literacy in Site 5

While I was researching in Site 5 I found remarkably few signs of public literacy; there was very little print – no street signs, adverts or brochures to be seen. Now and then a political poster was put up, or a small photocopied sign advertising Aids Day. Some residents made their own signs advertising services or goods. In most houses, the walls were papered with recent English newspapers, but no one whom I met in Site 5 ever bought a newspaper to read.

In Winnie's house a pile of eight books and pamphlets in English sat under a table. It included one women's romance, one booklet of recipes called *Food for the Soul* and two booklets on health issues and ANC matters. All of these were in English. The children's books were discards from households where Winnie had worked as a domestic worker and I noticed children looking at them once or twice. Her daughter and a lodger had read the thriller and the romance and discussed them. In one cupboard Winnie kept her tin of documents, ANC membership book and invoice book for her soup kitchen. At one point she brought out a box of papers from the ANC: agendas, resolutions and minutes (mainly in English, with a few items in Xhosa). On another occasion a group of ANC members was sitting in her lounge working on ANC posters advertising a local meeting. These were the only texts I saw in her house, and this was by far the highest number I saw in any house in Site 5.

Winnie's fluency in the three main languages of the Cape region initially enabled her to develop an important political role for herself in the community. For instance, she was one of the longest standing key members of the squatter committee which had become the official Civic Association (CA). She was also a member of the health committee and the preschool committee in Site 5, and of the Catholic Welfare and Development Committee (CWDC). Over a period of ten consecutive days when I visited her house, I calculated that she attended eleven meetings or functions.

Despite her own lack of literacy skills, Winnie's role in these meetings involved dealing with a variety of literacy practices. For instance, one night she told me she had to attend a commemoration meeting for an ANC marshal who had died in a fire in a nearby squatter area. I was later told that Winnie gave a speech in Xhosa and that photocopied sheets were given out with the words of *Nkosi Sikelel' iAfrika* (the national anthem) on them. I asked her about the photocopies, and she said that one day two senior ANC people came to Site 5 and were upset that people didn't know the words of the national anthem. 'So we took a copy to the ANC office and made other copies to give to the people.'

On another occasion Winnie told me that she was worried because the preschool teachers had come to her demanding an extra month's money (as it was close to Christmas time and they had not had a bonus). 'But I know that it was not written on that what do you call it?' (conditions of employment). Winnie was constantly involved in literacy practices such as these, initiating and organising them, yet she saw herself as 'illiterate'.

New South Africa, new literacy practices?

As Site 5 became more established and integrated into the surrounding infrastructure, new demands were being made of the leadership. Various bodies were involved in development in Site 5; in some ways they drew on old traditions, in others they brought in new discourses. Gradually, the oppositional anti-apartheid discourse of the organisations that had supported the squatters was being replaced by new discourses of reconstruction and development. There was a contrast between the CA, with its roots in the early years of local struggle, and the newer and powerful Development Forum (DF), which was set up to co-ordinate development efforts in Site 5. The CA met after dark, in the shack attached to the primary school. Proceedings were entirely in Xhosa, and I never saw anyone from outside Site 5 attending them. In contrast, the DF meetings were held in the primary school building in the afternoon and the proceedings were all in English, with minutes and agendas. It was attended by representatives from welfare agencies and NGOs, and by interested individuals from the surrounding white areas, as well as by representatives from the CA.

One incident at a DF meeting which sticks in my mind seemed to bring into focus the conflict between the old and new discourses in Site 5. Mrs Brown, a local white woman who owned a building company with her husband, had organised donations to construct the new primary school for Site 5 and had managed to procure fencing and roll-on lawn. She reported that the school committee wanted the men of Site 5 to spend a Saturday putting these in place, and asked if this could be discussed at the next CA meeting. The DF minutes (taken by the white ex-mayoress of a neighbouring suburb) duly noted:

> 4. Education: Community to assist with erecting fencing for school, school committee to progress. Need for liaison between school and civic committee stressed.

The clause structure and verb forms here are typical of English committee minute writing, but they are difficult for someone who is unfamiliar with such literacy practices to understand. In fact the minute did not seem to me to reflect the proceedings at the meeting, since the community had not yet agreed to assist and the CA representatives present at the meeting did not make any contribution at all to the discussion about the grass and fencing.

Three months later the fencing had still not been put up and the schoolchildren themselves had laid the lawn. It was reported that the men were not prepared to do the fencing unless they were paid. They needed to sit at the Four-Way Stop (a large crossroads near Site 5, where men wait to be offered casual work) on a Saturday morning, to try to pick up a day's gardening work in the white suburbs.

At the next DF meeting, Mrs Brown asked exasperatedly why the men couldn't do the work. For a few minutes there was an electrifying silence. Miriam, the preschool co-ordinator in Site 5, then explained:

> The men are angry that they should contribute to the school, when the community has been deprived of education and facilities for so long. They feel the DET [government department] should be taking over the school and providing these things.

Winnie added: 'And also the people are angry that they have to pay a lot of money to use the school for meetings.'

The discourse of reconstruction and development with its underlying assumption that 'we must all work together for the betterment of Site 5' is reflected in the DF minute, but for most of the Site 5 members the dominant discourses are still those of opposition and survival. The primary school, welcome as it is for the children, charges a high rental when its rooms are used by local groups; and as one young community leader explained to me, 'The community feels that this whole school has just been dictated to them.'

Winnie, who occupied such a key community role during the years of struggle, only made three brief contributions during the three DF meetings we attended together. I wondered why she contributed so little, especially as she is fluent in spoken English. When I considered her history, and scrutinised the DF proceedings more carefully, the reasons for her lack of involvement became clearer to me.

Winnie gained her confidence and her fluency in the situations of horizontal communication that I referred to earlier, in workshops among squatters, ANC gatherings and Civic Association meetings. Communication was largely in Xhosa, and there was little reliance on text. Events such as these were dominated by discourses of opposition and survival, with an ethos of collective participation. In these contexts, Winnie could draw on her great strengths in horizontal communication – her facial expressions, body postures and gestures, and her reliance on prosodic devices and narrative. In the DF, however, in the politics of the 'new South Africa', the oppositional discourse is disallowed in the cause of reconstruction. In the context of the rapid formalisation of Site 5, its incorporation into mainstream governance, its dependence on outside agencies for resources and the urgency of the reconstruction, vertical communication (that which takes place between squatters and dominant groupings) had rapidly become more regular and important. The DF was saturated with committee and other bureaucratic literacy practices in English. Contacts to obtain resources from outside the area were made in written English, with the DF acting as mediator.

Winnie was all too aware of the growing importance of being able to read and write in English. She explained how she wanted to get a job as a community worker in Site 5 so she could be paid for all the work she currently does informally. The fact that she was seen as 'illiterate' had excluded her from such a post. She had started attending the Site 5 night school every night where, as was common policy in South Africa, she had to learn to read and write in Xhosa before being allowed to start learning literacy in English.

Adults at the night school learning English worked exclusively from photocopied materials produced by an ESL (English as a Second Language) and Literacy Organization in Cape Town. Learners were taught basic comprehension skills, such as identifying the topic of a text and understanding relationships between paragraphs. I never saw any materials being brought in to the classes which were not part of the pre-planned curriculum: not one text, or even one written word from the context of the learners' lives entered the classroom. This can be contrasted with an experience I had with Winnie at home: when I went through an invoice for her soup kitchen with her, I found that she could actually read quite a few of the words on it.

What became clear to me was that a very particular type of schooled literacy was being promoted in the night school, which did not mesh with the existing literacy practices in the community, or with any of the learners' more specific reasons for wanting to attend the school.

I was disturbed by the way that powerful women like Winnie were being somehow positioned in the night school as deficient and incompetent. Winnie said that previously her children didn't know that she was unable to read or write. Now they did:

> He [the younger son] laugh now, he say 'Mama, are you Sub A [reception class]?' Sometimes I'm sitting here and write my things and he say 'Ooooh, look my mother, she's Sub A! Come, come and look.' If he roep [calls] his friends, I just close my door.

Conclusion

Unfortunately, the thrust towards modernisation in South Africa means that literacy (including English) is being seen as a commodity which must be delivered for the purposes of human resources development, rather than as a critical social practice in which power relations are deeply implicated. But so much is possible in the new political conditions in South Africa. Before 1994 there were two official languages, English and Afrikaans. Now there are eleven official languages, including Xhosa. This may start to make a small difference in places like Site 5, as long as development workers and literacy activists are aware of the particular relationships between languages, literacies and power in the South African context. If they are, they could swing the balance of power back towards the local community and seriously address its historical disadvantage. In contrast, literacy provision which draws on current support networks and existing social practices could strengthen learners' positions rather than undermine them, and the great strengths that were developed during the years of liberation struggle, such as empowerment, participation and democratic decision making, could be affirmed.

5 English at work

Neil Mercer and Almut Koester

5.1 Introduction

In Chapter 4 the focus was on varieties of written English and how they vary as a result of different contextual features. This chapter looks at both spoken and written English and how it is used as a language for work. In all the cases we discuss, at least one of the people involved is self-evidently doing what millions of people the world over do every day – using English to get a job done. In looking at English at work, you will see how the language is used in sequences which construct a **speech event** such as a business negotiation, and in shorter sequences, **speech acts**, such as giving instructions. You will examine examples where the language of work has its own specialised vocabulary and its own specialised written texts. You will also see that the language used to get things done is simultaneously contributing to the relationships established between people at work.

A tool for the job

The Russian psychologist L.S. Vygotsky (1978, p. 26) describes language as the most important 'cultural tool' that humans possess. The idea of language as a tool is useful because it focuses attention on the purposes and effects of using a language, and helps us see that the contrast between 'doing things' and 'just talking' is a dubious one. People achieve things through talk as much as through physical action.

To understand the ways in which English is used to get things done at work we need to look at how occupational or professional interests are represented in the dynamic structure and content of the language. That is, we must see how the English language itself is adapted to serve as a suitable tool for different kinds of work.

The structure of language events

ACTIVITY 5.1

Allow about
5 minutes

Read the following extract from a real conversation. What kind of business is being done?

Speaker A	Speaker B
We'd like to get some state business.	
	I will have to work out something, Joe, where you could visit with the trustees.
Do you control Mr Gordon?	
	He'll go along with a lot of the things I recommend.
How do you and I develop a relationship?	
	I have a public relations firm ... and I do business other than what I'm doing here.
I can give you $2,000 now, with a 50–50 split of the commission.	
	Keep talking.
I deal only with you. There's $4,000 a month possible in this.	
	We'll deal on a case by case basis. Can you handle X Insurance Company politics?
Here's $2,000. Let's shake hands on it. Do we have a deal?	
	We have a deal.
	There's 50 people I can send you. I have contacts in Boston.

(adapted from Shuy, 1993, p. 24)

The conversation in Activity 5.1, as you may have guessed, shows two people involved in negotiating a bribe. It comes from the research of a sociolinguist, Roger Shuy (1993), and is a conversation between an undercover agent for the American law enforcement agency the Federal Bureau of Investigation (FBI), Joe Hauser (Speaker A, who secretly recorded the talk), and a trade union official (Speaker B) who was a target of the FBI's enquiries. Roger Shuy has studied many such secretly recorded, clandestine conversations, and has offered the following analysis of the structure of an archetypal 'bribe' transaction.

Phases	Speaker A	Speaker B
Problem	We'd like to get some state business.	
		I will have to work out something, Joe, where you could visit with the trustees.
	Do you control Mr Gordon?	
		He'll go along with a lot of the things I recommend.
	How do you and I develop a relationship?	
		I have a public relations firm … and I do business other than what I'm doing here.
Proposal	I can give you $2,000 now, with a 50–50 split of the commission.	
		Keep talking.
	I deal only with you. There's $4,000 a month possible in this.	
		We'll deal on a case by case basis. Can you handle X Insurance Company politics?
Completion	Here's $2,000. Let's shake hands on it. Do we have a deal?	
		We have a deal.
Extension		There's 50 people I can send you. I have contacts in Boston.

(adapted from Shuy, 1993, p. 24)

Shuy claims that this 'phase' model can usefully be applied to all the tape-recorded data that he has seen presented by the FBI in bribery cases. Entry into each of the phases depends on the successful completion of the previous one. After some initial greetings (which might be considered to constitute a preliminary phase in themselves), a *problem* is presented by the first party. This usually amounts to a request for help. During this phase, the first party usually also checks on the other's authority and capacity to deliver. The next phase is the *proposal*, in which rewards are discussed and promises made. If things are going well, this phase may be used to build some kind of intimacy, with common acquaintances being mentioned, anecdotes told, and so on. The final part of the negotiation is marked by entry into the *completion* phase, classically symbolised by the handshake and expressions like 'We have a deal'. There may then follow an *extension* phase, with future possibilities being introduced.

Shuy's method of analysis is intended as a practical one, and its use has influenced the course of some court cases and retrospectively cast doubt on the validity of the verdicts of others. For example, in a number of US bribery cases involving politicians and other public servants it has been claimed by the state prosecution that the fact a public servant has even engaged in a conversation with a would-be briber is sufficient to show that they are corrupt. Shuy suggests that juries are often persuaded by this line of argument, because people generally assume that two people talking together in reasonable tones, without explicit disagreement, must have shared values and purposes. Those accused of corruption are then convicted on the basis of what he calls 'conversational contamination'. Shuy also comments that many American trial judges are unwilling to admit a linguist as an expert witness in court because they claim that any normal person can understand a conversation when they hear it, and that to analyse talk in depth is to impose false levels of meaning on 'common-sense' understandings. However, he shows that a more careful analysis of events may reveal that the attempted bribery did not follow the model pattern, that the accused person did not collude in the construction of a model event, and that the crucial stage of completion (in which 'the deal' is made) may never have materialised. An example is the following extract from a recorded conversation between a US politician (Williams) accused of corruption and an FBI agent (Farhart) masquerading as an Arab sheikh seeking residence in the United States. In earlier conversation, Williams has agreed to advise the sheikh on how he might best present his case to immigration, but with no suggestion of impropriety:

> FARHART   I will, for your help, uh, assistance, I would like to give you ... some money for, permanent residence.
>
> WILLIAMS   No. No. No. No, when I work in that kind of activity, it is purely a public, not uh, No, within my position, when I deal with law and legislation, it's not within ... *(telephone rings, interrupting)*. My only interest is to see this come together.

(Shuy, 1993, p. 32)

As Shuy comments, on this occasion a proposal for a bribe may have been made, but it was clearly rejected. However, his analysis did not save Senator Williams, who was convicted and imprisoned on this and similar tape evidence (none of which, Shuy suggests, was any more convincing about the senator's guilt than the example above).

Talk in its work setting

We have spent some time on Shuy's forensic analysis of tape recordings because it raises some interesting points about the use of the English language as a tool to get things done:

- Doing a certain kind of work is likely to involve the creation of distinctive patterns and content of discourse in the English language.
- The distinctive features of these language events may not be apparent to the participants, or even to a casual observer who listens to a recording of the event, but they can be revealed by an analysis which is based on an understanding of how the English language operates as a system and how it is used, in practice, in particular social contexts.
- The analysis of such non-obvious features of English in use can have practical applications.

Bribery may be an unusual form of work, but in this respect – that it is accomplished through certain distinctive ways of using the English language – it has something in common with a great many perfectly legitimate kinds of professional and commercial activity. Sometimes the distinctive, work-related features of the language are most obviously those of vocabulary: the 'jargon' or technical language of a trade or other occupation. (We deal with such technical language later in this chapter.) But sometimes, as in the case of bribery, the work-related quality of language may be more distinctively represented in the structure of an interaction, rather than the fact that technical English words are used. Shuy's analysis also demonstrates how language is used to construct and maintain 'working relationships', social bonds and commitments between people which develop through doing a certain kind of work and which may be closely bound up with the nature of the work itself.

Two types of language event

At this stage we would like to distinguish between two kinds of social event in which English can be used as a 'working language'. First, there are *events in which the people involved are members of the same, or a closely related, occupation, trade or profession*. Second, there are *events in which a working person is, as part of his or her job, dealing with a member of the public*. Do not think of this as a hard and fast distinction, but as a rough one which can be useful for understanding the nature of some kinds of 'working Englishes'. In the rest of this chapter we deal first with:

- **English among co-workers:** the Englishes associated with different worlds of work, different professions or occupations

  and then with:

- **English between experts and the public:** how English is used in interactions between those in different fields or professions and the general public; that is, between 'insiders' in a particular work English and 'outsiders'.

5.2 English among co-workers

In research on the use of English and other languages at work there has been a tendency to focus on occupations in which language constitutes the work to a great extent; one product of the work of lawyers and journalists, for example, is spoken or written language. It may be less obvious that language also plays an important role in 'getting the job done' for other kinds of occupation, such as manual, constructional ones and those which rely heavily on types of representation besides language (such as the plans and blueprints of engineers and architects).

Figure 5.1   Talk is an important 'tool of the trade' for the construction industry

ACTIVITY 5.2

Read 'Constructing the virtual building: language on a building site' by Peter Medway (Reading A). As you read, pay particular attention to Medway's use of the concepts of ideational function, interpersonal function and intertextuality.

Comment

You can see from Medway's research that the business of constructing a building is achieved to a great extent through language. It is not simply a matter of an architect drawing up plans and then handing them to the builder who converts them into three-dimensional reality. The whole process is one of explanation, interpretation and negotiation as the architect attempts to construct a 'virtual building' in advance of the real one, through conversations with builders and others involved. Medway uses Halliday's concept of the ideational function of language to explain this. But he also points to the **intertextuality** of the discourse – the ways in which various conversations, at different times and involving different sets of partners, are woven 'into a single multi-stranded web of discourse' which 'knits the diverse participants together into a discourse community'. He notes, too, the many different semiotic systems employed by those involved in the construction. (You may recall the different semiotic systems referred to in Chapter 4, particularly in the discussion of 'Reading the weather'.) Medway refers to Halliday's concept of the interpersonal function of language for establishing and monitoring relations in such a community. He shows, for example, that the architect's use of swear words in this conversation serves an emotional need, possibly expressing his annoyance.

It may seem surprising to talk about emotions in the context of work, but clearly emotions need to be expressed at work as well as outside it. In fact, interpersonal meanings are expressed in many aspects of workplace language. The degree of formality or informality of any interaction or text is a reflection of the relationship of the participants; and the use of in-group jargon, swear words or even vague reference to shared knowledge can all be devices for bonding and building solidarity. Furthermore, not all workplace talk is work focused: co-workers also engage in small talk and gossip which fulfil interpersonal needs. Finally, positive and negative evaluation (of jobs and people) plays a central role in workplace language, and the way this is expressed (e.g. directly or indirectly) is inextricably bound up with the relationship of those involved in the evaluation.

English as an international language for business and trade

English has been a language for 'getting things done' in many parts of the world, and not just among native English speakers. The use of English as a trading language – a **lingua franca** between people who have different mother tongues – goes back many years in some countries and, more recently, English has become the international language for business and trade. In fact, there are now many more people using English for business communication, whose mother tongue is not English, than people who use it as a native language. In being adapted to this use, a lingua franca may evolve into a new language variety with a simplified grammar and limited vocabulary. Elements of the grammar of one or more of the local mother tongues may be incorporated into the new variety, which is then technically called a **pidgin**. Pidgins sometimes eventually become the main language of some communities, rather than a specialised kind of 'work talk'. If this process results in children learning the pidgin as a mother tongue, the new language technically becomes a **creole**. A good example of work language which has expanded in this way is the Tok Pisin (talk pidgin) of Papua New Guinea. According to the sociolinguist Suzanne Romaine (1990), it was born in the colonial era. It was used first as a means of communication between the indigenous population and their European colonisers, but then became the most important lingua franca for Papua New Guineans, who have around 750 indigenous languages between them. The example below is an extract from a radio interview broadcast in 1972. The speaker is a student, and the written version of what he says represents a conventional, 'standardised' form of spelling. Healey provides both a 'word-by-word' translation into Standard English (in the second column) and a more thorough, meaningful translation (in the third column):

Mi salim eplikeson bilong mi na skul bod i konsiderim na bihain ekseptim me na mi go long skul long fama.	Me send application belong me and school board consider and behind accept me and me go to school of farmer.	I sent my application to the school board and then they considered and accepted me and I'm going to agricultural school.

(from Healey, cited in Romaine, 1990, p. 197)

Although English pidgins and creoles were first developed in parts of the former British Empire, English is now being used as a lingua franca on a global scale, and new forms of pidgin may be evolving. The Austrian linguist Barbara Seidlhofer (2001) and a team of researchers are currently examining the use of English as a lingua franca to see whether any simplifications or other systematic uses are occurring and whether a new kind of pidgin is emerging.

Intercultural business communication

Once a pidgin is established, the redefined meanings of some English words (e.g. in Tok Pisin *bihain* = *behind* as an adverb for creating past tenses) will become common knowledge to all involved, and pose no problem to the mutual understanding required for trade. However, even when business partners have established some variety of English as a common language, difficulties of comprehension may arise for other reasons. Helen Marriott (1995) has carried out research on 'intercultural business negotiations' – transactions which involve people from significantly different cultural backgrounds. Some of her data come from video-recorded talk between a Japanese businessman and an Australian cheese manufacturer, all in English even though the conversation was held in Japan. Here is an extract from their conversation.

J	And eh what your object to eh visit to me, is that eh introduce for eh this
A	We'd like to sell to Japan
J	sell to Japan
A	yeh
J	uh huh
A	or make it in Japan.
J	mm ah here yes
A	Either way, whichever is the best.
J	mm
A	Maybe make it here for um six months and eh if it's acceptable
J	ah six, six months
A	well we could send some samples from ⌈ Australia
J	⌊ in Melbourne uh huh
A	and just test the market (.) if it's good we could then make it in Japan
J	uh huh (.) uh huh
A	with a joint venture.

(Marriott, 1995, pp. 260–1)

Transcription conventions

- J = Japanese speaker
- A = Australian speaker
- deep brackets [indicate overlapping speech
- (.) indicates a pause

Marriott found that there were significant differences between the two men's behaviour in the interaction. The Japanese man often sought clarifications, and periodically offered summaries of information discussed. That is, he used strategies to check that there was shared understanding of matters being negotiated. After the recording, Marriott interviewed the two men to gain their views of how the transactions had gone. Both felt that the other had not talked in the ways they would have expected, given their business role. So, for example, the Japanese commented, 'in Japan maybe the salesman speak more, more explanation about the eh his company's and the condition of the trading' (Marriott, 1995, p. 263). The Australian, on the other hand, felt that the brevity and non-committal nature of the Japanese man's reactions to his comments (as in the extract above) left him feeling 'that I don't really know what he's going to do. It finished a little bit unconcluded' (Marriott, 1995, p. 262). Overall, then, the two men constructed rather different understandings of events from the conversation, and the Australian was left feeling much more dissatisfied with the encounter than was his Japanese partner.

Although the Japanese speaker was very ready to admit to inadequacies in his English, Marriott suggests that this was not a major cause of misunderstanding.

Instead, she suggests that the different expectations held and interpretations made about the conversation by the two reflected other, less obvious differences in their cultural backgrounds and experiences. To some extent, this may be a matter of Japanese and Australian people having different habitual conversational styles – ways of expressing intent, interest, and so on, through words and gestures which vary considerably across societies. But Marriott emphasises that explaining misunderstandings in terms of cultural experiences does not mean simply making generalised comparisons between Japanese and Australian ways of talking. In the international business world of today other cultural factors besides national origin might be important for shaping speakers' ways of 'talking business' in English, and for shaping their interpretation of events. The Japanese man worked in a large, international organisation: he had much more experience of intercultural business negotiations than the Australian; he had dealt a lot with foreign business people in Japan and had made several work trips abroad. The Australian, on the other hand, worked for his own small firm, had travelled little, and his previous work had not engaged him in these kinds of negotiation. In other words, the Japanese businessman was probably more familiar with the discursive practices of international trading, and so may have had a clearer and more confident set of expectations about the 'ground rules' for carrying on such a business conversation, and for predicting its structure and outcomes.

Figure 5.2 An international business meeting

However, many international business interactions occur without any problems of comprehension or interpretation. Gina Poncini's (2002) study of an Italian company gives an interesting insight into how successful intercultural business communication takes place. She studied the Italian company's meetings with its international distributors from twelve to fifteen different countries, at which English was used as a lingua franca. The company referred to as *Alta* below (not its real name) makes products for skiing and other outdoor sports. Poncini examined how business relationships were developed at meetings; for example, she shows how personal pronouns (such as *we*), technical terms and evaluative language are used to create a sense of group identity and build a positive relationship between the company and its distributors. These strategies show similarities with the political speeches discussed in Chapter 2. They draw on the resources of English to establish interpersonal relationships. The example below illustrates the way in which one of the company representatives uses evaluative language (highlighted) in order to build a positive image of the company:

> uh Edo yesterday explained to you that (+) our **success** (.) the **success** of *Alta* (+) has grown together (+) parallel (.) to the **success** of our athletes (++)
>
> **the the** best **example in this case is Rossi** (++) ((well known Italian skier))
>
> where Rossi (+) began to **win** (+) uh he **won** (.) thanks (.) to (.) *Alta* (.) to products of *Alta* (.) also- not only (.) of course ((smiles, almost laughs))

(adapted from Poncini, 2002, p. 361)

Transcription conventions

- (.) short pause under 0.3 seconds
- (+) pause of about 0.4–0.7 seconds
- (++) pause of about 0.8–1.7 seconds
- (( )) contextual information

Poncini suggests that 'the company speaker uses evaluation strategically to create a shared image of the company, its products, ... activities and strategy so that the image comes to represent what is highly valued by the group' (Poncini, 2002, p. 361). Poncini's study shows that national culture may not necessarily be an important factor in intercultural business interactions. It also shows that, even in a situation where English is used as a lingua franca, the language is not only utilitarian or 'instrumental', but also has an interpersonal dimension. Here positive evaluation is used to build a sense of group identity among participants with diverse national and cultural backgrounds. This illustrates the point made at the beginning of this section, that evaluation is one of the most significant types of interpersonal meaning commonly expressed in workplace language.

English for written business communication

Of course, a great deal of international business communication does not occur in face-to-face interaction, but across distances on the telephone, or in writing by letter, fax or email. In order to negotiate or take part in meetings in English, a good command of the language is required, but some types of written communication may be of a specialised and limited kind, and therefore do not require a high level of proficiency in English. Ulla Connor (1999) provides an interesting example of the use of English as a lingua franca in written business communication. She looked at faxes sent by a Finnish broker in the fish importing/exporting business. The broker she studied actually had a high level of proficiency in English, but simplified his language when dealing with less proficient business partners – for example, Estonian suppliers – as shown in the message giving instructions for delivery in Figure 5.3.

```
Barrels of head-off herring is OK.

Documents: Health/Sanitary/Quality certificates
  Certificate of origin

Your invoice to [Company name] should not
follow the truck. It will send to Helsinki.

Enclosed two documents will follow the truck.

Number of copies:
  Please give the truck driver two sets of orig-
inal documents and
  keep one set in your file.

[Company name] is asking as soon as possible a
set of documents to Helsinki by fax.

OBS! [Company name]'s contract is based on
100kg per barrel. Is that correct?

Best regards
```

Figure 5.3 Fax sent by Finnish broker to an Estonian fish supplier (Connor, 1999, p. 123, Figure 3)

The language used in the fax in Figure 5.3, consisting of short, simple sentences, contrasts with faxes sent to a Japanese buyer, which use more polite and sophisticated language, as shown in Figure 5.4.

These examples show that the Finnish broker adapted his use of English to the needs of the person he was corresponding with, a process known in

```
[Seller company name] has not
yet received any payments of
green roe. Could you please
check what is causing the
delays or when it has been
paid in Tokyo.
```

Figure 5.4 Fax sent by Finnish broker to a Japanese buyer
(Connor, 1999, p. 126, Figure 5(1))

sociolinguistics as **accommodation**. According to Connor, the level of English of the business partner is only one of the factors accounting for the broker's language variation. Other factors are the business partner's cultural background, the broker's own role in the interaction (as buyer or seller) and his relationship with the business partner. So, for example, his language is more polite in the fax to the Japanese buyer, because he is showing deference to him as the customer, but also because he believes (as he stated in an interview) that 'the Japanese are polite people' (Connor, 1999, p. 125). However, when the broker is in the role of buyer, the tone of his faxes is more direct and informal. In his interactions with the Estonian supplier, the broker is also acting as a kind of 'big brother' by explaining everything in detail and therefore trying to help the supplier, as a newcomer to the international market. Another interesting example of accommodation in the broker's correspondence (not illustrated) was the use of Estonian or Norwegian words when communicating with Estonian and Norwegian suppliers; for instance, he uses the term *mandel fisk* (literally 'almond fish') to refer to a type of fish they are both familiar with. This switching between languages, or codeswitching, occurred for a number of different reasons: 'in most cases for clarity, sometimes for fun or to create solidarity' (Connor, 1999, p. 122).

The above examples of spoken and written international business interactions show that the language used in such situations can differ in a number of ways from that of people interacting as native speakers of English. It may be simplified and more restricted, with an emphasis on clear communication and a tolerance of linguistic errors; and cultural factors may influence the interaction in a number of ways. Nevertheless, the examples also show that there is a great deal of variation in the level and function of the English used in such situations (even by the same writer or speaker), and that it fulfils both ideational and interpersonal purposes.

Jobs and jargons

Even people who speak English as their first language will often use a specialised variety of it, at least in terms of vocabulary when they are at work.

ACTIVITY 5.3

Allow about
15 minutes

Read the telephone conversation transcribed below and consider the following questions.

- What kinds of job (in general terms) do you think that the speakers do?
- Are they strangers, or do they work in the same business?
- How many jargon words do they use that are not part of your vocabulary for your own working life?
- Do you feel confident that you understand what they are talking about?
- Is it likely to be problematic, for the effective purposes of this working conversation, that the speakers use jargon?

Caller	Is Ellen there? It's Bill.
Switchboard operator	I'll put you through.
Ellen	Hello, Bill.
Bill	Oh, hi. Just a quick, um, query. Umm. You know, uh, with the CNS job.
Ellen	Yeah.
Bill	Umm, you know we were talking about the, the range which it's possible, the salary range?
Ellen	Yeah.
Bill	The two scales just join on, do they, end on? ⌐ Or ...
Ellen	⌐ Yeah.
Bill	... you know the discretionary range?
Ellen	Yeah, well ...
Bill	*[Interrupting]* Is that an overlap?
Ellen	Um. Strictly speaking it isn't.
Bill	Oh right.
Ellen	But we had someone appointed to the PTA ...
Bill	⌐ Yeah.
Ellen	⌐ who was earning above the top of the scale ⌐ where
Bill	⌐ Yeah
Ellen	... she came from.
Bill	Yeah.
Ellen	And that was a short-term post and she was allowed to be appointed ...
Bill	⌐ Aah.
Ellen	⌐ to a discretionary point, so that might be an option.

Transcription conventions

- deep brackets [indicate overlapping speech
- ... indicates continuous speech
- punctuation has been inserted to make the transcription easier to read

You may have guessed that this was a conversation between two people who work in the same business; they are in fact a manager (Bill) and an administrator (Ellen) in the same university. Their work often brings them into contact, and this is one reason why they can begin the conversation with few preliminaries or extended explanations. They both know the nature of each other's jobs, and in their conversation can build easily on the common knowledge of their shared workplace and of past conversations they have had on related topics (hence the use of expressions such as *you know we were talking about* and *you know the discretionary range*). They are continuing an earlier discussion of the point on a salary range at which an appointment could be made to a post in the university. The most obvious jargon words are the acronyms (CNS and PTA – Centre for Nursing Studies and Professional Training Area), which, because they are not real English words at all, would be completely incomprehensible to outsiders. Three-letter acronyms (TLAs) have become a common feature of business English. The phrase *discretionary range* is made up of two English words with established meanings, but the meaning for the speakers in this conversation depends on some very specific, shared knowledge about the financial working practices of British universities. Because the speakers' past experience has prepared them well for this conversation, the jargon used is certainly no problem. It is one normal feature of the English language being used efficiently as a specialised tool of work.

Of course, the use of jargon (the word itself seems to have entered English from French) often does create problems. Its use by professionals when communicating with a 'lay' person can result in non-comprehension and frustration (or, at the very least, irritation) on the lay person's part. In discussing many 'uses and abuses' of jargon, however, Walter Nash (1993) points out that jargon words and phrases often become incorporated into the mainstream of English language use. Some examples are *IQ* (from psychology), *programmed* (from information technology/mass media) and more recently *dysfunctional* (originally a medical term, but now frequently used to talk about a family or other types of groups or organisations with problems). A rather different kind of extension of the use of jargon English occurs when technical words are taken up as 'loan words' or 'borrowings' by speakers of other languages operating in specific areas of work. According to the Moscow-based journalist David Hearst (1994) 'business Russian' has incorporated such words as *lizing* (leasing), *bankrotia* (bankruptcy), *fond* (fund) and *privatizatsionny* (the meaning of which we leave you to guess).

Discourse community

In Chapter 1 Janet Maybin makes two important points about the language of 'everyday conversations' and the knowledge that speakers need to have in order to take part in them. First, *the meanings of words are shaped by the contexts in which they are used*; and second, the communicative success of almost all conversations depends heavily on speakers and listeners having some *shared cultural knowledge and understanding*. These points are very relevant to understanding how English is used as a working language, especially if we also make use of the concept of a **discourse community**. This concept has mainly been developed by the linguist John Swales. As Swales (1990) explains, the basic idea is that there are types of 'community' in which people do not necessarily live close together or even ever see each other face to face, but still share communications using a specialised '**discourse**' (here meaning the ways in which language, spoken or written, is used in the social practices of such a community). This discourse community may be geographically dispersed yet its members use spoken or written language, among themselves, to pursue some common goals in ways that distinguish them from other groups.

The concept of discourse community is helpful for analysing English at work, because it helps us relate the nature of specialised varieties of English to the shared experience and common interests of the groups of people who use them. Swales (1990) suggests that, to qualify as discourse communities, groups not only need a technical discourse but also common interests and goals. Even so, specific discourse communities may be hard to define. For example, although 'Joe' in Reading A is a member of the professional community of architects, the reading shows that he is also a member of a wider 'construction industry' community of discourse, in which some technical language, interests and goals are also shared.

ACTIVITY 5.4

Allow about
5 minutes

Think back through your own life experience. Have any of your activities involved membership of a group that used a distinctive variety of English? If so, try to list up to five vocabulary items that would not have been easily understood by people outside the group.

Genres

Swales also says that discourse communities use genres, which he defines as 'class[es] of communicative events ... which share some set of communicative purposes' (Swales, 1990, p. 58). This definition of genre expands on the one you read in Chapter 4, Section 4.5, and is useful in looking at the characteristics of different types of workplace interaction. Remember that at the beginning of this chapter you looked at the way in which conversations involving bribes follow a particular pattern. Many workplace genres have predictable structures, and they usually also have specialised vocabulary. But genres may also have other typical characteristics, including particular grammatical structures and a formal or informal style, and specific roles are often played by the participants.

ACTIVITY 5.5

Allow about
15 minutes

The extract overleaf is from a conversation one of us (Almut Koester, see Koester 2004 and 2006) recorded between two people who work in the back office of a US food co-operative. The bookkeeper, Ann, is talking to Meg, the new assistant she is training. This conversation is an example of a genre which occurs frequently in many different types of work: instruction giving. Read the transcript and answer the following questions:

- Who initiates the instruction-giving dialogue: the boss (Ann) or the subordinate (Meg)?
- Do you notice any particular patterns in the structure of the conversation?
- What role does each play in the conversation?
- Is there any specialised vocabulary?
- Do you notice any language (grammar or vocabulary) that is typical for instruction giving?
- How would you describe their relationship?

Comment

Meg, the subordinate, initiates the instruction giving in turn 1 by indicating that she has some queries (*I wanna ask you about things I wasn't sure about sorting*). Advance summaries like this of what an enquiry or meeting will be about are quite common in workplace or professional conversations. A clear pattern emerges in the talk, in that Meg asks questions or simply shows Ann the document relating to her query (turns 1, 4, 14), and Ann responds with instructions and explanations (turns 2, 5–9, 11–13, 15); Meg then acknowledges she has understood, usually by simply saying *okay* (turns 3, 6, 8, 10, 14, 16). The two speakers have clearly defined roles in this conversation: Ann as the instruction giver and manager, Meg as the one receiving instruction and training. The structure of the conversation reflects these separate roles; for example, we can see that Ann's turns are longer than Meg's, whose turns often consist of a single word. You probably noticed some specialised vocabulary to do with delivery and sales: *bill of lading, packing list, packing slip*. As for language typical of instruction giving, we find verbs such as *show, do, put*, and imperatives like *hang onto it* (turn 7), *the next thing you do* (turn 11). However, it is interesting that Ann often gives instructions in a more indirect way:

- *I would do this ...* (turn 11)
- *you can go ahead an' put it back in here* (turn 13)
- *we'll look through here ...* (turn 13)
- *let's treat that as an invoice* (turn 15)

1)	Meg	Before I get going to onto another computer, here I wanna ask you ... (Ann: Okay.) about things I wasn't sure about sorting. *[1.5 sec pause]* Bills of *la*ding?
2)	Ann	That is ... comes with every delivery an' it can be thrown away.
3)	Meg	Okay.
4)		*[Meg shows Ann something]*
5)	Ann	Uhm ... *that* is for the Save the Earth stuff, and ... I will- it will ev*en*tually probably get thrown away, but ... if you haven't come across a packing list for Save the Earth products
6)	Meg	Okay.
7)	Ann	hang onto it.
8)	Meg	Okay.
9)	Ann	'Cause I'm just- I'll show you what to do with it.
10)	Meg	Okay.

[a number of turns have been ellipted]

11)	Ann	Then the next thing you do is ... There *should* also be a packing slip for this one here. So ... I would do this ... staple that bill of lading onto that *in*voice, 'cause we know *those* two go together.

[9 secs pause]

12)	Meg	So they're all in this /?/

[8 secs pause]

13)	Ann	Okay, and ... just- assuming that our packing slip's gonna come from upstairs, you can go ahead an' put it back in here. An' then at- like at the end o' the month ... we'll look through here an' say wait a second. what happened to that packing slip an' figure it ⌈ out then.
14)	Meg	⌊ Okay. ... Alright. An' then: ... other things I had /????/ This ... uh- is this just a- d- do I just treat this-
15)	Ann	Hmmm ... let's treat that as an invoice for one case at twenty-seven bucks, ⌈ an' that's it.
16)	Meg	⌊ Okay.

Transcription conventions

- deep brackets [indicate overlapping speech
- ... indicates noticeable pause of less than 1 second
- ( ) around utterances interjected by a speaker within another speaker's turn
- /?/ indicates inaudible utterances: one ? for each syllable
- *italics* indicate emphatic stress
- the dialogue has been punctuated to aid understanding

This conversational, interactive way Ann gives instructions, even phrasing the instruction as a joint activity (*we'll*, *let's*), shows that the relationship between the two speakers is friendly and informal. This example illustrates the fact that genres have predictable structures and characteristics but can also vary; for example, in the language used and in who initiates the conversation (e.g. the instruction giver or receiver).

Speaking the same discourse

At the beginning of this chapter we suggested that it is useful to make a distinction, even if not a very firm one, between two general kinds of work-related language events. These are:

- language events in which only 'professionals' are involved (i.e. involving people who may well both be members of the same community of discourse)
- language events involving both professional and 'lay' persons (in which both participants are not likely to be members of the community of discourse for the work involved).

So far, we have dealt mainly with the ways in which English is used as a working language within certain discourse communities. In the next section we concentrate on the ways in which English language is used by 'professionals' as they deal with 'clients', 'customers' or other members of the public.

5.3 Working with the public

One obvious but nevertheless critical aspect of many communications between 'professionals' and 'lay' people is the extent to which the professional is willing and able to talk about relevant topics in a way that is clear to the uninitiated outsider. The issue here is not simply a matter of professionals remembering to avoid the use of jargon. For example, there is the well-known phenomenon of 'blinding with science' whereby a professional tries to maintain control and exert power over a lay person by deliberately not making allowances for lack of understanding, thus representing themselves as experts and the gatekeepers to powerful knowledge. Of course, some professionals may, out of force of habit or because of the technical nature of their activities, find it very hard to speak of their work in any language other than that of their discourse community.

In Section 5.2 we referred to Marriott's (1995) research on intercultural negotiations. Similarly, the lack of common knowledge and understanding between a professional and a client may not be confined to technical matters, but may be related to other differences in the cultural and linguistic experiences of the people involved. Roberts and Sayers (1988) have directly addressed this issue by recording and analysing job interviews and other similar interactions involving white, British English-speaking interviewers and interviewees who were immigrants to Britain (mainly from the Indian subcontinent) and for whom English was a second language. Their research was aimed at providing good equal opportunities training for interviewers who dealt with people of varied ethnic and linguistic backgrounds. Like Marriott, they found that problems sometimes arose because the speakers did not have the same shared understanding of the ground rules for carrying out this specialised kind of conversation. They also considered how an interviewee's lack of fluency in English affected the process and outcomes of the interview. You can read about some of the results of their analysis in the box below. (Note that supplementary benefit used to be a form of welfare assistance available in Britain, and that a supplementary benefits officer was a civil servant responsible for deciding people's eligibility for this.)

Keeping the gate: how judgements are made in interethnic encounters

In ... cases where interviewers have recognized second language difficulties as playing a role within the interview, there is a tendency to use the language factor as a reason for not clarifying misunderstandings. They assume that any of the candidate's talk which they did not understand was therefore meaningless, i.e. not meaningful for the candidate. Instead of clarifying such utterances, interviewers choose to ignore them. In this way they often fail to grasp where key points for the candidate are occurring, and the whole interaction starts to go wrong. As a case in point, see [the] example [below]. Here, an unemployed Bangladeshi worker was afraid that the amount of money he had managed to save was near the limit for supplementary benefit [eligibility]. He was persuaded to ask a supplementary benefits officer on one of our training courses [about this]. It was a risky thing to ask and he put the question indirectly by first stating how he was unemployed and living as best he could on little money but still managing to save small amounts.

Example

Int	What's your enquiry please, Mr. A?
Mr A.	Enquiry?
Int	What's your enquiry? What's your problem?
Mr A.	Me? Not problem, you know. Yes. Me, after three years, been three years, you know, unemployed.
Int	Three years unemployed, yes.
Mr A.	Unemployed, no money, you know.

Int	Not enough money.
→ Mr A.	Yes, if I saving next time any money, you know, ten pound, five pound, I keeping bank and building society.
Int	Yeah, I see. What sort of money do you have coming in at the moment?

The interviewer then goes on to ask a long series of questions to check whether Mr A. is getting all the benefit he might be entitled to, and Mr A. is never given the opportunity to ask his question about savings. The interviewer was quite happy at the end of the interview that Mr A. had come to check that he was receiving the correct benefit and was very surprised when we (the trainers) told him of Mr A.'s intended question. The key part of Mr A.'s introduction (marked → on the transcript above) where he begins to mention savings is also the place where the surface structure of his English deviates most from standard. It is also the only part of Mr A.'s introduction where the interviewer does not repeat back what Mr A. said. The interviewer had failed to understand the surface structure (here syntax and prosody) of what Mr A. said, and consequently disregarded its content and did not seek to clarify it. The interviewer confirmed this for us afterwards on viewing the video recording of this interview.

(Roberts and Sayers, 1988, pp. 130–1)

Roberts and Sayers suggest that problems of understanding in interviews are as likely to be caused by the ways in which interviewers react to an interviewee's lack of fluency in English, as by the lack of fluency itself. They also refer to the greater control that an interviewer usually has over the content and structure of the talk, so that interviewers can choose to ignore or pursue topics in ways that interviewees would not dare. Issues of power and control can also be important for understanding the structure and outcomes of any language event. We consider these issues in more detail in the next section.

Power and control in professional–client relationships

The following is a transcription of a telephone conversation one of us (Neil Mercer) had at home, at about 8.30 in the evening. I reached the phone too late to switch off the answerphone, which is why the conversation was recorded.

| ME | Hello [telephone number]. |
| CALLER | Hello. *[Conversation is then halted by the recorded message on my answerphone.]* |

ME	Sorry about that, I didn't reach it in time.
CALLER	Mr Mercer?
ME	Yes.
CALLER	I'm speaking from Holmes Insurance, we sent you a letter recently, and did you get it?
ME	Uh, um, I'm not sure, uh …
CALLER	We wrote to offer you a free consultation, with no obligations, on your personal finances. We are completely independent financial advisers, who can offer a wide range of insurance and investment tailor-made for our clients. Could we call and discuss this with you?
ME	Uhhh, no, no thanks, I think that we have, we don't need anything like that right now. If your letter turns up I'll read it. So thanks, cheerio. *[Hangs up quickly]*

Like many other people, I am plagued by what seems like an excessive amount of telephone selling (though I have no real standards of comparison). This rather informal evidence encourages me to believe that the call transcribed above was fairly typical in that it had the following characteristics:

1   As with all incoming telephone calls, I was the first speaker. Once I had spoken, the caller addressed me formally by my (assumed) title and last name, in an enquiring manner that begged confirmation.

2   Once I had confirmed my identity, the caller talked quickly and fluently in a 'sing-song' way that suggested either reading or performing a rehearsed script.

3   All the caller's turns ended with a question addressed to me. That is, having imparted some information, the caller then elicited information and a conversational turn from me.

4   I terminated the call.

On the recording I initially sound hesitant and confused, while the caller sounds relatively confident and 'in command'. Yet I terminated the call, because ultimately I have control. An unsolicited salesperson has no right to my time and in such encounters I can choose to have the last word. On the part of telephone sales staff, one of the earliest stages of their training must be developing a familiarity with the 'scripts' of their trade, with the intention that they can confidently and effectively deliver the message and interest their potential customers in their product. The risk of this strategy, however, is that hearing a script that is obviously prepared and rehearsed may alienate a potential client or customer, because they feel they are being set at a disadvantage, having to think and talk spontaneously without the benefit of such preparation. Early recipients of telephone sales calls, say back in the 1960s, were probably caught even more off balance, because such conversations then were novel events. They would not have had past experience to help them categorise the event and predict how it would unfold.

In a telephone sales encounter, control of the conversation may shift, at various times, between the participants. In some other kinds of encounter, the relative status and authority of the participants may be such that control remains much more consistently in one person's hands. One common and much researched kind of language event is the interaction between a doctor and a patient. Think of one particular kind of medical consultation, where a patient returns to the doctor for the results of an earlier diagnostic test. On the basis of casual reflection on our experience of such events, we may think of such consultations invariably having the following structure (after some initial exchange of greetings):

1   Patient (or patient's representative, such as a parent) asks what has been found out.

2   Doctor tells the patient.

In fact, research (such as that by Maynard, 1992) shows that events rarely follow this pattern. Patients rarely begin encounters with doctors with direct requests for information. Perhaps out of deference to the perceived status and authority of the medical profession, patients usually allow the doctor to organise and control the encounter. And doctors do not necessarily provide diagnoses in a straightforward, informative way.

Consider the following discussion between a doctor (Dr) and the mother (Mo) of a child who has been found to have severe learning difficulties. It is a simplified version of a transcription presented by Maynard. (This is not an initial consultation, but a discussion following identification and investigation of the child's problem by the doctor.)

Dr   What do you see as – as his difficulty?

Mo   Mainly his uhm: the fact that he doesn't understand everything. And also the fact that his speech is very hard to understand what he's saying lots
⌈ of time.

Dr   ⌊ right.

Dr   Do you have any ideas <u>why</u> it is? Are you: d ⌈ o you?

Mo   ⌊ No.

Dr   Okay I, you know I think we <u>ba</u>sically in some ways agree with you insofar as we think that Dan's <u>main</u> problem, you know, does involve you know <u>lan</u>guage.

Mo   Mm hmm.

Dr   You know both, his being able to under<u>stand</u> you know what is said to him, and also certainly also to be able to exp<u>ress</u>, you know his uh his thoughts, hh uhm, hhh in general his development.

(adapted from Maynard, 1992, pp. 337–8)

Transcription conventions

- deep brackets [indicate overlapping speech
- words spoken emphatically are underlined

Maynard suggests that a model of this encounter would consist of three turns, as follows (he uses the US English 'clinician' to refer to any consulting doctor):

1 clinician's opinion-query, or perspective-display invitation;

2 recipient's reply or assessment;

3 clinician's report and assessment.

(Maynard, 1992, p. 333)

He suggests that this model represents a generic conversational strategy (used by other 'experts' as well as doctors) for giving one's own assessment of a situation in a cautious manner, by initially soliciting the viewpoint of another interested party. The strategy is useful because it offers the doctor the possibility of *exploring* the patient's own understanding of the condition, *confirming* the patient's own perspective (which may well draw on earlier conversations with the doctor) and then *reformulating* the patient's explanation of events. The analysis of professional–client language has been an active area of research in recent years, and some research of this kind is described in Reading B by Jo Longman.

ACTIVITY 5.6

Read 'Professionals and clients: form filling and the control of talk' by Jo Longman (Reading B).

Notice how Longman discusses the processes of:

1 *filtering*, whereby a professional selectively responds to what a lay person says according to its perceived relevance to their work (note the links here with the research of Roberts and Sayers, 1988, presented earlier in this section)

2 *reformulation*, whereby a professional paraphrases and recasts the contributions of lay participants so that their content and style is in accord with the professional's conception of appropriate style and context. (And note here, too, the link with Maynard's, 1992, research on doctors and patients, discussed above.)

It is interesting to consider how well the practices of filtering and reformulating the language of lay people can be justified in different professional settings where a written account of events is generated by a professional person. It might seem, at first consideration, that any distortion of what has actually been said must be wrong, so that, for example, police officers who transform statements from suspects' spoken words into their own might well be considered to be fabricating evidence. However, although in most English-speaking countries formal interviews with suspects are tape-recorded and transcribed, police officers who are taking statements from witnesses and others at the scenes of crimes are not commonly required literally to *transcribe* what they are told. Rather, they are expected to use what the suspects said to prepare on their behalf a written statement. It can therefore be argued that a necessary part of a police officer's job is to use their professional understanding of the needs of the law court (and of the discourses of the legal community) to 'distil' the most relevant information provided by the suspects and present it in a suitable form.

In the case of the counsellors studied by Longman (see Reading B) a similar but perhaps even stronger justification for acts of filtering and reformulation can be made, because (as she explains) an explicit part of the role of counsellor is to act as a kind of public relations agent for clients, helping them to present themselves in the best possible light to trainers and potential employers through the 'Personal Training Plan' form. One could argue that the counsellors would be failing in their responsibilities to their clients if they did *not* filter and reformulate clients' statements in preparing the forms. The acts of filtering and reformulation can therefore carry quite different moral implications in relationships between lay people and professionals, according to the situation and the job being done.

5.4 Conclusion

One of the main points made in this chapter is that, as a 'tool' for many occupations, the English language takes on a range of distinctive forms. We can see the specialised nature of spoken and written 'working Englishes' in characteristic textual structures, syntax and vocabulary. We can also see that language used at work performs not only the ideational function of representing ideas, events, etc., but also the interpersonal function of developing and maintaining working relationships.

The concept of a discourse community and the use of specialised genres are useful for understanding the ways in which English is used in communications between professionals in a trade or other occupation. The discourses of professional communities may have characteristics which reflect the professional aims and goals, the social settings in which communication takes place, and the specialised nature of the knowledge shared by members. The ways English is used as a discourse of work can also be seen to embody social, emotive aspects of workers' identities and relationships, as well as the more obvious needs of effective information exchange. As in the rest of life, work-related language events embody issues of power, control and accountability. Understanding the use of English at work must include a consideration of these and other social and cultural factors.

READING A: Constructing the virtual building: language on a building site

Peter Medway
(Peter Medway lectures in English in Education at King's College, London.)

Specially commissioned for Mercer (1996, pp. 108–12). (Edited by Ann Hewings.)

Building a building is a physical process, a process of moving matter into new arrangements, so why should language come into it? Common sense and experience suggest a reason must be the need to coordinate the efforts of a sometimes large and shifting group of participants. Division of labour creates a need for language. People need to be told what to do, and to tell each other what they are doing, need to do and are about to do. And if the building process is not straightforward there is a need, too, for consultation and deliberation as well as instruction and information; people need to work out solutions together, and that implies using language. Sometimes the language is spoken, face to face or over the phone, and sometimes written, on paper or in electronic media.

So what exactly gets done in language, and how does the English language work to coordinate action? Evidence from recordings I made of a construction job in Ottawa, Canada, will provide some answers. On the one hand, talk and writing during construction are highly task-oriented; there is a pressing physical job to be accomplished, through content-laden, reference-heavy communications about hard facts and problematic situations (what Halliday (1994) calls the 'ideational' function of language). However, the participants are also always building, maintaining and enacting relationships, adjusting their utterances and texts to express those interpersonal recognitions of status, authority, expertise, dependence and the like on which the smooth running of the job depends (which Halliday calls the 'interpersonal' function).

The ideational aspect of language works mainly by encoding two sorts of reference, to entities (including things, people and abstract ideas) and to processes, relations and actions. These referential needs are realised in English roughly through noun phrases on the one hand and verb phrases on the other. As we would expect, the needs of particular contexts, such as a building site, require a repertoire of specific encodings for the things and processes of that world. Talking about walls, floors and wiring is different from talking about psychological traumas or international trade flows. At the most obvious level a vast number of architectural and building entities and processes will need to be nameable, as well as the size, extension, location and material properties of the elements of the building. There will be references to the way elements relate in space or to the way they are joined, separated and grouped.

We know that drawings fulfil many of the communicative needs of architects and builders, often much better than language could. (Try describing a complicated run of ductwork in words.) But some vital things only language can do. An example: an architect (let us call him Joe) was working on a building. ... At one point in his tour of the site, inspecting progress and being alerted to problems, Joe was led by Harry, the consultant responsible for heating and ventilation, to a spot on the third floor. A third member of the party was the site supervisor, Luc.

Harry had earlier phoned to tell Joe that the heating and ventilation ductwork had proved bulkier than anticipated, so that the planned space to accommodate it, between the ceiling (not yet installed) and the concrete slab above, would now be inadequate. Here is how the transaction opens.

1   Joe   OK, next.

         *[He looks up towards the underside of the concrete slab. Harry
         walks a couple of steps, pointing upwards. Joe and Luc
         accompany him.]*

2   Harry   <...>, right? <> the ductwork coming down that way
                       is supposed to <>

Transcription conventions

- <> indicates an inaudible word
- <...> indicates a short string of inaudible words

Harry's sentence probably finished with something like *is supposed to go through there*. Two forms of symbolic communication are in evidence: language and gesture. (It is easy to forget that pointing is a sign which has meaning only because of convention.) Here, as in a great deal of the communication in building construction, gesture works symbiotically with language, giving meaning to words; *coming down that way* has meaning because it is accompanied by a pointing movement. Language is here doing one of the things it can do best – refer to absent entities. (No ductwork has yet been installed.) The verbal resources by which this is done include the technical term *ductwork*, the verb phrases *coming down* and the second one that was inaudible, and, very importantly, those English resources used to specify and elaborate the verb phrase. The choice of *is supposed to* here gives the location, extension and direction of the ductwork the status of a reality that does not but should exist.

To Joe the solution seems immediately obvious: just lower the ceiling. In fact, Harry has already proposed this:

3	Joe	Well as you were saying yesterday on the phone, Harry that if *[9-second pause]* if we lower this part by three inches [Harry: yes] that will be fine, right?
4	Harry	This should be fine, [?because] the ductwork can be penetrating through there OK <>
5	Joe	Because this is at twenty-six hundred and this is twenty-seven seventy-five.
6	Harry	That's right.

(The dimensions are ceiling heights in millimetres.) So far, then, we have noted the simultaneous operation of two semiotic systems, and the key role taken by the array of resources for giving specificity to the verb phrase. Despite the shortness of the extract, there are two more important points to be made. First, what the transcript does not show, but the video recording does, is a crucial shift in reference and the introduction of a third semiotic system. What Joe was doing during that nine-second gap in his first utterance was spreading out on a waist-high pile of drywall sheets the roll of large drawings he had been carrying. From that point, his and Harry's 'deictic' references – to *this* and *that, here* and *there* – are not to the actual building but to its graphical representation. In fact, the entities for which the dimensions 2,600mm and 2,775mm are given are levels for a ceiling which does not exist. That raises the interesting question of what these deictic expressions refer to. Since the reference is neither to the actual building nor, presumably, to the piece of paper, it must be to the *planned* building.

In contexts where things are made or done and in which planning is a distinct operation, separate from execution and performed by different people, what is communicated to those who will realise the plan is a *representation* of the desired state of affairs. Like all representations, it is constructed with a system of signs – verbal and graphical signs in the present instance. What the participants talk about, though, is not the representation but the thing represented, even if that thing has no material reality. We might say that it has a *virtual* reality, and that Joe and Harry are talking about the *virtual* building. Similarly, since there is no ceiling, there is no question of anything in the actual building being lowered; the *lowering* will be to the *virtual* ceiling (it will be achieved simply by substituting one figure for another in the height indication on the drawing). The builders will lower nothing. They will just install the ceiling, but at a lower level than originally specified.

The remaining point is about 'intertextuality' (the way in which one piece of discourse implicitly or explicitly refers to another, often deriving part of its meaning from that reference). Joe makes a specific intertextual link through the clause *as you were saying yesterday on the phone, Harry.* Then *if we lower this part by three inches* is either a near-exact quotation or conveys the semantic content (i.e. the meaning) of part of yesterday's phone conversation. Thus the same semantic material, and possibly even the same verbal material (I can't say which because I don't have a recording of the phone conversation) is here getting recycled. And it may well be that Harry's initial noun phrase, the *ductwork*, is intertextual, too – the article *the* indicating a topic that has already been referred to. Intertextuality is of central importance in workplace discourse. It ties all the separate written and spoken communications into a single multi-stranded web of discourse (a *text* is a textile, something woven) and in the process knits the diverse participants together into a discourse community.

A bit later Joe says:

19   Joe   So let me look at the elevations [elevation drawings], I'll just study this whole area all over, I'll have to study this area over, because I know the lights, I mean my concern is A501. *[12-second silence]*

Something is nagging at Joe. His preoccupation is revealed by the way his discourse fails to move decisively forward. What is gnawing at his consciousness is revealed by that unexpected new verbal item, *the elevations*, that must have seemed to the other participants to have come inexplicably from nowhere. The elevation drawings, such as drawing no. A501, are different from the 'reflected ceiling plan' they have been looking at in that they show vertical features such as walls. In the twelve-second silence Joe turns up the drawing in question. Then he says:

Fucking lights. *[5-second silence]*

He stands up straight and looks at Harry.

It's right in front of the fucking window. *[3-second silence]* Yes, see the back here all, you see the back here? I think this is why this is set at twenty-seven fifty in the back so maybe we should just lower this portion.

To explain. *Lights* means glazing or windows. Elevation drawing no. A501 reveals an internal wall, the upper portion of which is glazed (i.e. a clerestory); it was some vague recollection of this that caused Joe to keep nagging at the problem, testing his partners' conversational patience to the limit. Lowering the ceiling would bring it below the top of this glass – clearly an unacceptable situation; hence Joe's frustration. That, Joe surmises, was why the ceiling level had originally been set (by him, but many months earlier) relatively high (2,750 mm) in that area.

Joe's swearing obviously serves an expressive need, but it has other dimensions. (Language rarely does only one thing.) First, the building site is a macho environment where language may be a way of declaring masculinity, an expectation with which even visiting male professionals may feel it useful to conform for the sake of 'street credibility'. But it may also have been Harry's presence that provoked the vehemence of the outburst, since it was Harry who originally supplied the incorrect ductwork dimensions which caused Joe to set the ceiling level where he did. At a subtext level of interpersonal meaning the expletive may be directed to some degree *at* Harry. Joe would never allow himself to respond with even semi-overt irritation to a mistake made by Luc, on whose cooperativeness he depends, showing constant concern to keep him sweet.

This contretemps shows incidentally how real was the virtual building, of which one element was the clerestory. Forgotten over many months, this had now re-emerged to block the straightforward action that had been contemplated.

The issue of the ceiling receives its final verbal expression, after much discussion between Joe and his boss in the office, in a written document called a site instruction, sent by the architect to the site supervisor:

> Lower ceiling @ corridor 327 as per attached sketch SK 26–01 and revise to acoustical lay-in tile as shown.

Like much of the spoken discourse, this written text works as much by intertextual reference as by overtly expressed meaning. The immediate participants, Luc, Harry and Joe's boss in the office, *recognise* in the words the same solution they have talked about. For Luc, for instance, the instruction is no instruction because he had already agreed he was going to lower the ceiling; the only question was about dimensions.

But there are other potential readers, a second audience waiting hypothetically in some unspecified future, shadowy at present but to be taken with great seriousness when or if they materialise. The management of the firm of contractors, the client's accountant, even some tribunal judge, could use the paper to allocate responsibilities and costs; Joe's *signature* confirms that the change was at the architect's orders. (The written act we learn to accomplish first, writing our name, remains the one with the most momentous possible consequences for our lives; think of cheques and confessions.) For this audience the text has to work differently, depending not on the conversations it reawakens but by the meaning of the words in themselves; functioning not as an awaited message (*Go ahead, Luc*) but as a device set to go off later, away from the context of its production and immediate reception.

The builders build a building with steel and concrete. Joe, with words and drawings, creates two other structures, one ideational, one interpersonal: a virtual building and a social network, a web of intertwined understandings, agreements and consents. Without both in place and constantly maintained, no building would happen; and both depend critically on language.

Acknowledgements

My thanks are due to the architectural firm and the individual architects who allowed me to study their work. They must remain anonymous: all names in the paper are pseudonyms. The research was carried out with the assistance of Stephen Fai as part of the study 'The relationships between writing in the university and writing in the workplace' funded by Strategic Grant 884–94–0030 from the Social Sciences and Humanities Research Council of Canada, with additional support from Carleton University Office of Graduate Studies and Research. I gratefully acknowledge also the assistance I have received in analysing the data from my colleague Dr Lynne Young.

Reference for this reading

Halliday, M.A.K. (1994) *An Introduction to Functional Grammar* (2nd edn), London, Edward Arnold.

READING B: Professionals and clients: form filling and the control of talk

Jo Longman
(Jo Longman is Roberts' Money Manager at the University of Nottingham.)

Specially commissioned for Mercer (1996, pp. 116–21). (Edited by Ann Hewings.)

The following professional client interview is from research I have done (Mercer and Longman, 1992; 1993; Longman and Mercer, 1993) on interviews in which professional advisers in occupational training (whom I call 'counsellors') are talking with their 'clients', who are people (usually unemployed) at the point of entering an occupational training scheme. The research involved the transcription and analysis of many hours of interview talk, recorded in many locations throughout Britain. In this paper I use data from one such interview to illustrate some of the features of 'interview talk' and explain how the English language, spoken and written, is used to define, construct and maintain the roles of the counsellor and the client and the relationship between them.

Background to the interview

The interview in question involved a counsellor who was a young woman and a client who was a man in his thirties. For both people, English was their first and main language. The interview lasted for 45 minutes, and took place within a British national vocational training scheme called Employment Training which operated from 1988 until 1993. This scheme was designed to facilitate the return of long-term unemployed people to the workforce by placing them in a suitable course of training. For clients entering the scheme, the first substantial contact was an interview with a counsellor whose job it was to:

1 elicit the client's preferences for specific kinds of work;

2 identify the client's relevant vocational strengths and weaknesses, special needs and so on;

3 propose suitable training.

One of the outcomes of the interview was a completed form which contained the information listed above. The form then had subsequent audiences: it went to a provider of training (known as a training manager) to see if they would accept the client on to their training programme; and it was also often used to 'sell' the client to an employer for a work experience placement at some point during their training. The completed form was officially meant to be owned and used by the client during their training.

This interview has a number of features which are typical of the interviews I recorded, and also of many other kinds of encounter between 'professionals' and 'clients'. These are:

- talk is the central vehicle for getting the business of the interview done;
- the participants have different 'internal' status within the interaction, i.e. one is a professional and the other is a member of the public;
- the participants have different 'external' status – in this case this is perhaps most noticeable in that the professional is employed and the client is unemployed;
- the participants follow certain conventions of English language use which distinguish the event from many other kinds of conversation.

Transcript

(The transcript begins about 40 seconds into the interview.)

	Client	Counsellor
1		Right, okay. What what what
2		prompted the interest why cars,
3		why motor
4	Uhh *[3 secs]* I just	
5	like tinkering about	
6	with cars more or less	
7	you know what I mean	
8		Do you do you own a car or, no
9	Not at the moment no	
10		But have you in the past?
11	Oh aye yeah	
12		Right so have you got a driving
13		licence?
14	Yeah I have yeah	
15		*[4 secs]* And you say you tinker
16		about with cars. Is that a sort
17		of like servicing and things?
18	Er well yeah just you	
19	know repairing them	
20	when they need it,	
21	y'know	
22		What sort of things have you
23		done you have done brake
24		shoes, oil changes?
25	I've more or less done,	
26	practically anything,	
27	on a car I can more or	
28	less do anything on a	
29	car as long as it	
30	isn't, y'know, one of	
31	these new fuel injected	
32	[things I'm a bit lost	[Mm
33	on the electrical side	
34		Right
35	When it comes to taking	
36	an engine out and	
37	putting another engine	
38	in I can do that sort	
39	of stuff. As long as	
40	it isn't, you know too	
	complicated	
41	or anything	
42	you know	

43	*[5 secs]* What what I'm trying to
44	do with you, it's an opportunity
45	for you to actually look at
46	Employment Training, you've
47	been through the basics. What I
48	need to go through with you is
49	the sort of area you need to go
50	into and then tie up any
51	previous experience you might
52	have which we can build on and
53	say he's this, he's done servicing
54	of cars, he's done brake shoes
55	etcetera, etcetera […] so we go
56	through the form and then I'll
57	write down the sort of bits and
58	bobs of what you've serviced *[6*
59	*secs]* it's in your spare time I
60	suppose
	[30 seconds later]
61	So if I put when you were working
62	as a taxi-driver you serviced,
63	your own car and, carried out
64	general maintenance
65	It may come to, er if I
66	get on a motor mechanic
67	course I'd maybe prefer
68	to do that [. I aren't
69	really sure yet. I'd [Mm
70	like to go back in
71	taxis more or less,
72	there's more money in
73	it, y'know [. I could [Yeah, yeah
74	do with the extra money

Transcription conventions

- [indicates overlapping speech
- the dialogue has been punctuated to aid understanding
- *[n secs]* indicates a noticeable pause (i.e. at a point or for a duration which it did not seem appropriate to represent by standard punctuation)

Three concepts are useful for analysing how the relationship between the counsellor and the client is defined, constructed and maintained through the use of spoken language: 'filtering', 'reformulation' and 'accountability'.

Filtering

One of the major themes throughout the whole of this interview is the client expressing doubts about his ability and level of experience. This includes not only his expertise in the central topic of car servicing and general maintenance (lines 4–7, 18–21, 25–33) but even his entire commitment to the idea of commencing training (in the last few lines). However, nearly all the information about his lack of knowledge and his uncertainty is 'filtered out' by the counsellor in that it does not find its way into the written record of the interview. What she actually recorded on the form (not included in the transcript here) were the following words:

> John is awaiting the outcome of an application for a taxi-driver licence and is considering a back-up plan in case this does not occur. His present experience as a motor mechanic has encouraged him to consider a career in mechanics or body repair. This he feels could be used as an alternative or supplementary income to taxi-driving.

Reformulation

The short extract from the written form quoted above is also interesting because the language is so strikingly different in style from that used by the client. Of course, any rendition of the meaning of English speech into writing, other than transcription, is likely to effect some change of meaning. But remember that the completed form is meant to represent the client's past and present situation, to communicate this to trainers and possible future employers, and to be *owned* by the client. Throughout the interview, the language the client uses is hesitant and uncertain (*I've more or less done, more or less, as long as it isn't, I'm a bit lost*, etc.). The counsellor's written version makes him sound better organised than how he represents himself during the interview. So, as well as filtering out information about the client's uncertainty, the counsellor recasts or *reformulates* the client's statements, recording the information he provides in a way that makes it more 'suitable' (from the counsellor's perspective) for the form. In this case (as in many others I have observed), this means choosing words that are more definite, positive, formal or technical than the words that are spoken by the client. For example, the client in this interview initially describes his experience with cars as *tinkering* (line 5) and the *just* at the beginning of the sentence has the effect of making his experience seem less formal or technical. The counsellor attempts to reformulate the words that the client has used to describe his experience by suggesting *Is that sort of like servicing and things?* (lines 16–17). The use of the word *servicing* in this instance has the effect of making the client appear to be more technically and professionally competent than someone who simply tinkers around with cars in his spare time.

Reformulation is symbolic of the relative power that the counsellor has over the final words that are written down as the material outcome of the interview.

Accountability

Reformulation of clients' words by counsellors is a very common occurrence in these interviews, and highlights the importance of the completed form for the professional accountability of the counsellor. Counsellors know that the form may reach professional audiences – trainers, possible employers, possibly future counsellors in the client's projected future. They know that these audiences will judge them, as may the client, by the quality of form they produce. Of course, counsellors are also accountable to their clients, and every client will be expected to agree and sign the form at the end of the interview. For this reason, one sometimes finds counsellors *accounting for* their form filling to the client in the talk of the interview. A good example is the long statement by the counsellor in lines 43–60.

The complexity of the counsellor's role in handling information provided by the client is apparent from the contents of the official manual of practice for these interviews (Training Commission, 1988). There it says: 'Your job is to be the client's advocate: to encourage each individual to present him or herself in the best possible light' (Training Commission, 1988, p. 9). There is an implication here that in completing the form the counsellor *is expected* to filter out and reformulate information wherever necessary so as to create on the client's behalf a suitably positive image of the client as a potential worker.

Conclusion

Throughout these kinds of interview the way in which spoken and written language is used reflects a tension for the counsellor between achieving the institutional language business of the interview (i.e. getting the form completed, showing the client in the best light to other audiences, etc.) while at the same time keeping the interview process 'client centred' so that the client's concerns are addressed, all within very constrained time limits. Overall, however, the responsibility for resolving this tension, and the power to achieve that resolution, can be seen to rest with the 'professional' rather than the 'client'.

References for this reading

Longman, J. and Mercer, N. (1993) 'Forms for talk and talk for forms: oral and literate dimensions of language use in employment training interviews', *Text*, vol. 13, no. 1, pp. 91–116.

Mercer, N. and Longman, J. (1992) 'Accounts and the development of shared understanding in employment training interviews', *Text*, vol. 12, no. 1, pp. 103–25.

Mercer, N. and Longman, J. (1993) 'Language events with two dimensions: the relationship between talking and writing as exemplified in a set of counselling interviews', *Changing English*, vol. 1, no. 1, pp. 154–67.

Training Commission (1988) *The Employment Training Interview: Identifying Personal Strengths and Past Achievements*, Sheffield, Training Commission.

6 Market forces speak English

Sharon Goodman

6.1 Introduction

This chapter examines the concept of 'border crossing' as it relates to uses of different forms of English. **Border crossing** is the term used by some linguists and sociologists to describe what they identify as a phenomenon of post-industrialised societies: that a complex range of new social relationships is developing, and that behaviour (including linguistic behaviour) is changing as a result (Fairclough, 1996). Forms of English associated with one situation are crossing the borders into new ones: informal English, for example, is said to be crossing into professional relationships, and 'advertising English' migrating into public information campaigns.

Working practices worldwide are changing to suit the needs of a 'global economy', and changes in the various relationships that English speakers have with other speakers are said to be bringing about these new uses of the English language. A decline in manufacturing and heavy industry in many countries has engendered the rise of the service sector, so the language forms used at work are different, as are people's relationships inside and outside the workplace. Norman Fairclough, for example, believes that traditional, hierarchical social structures are becoming far more fluid and precarious than they once were. Relationships based automatically on authority, as well as personal relationships based on family duties and obligations, are in decline: 'people's self-identity, rather than being a feature of given positions and roles, is reflexively built up through a process of negotiation' (Fairclough, 1993, p. 140).

Analysts working in this area locate English language border crossings in the context of wider social, political and economic changes. These changes have consequences for the forms of English that speakers use, and the range of contexts in which they use them. This chapter looks at the phenomenon of border crossing in English. In order to judge the extent to which English forms are migrating into new contexts, the chapter considers aspects of verbal (and visual) language, focusing particularly on informalisation and marketisation.

- **Informalisation** Are informal forms becoming more frequent in English? The argument put forward by some linguists is that the boundaries between language forms traditionally reserved for intimate relationships and those reserved for more formal situations are becoming blurred. Professional encounters, for example, are increasingly likely to contain informal forms of English: they are becoming 'conversationalised' (Fairclough, 1994). Institutions, too, such as the state, commerce and the media, are increasingly using less formal, more conversational styles. In many contexts, then, the public and professional sphere is said to be becoming infused with 'private' discourse. This issue can be considered from two points of view. On the one hand, it could be argued that using more conversational, 'everyday' English in a widening range of contexts is a good thing, because it allows people to understand and participate in interactions more easily – for example, when talking to a solicitor, or listening to a political interview on the radio. The counter-argument might be that using 'the language of the people' allows those in positions of power, such as government officials or politicians, to imply the existence of a friendly relationship between themselves and 'the public' where no such relationship actually exists. It could therefore be seen as manipulative.

- **Marketisation**   A related issue is that 'advertising language' is seen to be crossing over into the domain of 'information'. Government documents and information leaflets, for example, may use styles of verbal English and visual presentation more commonly found in commercial advertising. English texts are therefore becoming increasingly 'market-oriented', or marketised, subject to political expediency and/or commercial pressures. The chapter builds on discussions of advertising in Chapter 2, considering examples of 'real' advertising and selling techniques compared with institutional texts, drawn mainly from Singapore and Britain, which use similar devices. How do these texts use English to 'sell', and what are they selling? How do they attempt to position their readers in certain ways, and what strategies do people develop in order to resist this positioning?

If the processes of informalisation and marketisation are indeed becoming increasingly widespread, then this implies that there is a requirement for English speakers generally not only to deal with, and respond to, this increasingly marketised and informal English, but also to become *involved* in the process. For example, people may feel that they need to use English in new ways to 'sell themselves' in order to gain employment. Or they may need to learn new linguistic strategies to keep the jobs they already have – to talk to 'the public', for instance. In other words, they have to become *producers of promotional texts*. This can have consequences for the ways in which people see themselves. What happens to a person's 'sense of self' in an environment in which certain forms of English have to be used, and other forms are discouraged or banned altogether?

In this chapter I first consider some of the forms that informal and marketised English can take. I then look at how such linguistic forms can be used – and resisted – in a world that is becoming increasingly complex and where a multitude of new types of social relationship is developing. The focal point throughout is border crossing between forms of English that traditionally have been seen as distinct – although in practice they probably weren't – between formal and informal; public and private; informative and promotional.

6.2 Informalisation

To examine the claim that people are making more use of informal styles of English, we can consider how some of the markers of informal English might be crossing into situations more traditionally associated with formal English forms.

Some markers of informal English

In Chapter 1 you considered some of the markers of informal, conversational English. You may find it helpful to reread Sections 1.2 and 1.3 of that chapter at this point. Informal English varies, of course, across countries, cultures and contexts, but a starting point might be the following, which are increasingly likely to occur in sales or traditionally more 'formal' exchanges.

- Terms of address: a key area of informalisation. It may no longer take months (or even years) of familiarity for speakers to address each other by first names – people seem likely to use first names at an initial meeting, and rarely ask permission to do so. Do you think this matters? How would you (or do you) feel about being on first-name terms with your doctor, parliamentary representative, tax collector or clients?

- Pronouns and names: unlike many languages, English no longer distinguishes between familiar and formal pronominal usage, except in certain regional dialects. But names themselves are adapted or shortened (*Richard* becomes *Rich* or *Ric*) or replaced by nicknames. Diminutive suffixes (*-ie* or *-y*) are used, thus *James* becomes *Jamie*. As these are associated with childhood names, they convey an impression of intimacy and familiarity. Salespeople have realised this and often attempt to turn it to their advantage: many now use the shorter version of their name when introducing themselves to customers.

- Contractions of negatives (*wouldn't*) or auxiliary verbs (*he'll*): associated with less formal, often spoken English, these are increasingly likely to occur in writing.

- An increased use of more informal vocabulary, such as colloquialisms and slang forms even in professional encounters: *this guy comes up to me and he says* … .

- The use of active rather than passive verbs: the active voice is more common in spoken (usually more informal) than in written English. *We carried out an experiment* is more informal than *An experiment was carried out.*

- Intonation, too, can be used to signify informality: think about how you answer the telephone in different situations. Do you use different 'voices' to talk to friends, and to colleagues or officials?

It is these sorts of division that some believe are changing and breaking down. We can view the issue of informalisation from two angles. On the one hand, relationships built and conducted on an informal basis can be beneficial to both parties. Seeing yourself as a 'friend'– with the rights that the status of 'friend' affords you – can be an empowering experience. On the other hand, the speedy establishment of this kind of informal relationship can have disadvantages. In cases where a degree of distance is subsequently required (e.g. if you need to make a complaint) it may be much harder to make the required shift – to put things back on a professional footing.

ACTIVITY 6.1

Allow about 10 minutes

Think of some of the people you have spoken to in the last day or two. How did you address them, and how did they address you? To whom did you use, or avoid using, colloquial language or slang? Why? Can you identify any changes in your use of different styles of English, by thinking back to ten, or perhaps twenty, years ago?

There may be many different reasons for adopting an informal or conversational style of English. Between intimates, or 'equals', informality can serve to build and maintain social bonds. It can also be used deliberately to make writing or speech more accessible to an audience. You'll find examples of contractions, for instance, in this chapter and others in the book.

Formality, on the other hand, can be used as a resource to create and maintain professional relationships, or to keep people at a distance. What happens, though, when institutions, or those in authority, use informal language to speak to those who are not on an equal basis with them? Some aspects of this are not new: the use of first names by managers when addressing their 'subordinates', for example. But there are other informal English forms that seem to be increasingly common in a widening range of contexts.

Informal English in the public and professional domain

Official or institutional English is generally associated with a formal, impersonal style. An impersonal style is significant as it establishes a 'top-down' relationship of power, in which the 'official' is addressed as, and perceived as, being in control of the exchange. Thus an impersonal, formal style of English can be instrumental in creating and maintaining hierarchical relationships (see Fowler, 1991, p. 128). Government officials, lawyers and public broadcasters are just a few of those who traditionally have been associated with this style of English.

In recent years there have been attempts to simplify the language of institutions with a view to making it more straightforward and comprehensible to 'the public'. Ernest Gowers's attack on what he saw as the incomprehensible 'bureaucratese' or 'officialese' he encountered while working in the British Civil Service, resulted in the publication of his book *Plain Words: A Guide to the Use of English* in 1948. There have since been many revised editions (as well as similar publications), and Gowers's book is still widely consulted by officials, journalists and others who wish to write as clearly and as concisely as possible. 'Plain English' does not necessarily entail informality, but connections can be made.

'Plain English' has not been uncontroversial, however. Deborah Cameron (1995, p. 64), for example, notes that debates over 'style' and 'clarity' have been going on for centuries, and that such debates 'have a history and a politics'. She describes the ways in which speakers try to keep a language 'clean' and free from corruption, and notes that modern technology is also routinely harnessed in the quest for 'good' English prose, with the wide availability of computer programs that check style and grammar. Cameron questions the assumptions underlying these software programs, pointing out that there are often moral and 'class' issues behind movements for changes in English style. In discussing the rise in popularity of 'plain English', she notes that, symbolically, it is seen as in opposition to elitism: 'It is not acceptable in modern society for class or professional elites to address people in a way they find unintelligible, pretentious or suggestive of very distant and authoritarian social relations' (Cameron, 1995, p. 68).

Whatever the motivations and moral issues here, the 'plain English' debate has undoubtedly been influential in making the English of official documents and newspapers more comprehensible to the public and non-specialist audience. A parallel tendency is the increasing use of informal forms of English in the public domain, whether in letters from government departments, in telephone calls between professionals or in political speeches. Official or 'public' English is increasingly harnessing the linguistic resources of informal or 'private' discourse. Look back through the list of informal markers in the previous subsection – how many of these would really seem out of place now in a professional encounter, or a public speech? Some of these informal markers seem relatively insignificant. (Does it really matter, for example, if a politician says *he'll* rather than *he will?*) However, the increasing occurrence of informal English *itself* in these situations can mean that an overall impression of informality can be built up over time, and can leave you with the feeling that you have just been listening to a friend.

It is not necessary for an entire exchange, or speech, to be presented in an informal style for this impression to be conveyed. Textual cues can function to *foreground* the impression of informality: a small segment of informal English in an otherwise formal document or speech can be sufficient to convey an overall impression of informality.

Deborah Tannen (1992, p. 32) observes that conversation (ordinary talk) can 'create interpersonal involvement and meaning'. Because informal language forms are traditionally reserved for, and associated with, more intimate relationships, they can – when used in the public domain such as the media – be seen as implying a social solidarity with listeners, a claim to share their point of view and concerns. As I mentioned in the Introduction,

Fairclough, in discussing trends in Britain in the 1990s, suggests that traditional hierarchical relationships are in decline (i.e. people no longer automatically respect others simply because they hold a government post, or other official position) and he therefore sees the use of a conversational style as significant. He analysed the script of a BBC radio interview in some detail (Fairclough, 1995, pp. 142–9), looking at a section of the *Today* programme, which is broadcast in Britain every morning except Sunday on BBC Radio 4. He focused on the language of the presenters during a political interview, and noted many instances of colloquial English, as well as inclusive pronouns such as *we* and *our* (which imply that the presenter shares the same world and culture as the listeners) and a general informality of style. The presenters used discourse markers associated with conversation, such as *oh*, *well* and *right*, and shortened words, such as *because* to *coz*. Fairclough sees the BBC presenters as aiming to create a sense of linguistic (and, by extension, social) solidarity with the listening public. By using informal language in a radio interview – as well as by explicitly claiming to put forward the views and concerns of the listeners – the interviewer is creating a sense of 'community'. It may also be significant that the activity the presenter is using the language for – giving politicians a hard time – means that audience approval is even more likely.

Fairclough's analysis demonstrates the tension between the standpoints reflected in both formal and informal discourse. As he puts it elsewhere:

> ... [this illustrates] an important contemporary tendency: for the informal, conversational language associated with face-to-face interaction and group interaction in more private spheres of life to shift into public and institutional spheres ... There is a deep ambivalence about the contemporary 'conversationalisation' of language, as we might call it, in its implications for power: on the one hand, it goes along with a genuine opening up and democratisation of professional domains, a shift in power towards the client and the consumer. But on the other hand, conversational style provides a strategy for exercising power in more subtle and implicit ways, and many professionals are now trained in such strategies.

> (Fairclough, 1992, pp. 4–5)

A related issue concerns the reception of the discourse. Who is the real addressee in such broadcasts? A radio interview, of course, means that the politician is not the real addressee, even though he or she is being directly addressed by the presenter. There are many other people listening. There may be other interviewees present in the recording studio awaiting their turn. Often, in both radio and television broadcasts, a studio audience is present. Then there is the listening audience at home. This is a wide, fragmented audience, which can be local and international simultaneously. Who, then, is speaking to whom? Is the interviewer addressing the politician? Are 'we' (the public) addressing them, through the interviewer who is putting questions on our behalf? And is there any way of knowing who is listening?

ACTIVITY 6.2

Allow about
20 minutes

Try to listen to a short radio or television interview. How do the interviewer and interviewee address each other? Are any abbreviated names, or nicknames, used? What markers of formal and informal English are there? Are there any colloquial words, or slang? What signs are there in the language that this is a conversation designed to be overheard (by the audience)?

The use of an informal style is not necessarily a practice to be regarded with suspicion, of course. New journalists at the BBC, for example, are encouraged to write their stories in an informal and friendly way: 'Write a story as you would tell it to a friend – but without the ums and ers' (said by a trainer to a group of journalist trainees at the BBC, in my hearing). The aim throughout their training is to develop 'good, spoken English' – language that is clear, informative and accessible.

I now turn to look at another example of border crossing. To what extent is the language of advertising being used in spheres associated with information or politics?

6.3 The marketisation of English

Many of the forms of informal English discussed in Section 6.2 are widely used in the discourse of sales. This is because the seller hopes that being friendly to the customer will mean a greater chance of a sale. In 'sales English' there are also linguistic devices designed to persuade customers to buy the product – to convince them that a particular need will be fulfilled by purchasing it (see also Chapter 2). These can range from the use of slogans in advertisements, which may be alliterative or 'catchy' and thereby stick in the customer's mind, to specific ways of speaking to customers face to face to convince them to buy. It is worth considering a few aspects of sales language, before turning to look at how these same strategies can be used by institutions not explicitly aiming to sell, such as public-information campaigns or government documents.

The English of sales

Sales personnel are often trained by their employers to speak effectively to their customers, and sales interactions often take place on the basis of scripts which salespeople are expected to follow as closely as possible when they speak to customers. Below is an example of one of these sales scripts, which covers the initial telephone call from a financial services sales consultant to a prospective client (the 'prospect'). The script is given to employees by a firm of insurance and pensions consultants operating in English, worldwide.

First telephone call: how to approach your prospect

CONSULTANT	Mr Brown?
[PROSPECT	Yes?]
CONSULTANT	Good morning, sir.
[PROSPECT	Good morning.]
CONSULTANT	My name is [employee's name] from [company name]. You may have heard of us?
[Wait for reply]	
	[Softly] Would you allow me to explain why I'm calling you this morning?
[PROSPECT	Yes.]
CONSULTANT	We are a company of international insurance and pensions consultants. I live and work here in [prospect's town/city].
[Pause]	
	Within [company name] my job is to advise people on investing for their future ...

This is an example of a 'cold-call' script – where the salesperson telephones the prospective client, often at home during the evening or weekend, without prior arrangement. (It has a lot of similarities with the telephone interaction reported by Neil Mercer in Chapter 5.) The interaction is intended to lead to the client agreeing to an appointment to discuss things further. You can see that the employee is explicitly told, step by step:

1 *what* to say

2 *how* to say it ('Softly')

3 *when* to say it ('Pause'), and

4 how the prospective client is likely to react.

There are linguistic strategies for personalising the encounter, too: 'I live and work here in ...'. The place-name is always the town or city where the client lives, and the deictic word *here* functions as a claim to proximity. Claims to a shared world are an important means of establishing personal links between client and salesperson, so deictic markers are widely used in sales English.

Cold-calling (or cold-faxing, increasingly) in order to sell products or services is still one of the most common forms of sales approach, despite the phenomenal rise of advertising via email and the internet. The problems facing people on the receiving end of a cold-call are twofold. One is that they may not be aware of some of the persuasive techniques being used; a second is that the sheer speed of these sales interactions – face to face or by telephone – means that the time for reflection is minimised, as you may remember from the cold-call example in Chapter 5. Persuasive sales techniques can be difficult to deflect. (This is why many countries now make it a legal obligation for a company to provide a 'cooling-off period' before such a sale is confirmed, to allow consumers to reflect on their decision to purchase.) That said, the 'hard sell' is perhaps becoming less successful than it once was – consumers have become more accustomed to it and have developed strategies to deal with attempts to make them part with their money, as you read in the account by Neil Mercer in Chapter 5. Later in this section I will be looking at some of these strategies of resistance.

The next stage in the sales encounter that we are looking at is the first meeting. The client is again referred to in the company literature as a 'prospect', and the salesperson is told that the purpose of this meeting is to 'educate the prospect about the necessary process'. There are three words here – containing interesting assumptions – that may jump out at you: *educate, prospect* and *necessary*. Who 'educates' whom, and for whose benefit is this 'education' given? What does it mean for the client to be seen as a 'prospect', with all the implications contained in that somewhat impersonal word? And 'necessary' for whom?

Again, the entire conversation is scripted:

> CONSULTANT   Is all that clear to you, Mr Brown?
>
> *[Wait for him to reply]*
>
> Are you happy so far?
>
> [PROSPECT   Yes.]
>
> CONSULTANT   Good.
>
> *[Remember to smile]*

One significant element of this type of discourse is that the script prescribes turn taking. Employees are told, for example: 'Don't thank him and he'll thank you!'

Throughout, it is the salesperson who is supposed to be in charge of who speaks, and when. Questions are, furthermore, put to the client in ways that prescribe a certain response (usually positive). Questions can even be designed so that the customer grants permission for a further sales pitch:

> CONSULTANT   May I just explain what our Special Care policy covers?
>
> [PROSPECT   Yes.]

By the time of the second meeting between the client and the consultant, first name terms are to be used. The pronouns have also shifted in this second meeting, client and salesperson now being presented as partners in a joint endeavour:

CONSULTANT   Fine, John, well *we've* actually got an agenda for today's meeting. If you recall, John, when *we* finished last time *we'd* worked out that your most important concern was ... [emphasis added].

As I noted earlier, pronouns can be highly significant because they can be used to signify, or imply, intimate relationships. Goodin describes the use of inclusive pronominal forms such as *we* and *our* as 'hidden co-optation'. Here he is talking about the linguistic strategies employed in political speeches:

An important aspect of appealing to audience prejudices is the orator's claim to share their perspective ... The 'language of participation' in general, and the word 'we' in particular, figure importantly in this process. Use of the first person plural implies a unity between the speaker and his audience that is typically a fraud.

(Goodin, 1980, p. 105)

ACTIVITY 6.3

Allow about 15 minutes

Below is a section of a speech from *Animal Farm*, George Orwell's satirical novel criticising the Stalinist regime in the former Soviet Union. At this point one of the leaders, a pig named Major, is trying to rouse the other animals to rebel against the authority of humans. He uses many linguistic strategies common to political speeches and other types of discourse where the aim is to persuade the audience of a certain point of view. As you read, note carefully Major's use of pronouns and other inclusive devices.

Now, comrades, what is the nature of this life of ours? Let us face it, our lives are miserable, laborious and short. We are born, we are given just so much food as will keep the breath in our bodies, and those of us who are capable of it are forced to work to the last atom of our strength; and the very instant that our usefulness has come to an end we are slaughtered with hideous cruelty. No animal in England knows the meaning of happiness or leisure after he is a year old. No animal in England is free. The life of an animal is misery and slavery: that is the plain truth.

(Orwell, 1987, p. 3)

Comment

There are many claims to solidarity in this speech, which is not surprising as Major is trying to convince his audience that he shares their concerns. Words such as *comrades*, as well as pronouns such as *we* and *our*, are used. As you read in Chapter 2, these are typical features of political speech making. Note also the high **modality** (claims to truth) in the extract above. By using unmodalised declarative sentences (e.g. *Let us face it, our lives are miserable, laborious and short*) the ideas in the speech are presented as truth or facts.

Similarly, there are generic statements (statements that make a claim to a universal truth) such as *The life of an animal is misery and slavery.* The use of the present tense aims to tell the animals in the audience how the world *is*, rather than how it might be, or might appear. This speech is therefore highly **monologic** – that is, it attempts to suppress any interpretation of events or the world, other than the one given. ('Monologic' is a term associated with the Russian theorist Bakhtin. It refers to 'single-voiced' dialogue, where the author's voice is dominant: see Bakhtin, 1981.) It is not only spoken discourse that uses these techniques – you will probably be able to find many examples for yourself in almost any daily newspaper. *We* and *our* are particularly common in the press, and function as devices for creating a shared point of view between the paper and its readers.

Multimodal sales techniques

Written and electronic texts are becoming increasingly multimodal – that is, they use devices from more than one semiotic mode in a single text (words and pictures, or pictures and sound, for example). Many written texts also incorporate visual or verbal elements that suggest speech, rather than writing. Speech is generally more informal than writing, so devices used in print to imply speech can be seen as another aspect of informalisation. They are also part of increasing multimodality: the two modes (or channels of communication) – speech and writing – appear in the same text.

Written texts can use a variety of visual elements to imply spoken English. These can include the following.

- Typographical devices, such as changes of case, size and emphasis, can be significant. Typeface change can also be used to imply contrastive stress in the clause.
- Speech bubbles can be used to suggest people, or characters, actually speaking.
- Punctuation: parentheses in a printed text can suggest that the 'speaker' is thinking on his or her feet; exclamation marks and question marks can imply speakers interjecting or disagreeing with one another.
- Triadic structures (presenting a proposition in three parts, as in *our lives are miserable, laborious and short* in the extract above from *Animal Farm*) are a rhetorical device traditionally associated with public oratory, and therefore reminiscent of speech. (Three-part lists are discussed in Chapter 2.)
- Semi-phonetic representations of non-standard English (*wot, yer*, etc.) are widely used in popular newspapers and comics, and give a strong impression of speech styles, and of social values associated with those styles.

- Intonation can be implied visually by, for example, repetition of letters (*b-b-but*) or changes in font size. Suspension points (...) can imply a speaker's voice trailing off.

Markers of spoken English in written texts will be revisited in examples later in this chapter.

Advertising in all media has used multimodal strategies for a long time. Figure 6.1 shows an advertisement that dropped through my letter box, which uses many visual and verbal strategies in order to persuade me to respond to it. It contains examples of border crossing between spoken and written English, formal and informal styles, and printed and electronic communication. It is printed on glossy paper, but is made to look like a computer printout, presumably to imply and emphasise how urgent it is – they haven't had time to print it on company letterhead! In case I missed the visual 'hole marks' printed down both sides of the paper, the company has added *COMPUTER PRINT OUT* in words at the top of the page, and informed me that the *Data run commenced 8.05am*. The omission of *at* implies haste, and is potentially intertextual with newspaper headlines, which routinely omit prepositions and auxiliaries. Is the customer intended to be impressed by this evidence of such early working hours? Does *8.05* imply that I was almost at the top of the list that day, and therefore a priority?

I am then told that I have been allocated an award, a stereo hi-fi, but the exact description of my prize is crossed out with a line of Xs, and the words

La Redoute would prefer to surprise you!

printed as if handwritten below. There are several double bluffs here, typical of a more aware, knowing relationship between companies and consumers. I know, and the company knows that I know, that it wants me to buy something. All parties also know that if the company had really wanted to cross something out, it would simply have erased it from the advertisement during the printing process and left no trace. But the company wants the connotation of urgency, so has *added* something to make it look *deleted*. This also creates the impression of additional agency: it looks, visually, as if a harried supervisor has rushed over and corrected the work of a careless employee, who is obviously unaware of my importance as a customer.

The 'data run' apparently finished at 8.15 a.m. – rather a long time, on reflection, for such a short printout – but of course that is not the point. To validate the fact that I have been allocated an award, a company stamp has been applied (very carefully positioned so as to appear rushed and smudged). High modality is therefore portrayed visually. The designing of this advertisement as a computer printout carries with it all the connotations of speed and urgency that are presumably meant to imply, by extension, the efficiency with which the company will treat me as a customer.

Experienced consumers are generally aware of most of these sales techniques, and recognise them for what they are. But what happens when government

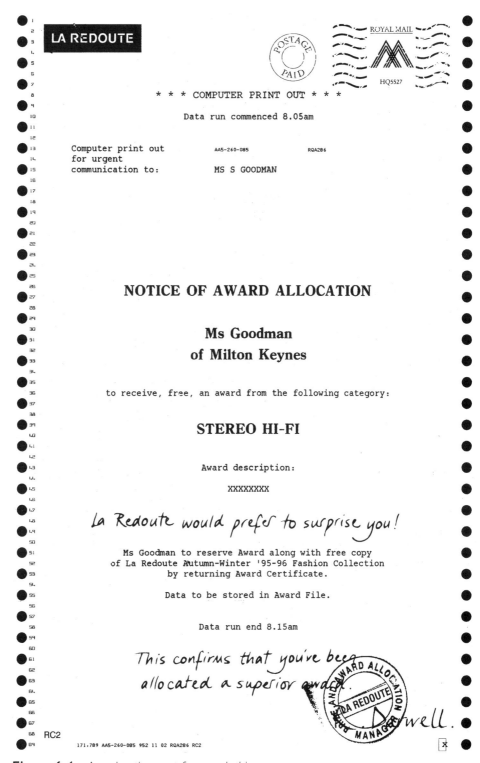

Figure 6.1 An advertisement from a clothing company

circulars, public-information leaflets and even tax forms use the same devices? The use of a conversational style and of 'advertising techniques' in these texts is becoming increasingly widespread. In a sense the Campaign for Plain English, by encouraging official institutions and companies to put documents into forms of English that all citizens can readily understand, together with the growth of mass-media advertising, has opened up new possibilities for persuasion. Is an informal style of presentation to be welcomed because it makes the text more readable, lively and accessible? Or is it to be regarded with suspicion, because it aims to create a 'friendly' basis from which to convince us of the need to part with our money or to espouse a political viewpoint?

The marketisation of official English

That political speeches are often infused with the language of selling is widely recognised. Modern electoral campaigns often make use of commercial advertising agencies, so much so that elections in the USA and Western Europe are commonly described as 'a battle between rival advertising campaigns' (Wernick, 1991, p. 140). In the UK, the 'packaging' of political parties and political agendas to make a particular point is often referred to as 'spin doctoring' and widely denounced by journalists who believe information is distorted and designed to manipulate, or mislead, the voters.

Promotional discourse is increasingly used to 'sell' government policy. Deductions from citizens' earnings to pay for public services such as road-building programmes or hospitals are not, of course, voluntary. But these days, such policies are 'advertised' – that is, they are put into the public domain in the format of advertising, rather than as information. The function of 'advertising' them, therefore, has more to do with winning the public's approval than with selling in the traditional sense. Look at these examples:

> HIGHER Sum Assured ... LONGER Protection ... LOWER Premium ...

> TRIPLE cover from one plan ... vital protection for you and your family

These are taken from printed newspaper advertisements, from two different organisations. Both appear to be selling insurance. One, however, is from a government scheme in Singapore, whereby taxpayers compulsorily contribute from their earnings on a regular basis to pay for the public health service. The other is from a private British insurance company. Which is which?

We will return to the first of these two (the government one) later, where the complete text will be considered as a multimodal example of border crossing between 'advertising' and 'information'.

Figure 6.2 shows a page from a Department of Health leaflet published by the British government. The aim is to encourage people to increase their consumption of fruit and vegetables. There is evidence of marketisation and informalisation here, as the leaflet shares many features with traditional

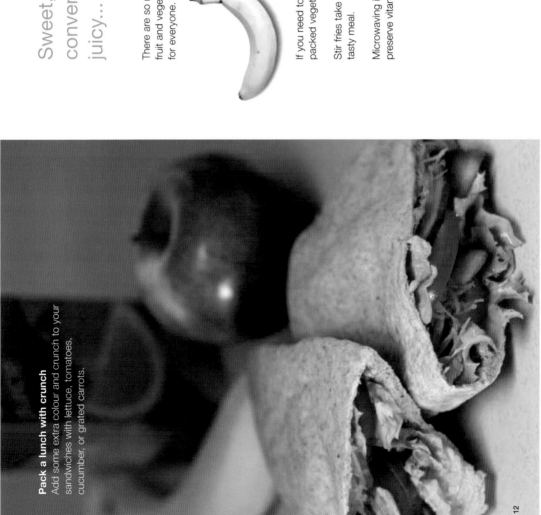

Sweet, colourful, convenient, juicy...

There are so many different types of fruit and vegetables that there's something for everyone.

And they're even easy to eat when you're on the move.

Need to fill a gap before dinner? Have a piece of fruit or if you prefer savoury snacks, try some refreshing celery or a crunchy carrot.

If you need to fix dinner in a hurry, frozen, canned or pre-packed vegetables are quick and easy to cook.

Stir fries take only a few minutes to prepare, and make a tasty meal.

Microwaving is a quick and easy way to cook and helps to preserve vitamins.

13

Pack a lunch with crunch
Add some extra colour and crunch to your sandwiches with lettuce, tomatoes, cucumber, or grated carrots.

12

Figure 6.2   A page from a Department of Health leaflet, 5 A DAY: *Just Eat More* (fruit & veg)

advertising. It contains professionally photographed images and uses full colour to attract our attention. A catchy, alliterative 'slogan' ('Pack a lunch with crunch') is used. Contractions such as *there's*, *they're* and *you're* imply casual speech.

Other government campaigns have adopted many of the tenets of commercial advertising: they make full use of colour, they may include devices such as 'bullets' to set out points, and there are often logos as well. Logos are a strong clue to marketisation in many written texts produced by institutions. Unremarkable in advertising, where brands need to be instantly recognisable, nearly all government departments and public service utilities worldwide now have them.

Striking examples of border crossing between advertising and information are shown in the two texts in Figures 6.3 and 6.4.

Figure 6.3 is part of an advertisement for a shopping complex in Singapore. The advertisement shows a streetscape, in full colour, with speech bubbles emanating from various parts of the shopping centre. We therefore have crossovers here between visual and verbal, and spoken and written, English. There is much that one could say about the positioning of the reader here: who is actually supposed to be speaking? Note that there are no people actually depicted, only their speech. It could be argued that the readers are supposed to 'fill in the gaps' and imagine the voices of excited people exploring their shopping centre – or even to 'become' those people themselves in their imagination. It can therefore be seen as a device for *involving* the readers in the text. Speech, and particularly informal speech as we have seen, plays an important role in constructing a sense of personal involvement. Here speech is not only implied, it is visually depicted. The text's cartoon-like presentation provides another clue to informality: cartoons are associated with childhood and leisure time, rather than the adult world of work. They are therefore familiar and reassuring.

Now look at Figure 6.4, where you will find what appears to be a very similar advertisement. The same device of speech bubbles is used, and this time we see both people and cartoon characters interacting with each other. This, however, is not a normal advertisement. It is a notice from a Singapore government department that takes contributions from citizens' earnings for its state savings scheme. Citizens cannot choose whether to contribute to the Minimum Sum Scheme (as they can to visit the new shopping centre). This, then, has more to do with explaining government policy and setting out the new regulations than with advertising in the more usual sense. Its layout, and visual and verbal use of language, can be seen to cue the reader's background knowledge of advertisements and advertising genres. The reader may therefore bring very different assumptions to this text than to a plain, official-looking document.

JT IT.

ining.

the Bugis MRT, it's

on ... everybody will

ion.

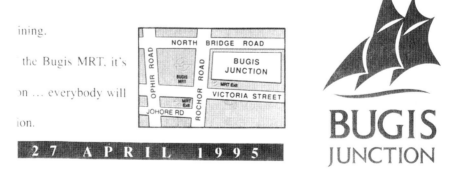

Figure 6.3   Extract from a shopping centre advertisement

Figure 6.4   Part of a public-information notice issued by the Singapore government

ACTIVITY 6.4

Allow about
20 minutes

Turn to Figure 6.5. The text here looks even more like an advertisement. Issued by the same government department in Singapore that issued the notice in Figure 6.4, it has the layout of a company newsletter. Consider the visual layout as well as the linguistic forms. What advertising strategies, or forms of marketised discourse, can you find in this text?

Comment

Some of the most striking elements are the triadic structure, HIGHER ... LONGER ... LOWER, and the use of cartoon characters to 'sell' this savings scheme. In addition, there is the promise of a prize in the bottom right-hand corner.

We can view the use of this style of presentation positively or negatively. On the one hand, it makes the information clearer, less intimidating and easier to read. On the other, readers may feel that the production of expensive 'advertisements' to disseminate public information is not something to be welcomed.

ACTIVITY 6.5

Read 'Selling in Singapore' by Anthea Fraser Gupta (Reading A), in which Gupta provides a practical analysis of marketised texts in Singapore. The reading discusses the stylistic devices used by the producers of two Singaporean texts, one promoting a government housing scheme, the other a private shopping centre. Both texts draw on styles found in other texts, and have certain similarities such as the use of a cartoon format and of ethnic and gender stereotypes. In addition, Gupta notes that each text has influenced the other in its style of presentation. The process is therefore two-way: each has an effect on the other.

We have been looking in this section at some of the strategies that can be employed by speakers and writers wishing either to persuade an audience of their point of view, or to sell them something, or both. We come now to the strategies that clients, readers and audiences use to reject these persuasive devices – to refuse their positioning in the discourse.

Resisting the sales pitch

Some of the points made so far may seem to suggest a passive, 'acted upon' consumer (or reader, or viewer) who is being subjected to the malign influences of politics and industrial expediency. While there are many linguistic strategies for attempting to position readers in certain ways, the

Figure 6.5 Singapore government newsletter

readers/receivers of a text are not as defenceless as they may appear. The increasing sophistication of consumers means that many of the traditional or established sales pitches may not be as effective as they once were. A complex situation arises where consumers are no longer the 'dupes' of the persuasive devices of the professional seller. They develop skills to deal with unwanted salespersons. These may include subverting attempts to make the customer initiate the 'thank yous' in an exchange, or waiting on the telephone line until the seller is finally forced to say goodbye – contrary to all the rules of the training manual. Junk mail, too, seems to be almost universally regarded with suspicion. Certainly anything in my house that is printed with the words 'Urgent Communication' is immediately thrown away! Those who do actually order goods from these companies may deliberately misspell their name on the order form, so that when further unsolicited mail arrives its origin can be traced. Junk also arrives by email, and is often automatically deleted by a 'spam filter', a piece of software which identifies unsolicited advertising and removes it from the user's inbox before it is read, or even noticed.

Here is the final part of the pension consultant's sales script that you looked at earlier in this section. You may find that it raises some questions about the power of the client to subvert sales techniques.

CONSULTANT	I trust this meeting has been useful?
[PROSPECT	Yes.]
CONSULTANT	Fine. Could I ask you for your help with something, John?
[PROSPECT	Yes, of course.]

[Remember: he can't refuse!]

| CONSULTANT | You realise that I can only help people by meeting them. You can help me to help more people by giving me the names and phone numbers of people you know – business partners or friends. OK? I'll just wait a few minutes while you fill this sheet in. |

[Remember: you are in control. Let him thank you.]

How effective do you think this strategy would be? How many people would happily give the names of their friends (more 'prospects'!) to this salesperson, even if the request were put in terms of a favour? It is highly likely that many people would resist. It also seems to me that the method of introducing this request to the client is likely to trigger resistance even before the favour is asked. Background knowledge on the part of the client, and awareness of the present situation, will inform the client immediately that doing a favour for the salesperson is likely to have financial implications. In this case there are social consequences, too – how many friends would the client still have after releasing their names and telephone numbers?

ACTIVITY 6.6

Allow about
15 minutes

Reread the extract above from the pension consultant's script, noting the use of conversational English, and the linguistic indications of the relationship between the participants.

- If you were the salesperson in this extract, what could you do linguistically to ensure the success of your sales pitch – to get those telephone numbers?
- If you were the client, how could you resist? Assume that you want to stay polite!

The client, then, is far from powerless. Wernick, too, notes a complexity in this type of interaction, saying that consumers have developed 'a hardened scepticism about every kind of communication in view of the selling job it is probably doing' (Wernick, 1991, p. 192). Just as television viewers often develop strategies for deflecting advertising – such as leaving the room to make a cup of tea – so those on the receiving end of promotionalised official discourse may also develop strategies for 'talking back'. Readers become sensitised to the 'buzz-words' of advertising and to lexical changes, especially as these issues are often discussed by the very media in which they occur. People quickly learn that when a company announces a decision to *downsize*, this means that it is going to make redundancies among its workforce. In the UK, train passengers were renamed *customers* some time ago, and patients in health centres may now be called *clients*. There are always widespread discussions (and often derision) about such attempts at renaming. You may be able to think of more examples from your own context. Readers or audiences cannot, then, simply be manipulated by language designed to persuade, or which repositions them as consumers. Corner states that a theory of straightforward top-down manipulation is in any case unsustainable:

> ... any idea of influence as linear transmission, the direct reproduction (by manipulation, implantation etc.) in the viewer of certain attitudes, is radically put into question by a theory of meaning as contingent on interpretation. For a start, the very fact of *variation* works against the idea of any uniform influence, while the emphasis on 'activity' works against that characterisation of viewers and readers as essentially passive which has been a feature of theories of 'heavy influence' (including theories about ideology).

> (Corner, 1995, p. 137)

He notes, however, that producers of texts will *try* to create preferred meanings (to indicate the way in which the text is to be read) even though they cannot guarantee success. The extent to which they can hope to succeed depends on a variety of factors. Cameron (1995, p. 71) believes that the creative inferential abilities of readers have been vastly underestimated, and that they readily untangle ambiguities when they encounter them. She commented, for example, on the vocabulary used in the press in the USA and Britain during the Gulf War in 1991, where phrases such as *collateral damage* were used instead of *civilian casualties*. Such euphemisms are intended to dehumanise war and obscure the fact that many thousands of people die. Cameron argues that when faced with a meaningless phrase such as *collateral damage* people will not simply dismiss it as meaningless. If they cannot see the meaning, they will infer one – and they will infer not only the meaning (that civilians have died), but also that *the phrase was designed to conceal this fact*. They will therefore be doubly angry (Cameron, 1995, p. 73).

So far I have looked at some ways in which commercial enterprises and institutions address or position their customers and readers, and ways in which such positioning can be resisted. I now look at similar interactions from the point of view of the employees – those who use these forms of English at work. In Chapter 5, you read about difficulties between expert and lay users of specific types of English used to get things done. In the next section, I will consider some aspects relating to the specific training in language or 'communication skills' provided by companies and service industries for their workforce.

6.4 Designing the language of employees: 'speaking another language' at work

Commercial institutions of all sorts train their employees in how to talk to 'the public' or to their clients. The script in Section 6.3, used to sell financial services, is one of these. Language training at work can also include such things as the type of greeting to be used:

> Good morning, Jackie speaking, how may I help you?

Or repetition of the company name at the end of the encounter:

> Thank you for calling [company name].

Service encounters are particularly likely to proceed according to a script, which may in some instances be laid down word for word by the company. Hochschild (1983) cites an example where an American company ensures that its workers speak to customers according to company guidelines. Cashiers at a store in St Petersburg in 1982 were brought into a courtesy campaign: if the cashier didn't greet the customer in a friendly way and say *Thank You for Shopping Winn–Dixie* sincerely, the customer received a dollar (Hochschild, 1983, p. 149). Anyone who has ever been to a fast-food restaurant, or telephoned a mail-order company, will have heard an institutionalised script in some form. Furthermore, companies that trade worldwide, such as fast-food restaurants, often use the same scripts in all their outlets. This adds a global element to the scenario, as customers in Dubai, Hong Kong and the USA may be spoken to by employees in exactly the same way.

Hochschild studied working practices in a particular service industry, Delta Airlines, based in the USA. She looked closely at the work of Delta's flight attendants, at the language of their training programmes, and at the ways in which the (largely female) workforce was trained to deal with difficult passengers. She noted that the use of customers' names was a technique explicitly taught: 'Attendants were urged to "work" the passenger's name, as in "Yes, Mr Jones, it's true the flight is delayed." This reminds the passenger that he is not anonymous, that there is at least some pretension to a personal relation' (Hochschild, 1983, p. 111).

In another study, Cameron looked at the language used in British call centres, which most people now have to deal with when buying something, or contacting their bank or electricity supplier. Cameron (2000, p. 98) notes a high degree of both *codification* (the way employees must speak to customers is strictly laid down, often word for word) and *surveillance* (exchanges between call centre employees and customers are recorded, to ensure that employees are following the script accurately).

It is not just in explicitly commercial institutions that such change is happening. For Wernick, the rise of commercial culture combined with mass-media advertising has led to 'culture' itself becoming a commodity (Wernick, 1991, p. 185). The political arena has provided the impetus for this change in the UK. An increasingly market-oriented political agenda has meant that it is expedient to rename *students* as *customers* (as with the train passengers I mentioned above) – particularly as budgetary changes have meant that, for example, an additional student per course is worth a certain sum of money to an educational institution. Walsh notes the following: 'The system that is emerging is based upon market principles and the idea of the citizen as consumer. Competition is to replace authority as the basis upon which decisions are made, and in ensuring that there is adaptation to changing circumstances' (Walsh, 1994, p. 201).

That institutions and governments have introduced lexical changes for financial or political reasons is one aspect of this scenario. The problem for those working in what used to be considered as public services (education, public transport, local administrative bodies) is that, to some extent, they eventually have to use this language themselves, and in some way that must imply taking on board the social values encoded within it. I once telephoned an organisation listed under 'Educational Services' in the telephone book. Unsure whether I was speaking to a school or a related institution, I asked what they did. 'We are providers,' was the reply, 'and we have about 350 teaching units.' This apparently means that it is a school, with 350 pupils! Funding concerns and a falling birth rate also mean that schools and universities need to fight for students. If education becomes a 'product' that is sold to 'consumers', then teachers find themselves under pressure to see themselves as 'salespeople', needing to promote both their courses and their own expertise.

To a greater or lesser extent, in fact, we are all somehow involved in selling. If you were responding to an advertisement for a job, or trying to persuade somebody that extra financing was needed for a project, the chances are that you would need to 'sell' yourself or your idea. Wernick believes that we must take this into account in understanding changes in society. It is not enough to consider the question only from the side of reception, the ways in which the public is addressed. We must also look at the ways in which people are all, increasingly, becoming involved in the *production* of promotional texts:

> ... from dating and clothes shopping to attending a job interview, virtually everyone is involved in the self-promotionalism which overlays such practices in ... everyday life.

> At one level or another, then, and often at several levels at once, we are all promotional subjects.

(Wernick, 1991, p. 192)

ACTIVITY 6.7

Read 'The marketization of public discourse: the universities' by Norman Fairclough (Reading B). This is Fairclough's account of the linguistic strategies he had to use in order to be promoted at work. As an academic in a British university, he analyses how marketisation is becoming routine in the linguistic practices of British higher education.

Comment

Fairclough feels a deep ambivalence about the activity he had to become involved in: 'selling himself'. What other situations now require the use of the same promotional linguistic strategies? Is it a reasonable assertion that you must 'sell yourself' in an increasing range of contexts: in job interviews; when renting accommodation; when arranging a mortgage? Wernick believes that many social encounters now require people to behave (both socially and linguistically) in these ways, and voices his concern about the possible consequences. He refers to this phenomenon as producing a 'profound problem of authenticity' (Wernick, 1991, p. 193) – in other words, people don't know who they are any more: 'If social survival, let alone competitive success, depends on continual, audience-oriented, self-staging, what are we behind the mask?' (Wernick, 1991, p. 193). Do you agree that people increasingly need to become involved in self-promotion? If so, do you think this is a good or a bad thing?

We can link questions of 'self' in marketised English to questions of identity in globally structured industry. English is becoming increasingly important for all employees in transnational companies, as noted in Chapter 5. In some companies, employees are permitted to speak only English at work. Tollefson

(1991) believes that the imposition of English on employees in transnational companies, and a corresponding ban on the use of local languages, can have a fragmenting effect on employees' sense of identity: 'What we do is what we feel we are. Therefore when individuals are not permitted to use their own languages at work, they are alienated not only from their work and the workplace, but from themselves' (Tollefson, 1991, p. 207). If this is true when different languages are at issue, then it may be true, at least to some extent, in companies in which there is a requirement to use marketised English at work, or to follow scripts laid down by company regulations.

Both informalised and marketised English can be seen to throw into the arena all sorts of issues about agency – about 'who does what to whom' – in these situations. It would be somewhat simplistic to assume that the sales techniques in the scripts given earlier simply aim to produce the desired response in the client, persuading him or her to buy the product. That is of course one function, but equally important is the positioning of the *employee* – the salesperson – by the discourse. The script is a complex interplay of instructions from the company to the employee, and from the employee to the client. There are unseen people involved in the immediate interaction between the 'prospect' and the salesperson, such as the investment company, perhaps a parent company and almost certainly shareholders.

The 'prospect', too, of course, draws on his or her knowledge and experience of sales interactions in dealing with the current situation. Who, then, actually holds the cards? The answer seems to be that all the participants, whether present or implied, have a certain amount of power in this interaction. It is not simply a case of the seller 'acting upon' the buyer – even though this may seem at first to be the case. The salesperson, too, is subject to pressures, and needs to behave linguistically according to company guidelines, in order to do the job and achieve certain goals. And this involves not only *saying* certain things rather than others; it involves, to some extent at least, *believing* them. Cold-calling is a difficult and somewhat emotionally threatening task, and employees, once trained, are more or less left to their own devices. The job requires high levels of motivation and commitment, and employees who appear half-hearted are not going to succeed. The employee, therefore, is co-opted into the exchange, just as the customer is. The forms of English used are an important element in the process: the pronouns *we* and *us*, the use of first-name terms, deictic markers – all these create an involvement between the customer and the salesperson, which can act on the salesperson's sense of self, just as much as the customer's.

Some cases of institutional language design, then, can have consequences for the employee as well as for the customer. These come from being required (sometimes by contract) to speak in certain ways rather than others, to respond according to a script, and to use the same script as every other employee. Customers, too, may be left wondering whether they are dealing with an individual or an institution. As I noted above in the example of the fast-food restaurant, they may, for instance, get the same response, in the same words, from different company employees, in different branches, even in different countries.

6.5 Conclusion

In this chapter I have outlined some of the changes in English use that are occurring in increasingly post-industrialised societies. Informalisation and marketisation in English are the result of many interconnecting factors, some political, some social, some local, some international. These include the decline of industry-based employment and the rise of the service sector, the need for political and commercial institutions to gain public approval or to meet expectations of accountability for policies and financial imperatives, and the need for many English speakers in general to adopt these changes in the language they use, in order to remain employed or to become employable. These factors are not clear-cut and distinct, and neither are the merging and emerging forms and uses of English: rather, they connect and intersect.

No one person or institution is in control of these types of English border crossing: they are neither completely top-down nor bottom-up. Informalisation and marketisation can be seen as good or bad, depending on your point of view. If a government circular or broadcast interview addresses readers or listeners in an informal, friendly way, this can be seen as a benefit if it allows them a greater degree of comprehension or involvement in the interaction. It can also, however, imply a basis of social solidarity with the audience, which may well be fraudulent in the wider context and may simply generate deeper cynicism.

In addition, it may be that the sheer amount of informal and marketised English produced by institutions will have similarly fragmented effects: 'consumers' will become adept at decoding it and will therefore develop skills for deflecting its potential influence. They will also learn to adopt similar promotional or conversational strategies themselves when dealing with those institutions. These same strategies can, after all, be adopted by the relatively power*less*, in their interactions with institutions – once people are aware of what those strategies are and how to use them. Furthermore, they will have to hand not only linguistic resources, but multimodal ones. It is not only institutions and commercial enterprises that have access to the increasingly sophisticated technology required for the production of glossy, professional-looking documents, after all.

READING A: Selling in Singapore

Anthea Fraser Gupta
(Anthea Fraser Gupta is a Senior Lecturer in Modern English Language at
the University of Leeds. She taught at the National University of Singapore
for 21 years.)

Specially commissioned for Goodman (1996, pp. 169–77).

Commercial organizations and the government build on common techniques
to promote their products or services and to create an acceptance of
government policies in Singapore. They also build on and develop stereotypes
and myths of Singapore, its history and its people. The two cartoons examined
here appeared in the *Straits Times*, Singapore's leading English language
newspaper, in 1995, and portray a similar image of Singapore, manipulating
images of ethnic identity, gender and language. The texts cannot be
understood without prior access to these stereotypes, which allude to other
cartoon and media sources, including those portrayed in comic strips, in
textbooks and on television.

Figure 1 shows 'Kampong Days 1965', an advertisement for a shopping mall
(Northpoint) in one of Singapore's large government housing estates (Yishun).
'The House-hunters', in Figure 2, is a lavish, full-colour spread, which guides
Singaporeans through the complexities of applying for government housing.
Eighty-five per cent of Singapore's population were living in housing
development board (HDB) flats in 1990 (Lau, 1992b, p. 16): the procedures
concern nearly the whole population of Singapore. Although apparently
designed by staff from the *Straits Times*, 'The House-hunters' appears to be a
public service announcement: in Singapore the media are regularly used for
public-service announcements in this way.

'Kampong Days 1965': a commercial advertisement

'Kampong Days 1965' manipulates an icon of Singapore: the kampong. The
term *kampong* (from Malay *kampung*, 'village') refers to an area of traditional
housing, sometimes but not necessarily rural, where houses were (and in one
or two places, are) made of wood and roofed with tin or attap thatch. The
mythic landscape is said to have been recreated at a promotion of a shopping
mall inside one of the government housing estates that represent modern
Singapore.

Figure 1 'Kampong Days 1965' (*Sunday Times*, 17 September 1995)

The advertisement manipulates both the English text and pictures to recreate the mythic past of kampong life – a source of nostalgia. The two main characters of the cartoon text are a stereotypical Chinese and a stereotypical Malay, both middle-aged males. They are ostensibly reflecting on their shared kampong youth, and the most striking feature of their language is the incorporation of many words, mostly of Malay origin, that are seldom used in modern Singapore English, and which refer to games played in the kampong past. Another mythic figure, a nonya (a woman from the ethnic Chinese community of long residence in the Malay peninsula, with distinctive customs of language, dress and culture), is represented in one frame.

Further examination reveals a much more complex text. The time reference is complex. On the one hand, the middle-aged men are supposed to be in present day Yishun, and they are holding plastic carrier bags; yet they are dressed in a way (the Chinese man in shorts and singlet, the Malay man in sarong and songkok [a traditional hat]) that is seldom seen in the modern environment, but would have been more common in the adults of the kampong past. Similarly, on the one hand the archaic vocabulary of their English is supposed to recall the past, yet on the other, the Singaporean reader knows that the real kampong children of the past would have been unlikely to talk to each other in English. The magician who appears in the imagined kampong is actually in the present time period – a magic show is advertised below.

The nature of the recreated kampong does not correspond to that of the real kampong that formerly occupied the site of the present shopping mall, nor indeed to any actual kampong of Singapore's past. The promotion that is advertised here includes pictures of the historical kampong, which was a Chinese kampong specializing in pig farming. Most historical kampongs were ethnically homogeneous (Malay or Chinese or Eurasian). However, modern housing estates are (by government policy) ethnically mixed. The imagined kampong reflects the multiracial aspect of the modern Yishun, not the ethnically segregated housing of the historical past. In the picture of the kampong, the humans are identified as multiracial, while the animals portrayed do not include pigs and dogs, which were ubiquitous in Chinese kampongs but absent from Malay kampongs. The animals shown are the racially inoffensive cats, ducks, chickens and a cow. The cow has a European appearance and is historically implausible.

'The House-hunters': a public-information advertisement

'The House-hunters' takes the form of a cartoon narrative of a coach trip, with a tour guide who explains to passengers as they move around Singapore the complex rules for applying for flats. In the original advertisement, from which the frames in Figure 2 have been selected, only three frames show scenes exterior to the coach. One frame shows the coach setting off, while an Australian couple (thrown off for being foreigners) watch it depart. The HDB skyline is shown on the horizon, although the hen in the foreground appears to suggest that we are in a non-HDB area. Another exterior frame shows a stereotypical 'mature estate' while a third portrays a private condominium, to illustrate the future HDB 'executive condominiums'.

The focus of the text, then, is on the passengers in the coach; these visually and linguistically represent Singapore types who fulfil certain of the requirements of HDB buyers. As in 'Kampong Days 1965', care is taken to portray multiracial Singapore, with characters being visually identified for race. In this text, ethnic identity is conveyed mostly by skin colour, with the Chinese (the tour guide and eighteen of the passengers) being portrayed as pink, and the Indians and/or Malays as dark brown. The Australians are portrayed with the same pink skin as the Chinese, but with blond hair. A dark-brown couple is identified as Sikh by means of dress, as the man wears the instantly recognizable turban, while the woman has a pigtail and a puttu on her forehead. There is a hint of her wearing a sari or a dopatta, in the material across her right shoulder. No other characters are identified ethnically by dress, with all other males portrayed in trousers and T-shirts, and all other females (implausibly) in dresses. Although Sikhs (known in Singapore as 'Bengalis') are a small minority among Indians in Singapore (officially only 7 per cent of all ethnic Indians in 1990; Lau, 1992a, p. 57), they appear in disproportionate numbers in the media, as the turban creates an instant recognition. They also (it must be said) feature in nursery rhymes, as bogeymen, and as figures of fun, as in the following news item:

British–Bengali Bungle

British health workers carrying out a survey about psychological wellbeing were puzzled by the results they were getting from the Bengali-speaking population in a London district.

According to *New Scientist*, all became clear when they realised that they had failed to check the translation into Bengali of the self-administered questionnaire.

The respondents must have been equally confused. 'I'm feeling on edge' became, in translation, 'I'm walking along', 'I'm finding it hard to make contact with people' turned out as 'I don't have a phone and can't write', and 'I feel there is nobody I am close to' became, regrettably, 'All my immediate family are dead.'

Happily, the questionnaire has since been corrected.

(*Straits Times*, 1 June 1994)

Unusually, there is no clear representation of Malays. As eighteen out of the twenty-three coach passengers, the Chinese are represented in a proportion as close as possible to their actual representation in the population (officially 78 per cent in 1990; Lau, 1992a, p. 5). This care over multiethnic representation is characteristic of all governmental materials.

The skin differences between Chinese and Indians/Malays are exaggerated visually in this cartoon, as is usual, with Indians and Malays being portrayed as of darker skin colour than is plausible (notably in the case of a Sikh family, for

example), and the Chinese being portrayed as paler than is plausible. Sex roles are clearly demarcated, both by dress and by behaviour. Serious questions are put in the mouths of both males and females, but two Chinese females are shown in the stereotypical role of nagging wife – one demands a 'long-overdue first anniversary diamond ring' and another (not shown here) rebukes her husband for admiring a scantily dressed younger woman. Conversely one Chinese male is shown as obsessed with gambling, and another as lecherous. The only children are fat, greedy boys. These are all intertextual references: they recall familiar stereotypes from other texts (see, for example, the cartoon in Figure 3).

Figure 2   Part of 'The House-hunters' (*Sunday Times*, 17 September 1995)

Figure 3   A popular stereotype: the Chinese love of gambling

The explication of the HDB rules is given by the tour guide, portrayed with sunglasses and permed hair. Visually, this guide reminds the acculturated reader of the smooth guides and salesmen common in comic strips and in television comedy (for an example see Figure 4). This seems an inappropriately negative stereotype to invoke here, and may be intended to be humorous.

In the speech bubbles of 'The House-hunters', characters generally speak Standard English. All questions and answers relating to the HDB rules are in resolutely formal Standard English. For Chinese male characters, this may be Standard English with one of the pragmatic particles (*ah*, *lah*) associated with the non-standard variety usually known as Singlish. Singlish is regularly quoted as an emblem of Singapore (as, for example, in the National Day Issue of the *Straits Times* for 9 August 1994). In 'The House-hunters', two Chinese males are portrayed as speaking only Singlish (although in reality, many speakers switch between Standard English and Singlish; see Gupta, 1994). However, these two characters are given no substantive comments: Singlish is a possibility only for asides, which are intended to lighten the tone of the cartoon, and which also relate to our expectations of a cartoon strip. While his wife asks for information, one man makes a personal response in Singlish

Figure 4   Another familiar stereotype: the tour guide

(*Wah – not bad: live near parents can get extra money, and also use them as babysitters*). In another couple's interaction, the man again uses Singlish (*But cheap or not?* and *Got one-room only? Don't want to pay so much, lah!*) while the woman uses Standard English for both her substantive remarks and her asides (demanding a diamond ring).

At other points English is manipulated to invoke a foreign national identity. As the coach leaves the Australian foreigners behind, its passengers are shown calling the stereotypically Australian *G'day mate*. As in the case of the Sikh family, it would appear that Australians have been chosen because of the possibility of linguistic satire of this type.

Like 'Kampong Days 1965', 'The House-hunters' is a self-conscious portrayal of multiracial Singapore. A striking omission from the content is any reference to the racial policy of HDB allocation, which aims to keep blocks, sections of estates and whole estates racially mixed within a fixed proportion. This has been the subject of much discussion (Ooi *et al.*, 1993; Tremewan, 1994) and is seen by many as discriminating against the minorities, who have a need to congregate in order to have sufficient numbers for ethnically based cultural events. The majority Chinese will always have such numbers.

Advertising techniques

The fostering of consent to government policies and the conscious creation of an ideology for Singapore has long been a major concern of the Singapore government (Tremewan, 1994, p. 2f.; Chua, 1995). The primary aim of 'The House-hunters' is to inform readers of the rules and to convince them that these rules are beneficial. A secondary aim is to portray a harmonious multiracial Singapore. 'Kampong Days 1965' is attempting to persuade readers to visit a shopping mall. In both texts the use of an informal format encourages readers to read the text, which looks attractive and raises expectations of humour. Both texts use elements from Singlish, a Singapore identity marker. However, in both cases the conversationalization turns out to be superficial: Standard English remains the vehicle for the substantive content. Gender roles are clearly distinguished, with men being more central than women. Both texts choose characters with care to convey the impression of a multiracial Singapore, and use icons of skin colour and of dress that exaggerate ethnic stereotypes to allow for instant recognition. They are operating in the same mythic Singapore. In the real Singapore, sex roles are less clearly defined, dresses are not the sole (or even the principal) dress style for women, and the colour difference between Chinese and non-Chinese is not so sharp. The mythic Singapore has been created partly from the official ideology of a multiracial Singapore, where men are the head of household, and partly from popular cartoons published in both Singapore and Malaysia, which build on stereotypes and strengthen them.

Although the public-service advertisement would appear to be using many of the norms of advertising, it could be said that the government strategies have also influenced the commercial advertisement. The portrayal of multicultural Singapore is conscious and obligatory in government publications, but commercial advertisers are at liberty to represent whatever individuals they wish. However, the minorities are sensitive to their own visual absence and are likely to react negatively to advertisements in which they do not appear. This advertiser is building on government documents in its consciously multiracial portrayal. The influence is not in one direction only.

Acknowledgement

I would like to thank my English as a World Language class (1995) for their full discussion of this text, and especially the following, who contributed important points: Imelda Chang; Caroline Ching; Feisal Abdul Rahman; Harn Siow Ping; Patricia Ho; Dinah Ong; and Laura Yzelman.

References for this reading

Chua, Beng-Huat (1995) *Communication Ideology and Democracy in Singapore*, London, Routledge.

Gupta, A.F. (1994) *The Step-Tongue: Children's English in Singapore*, Clevedon, Multilingual Matters.

Lau Kak En (1992a) *Singapore Census of Population 1990*, Statistical Release 1, *Demographic Characteristics*, Singapore, Department of Statistics.

Lau Kak En (1992b) *Singapore Census of Population 1990*, Statistical Release 2, *Households and Housing*, Singapore, Department of Statistics.

Ooi Giok Ling, Siddique, S. and Cheng, S.K. (1993) *The Management of Ethnic Relations in Public Housing Estates*, Singapore, Institute of Policy Studies/ Times Academic.

Tremewan, C. (1994) *The Political Economy of Social Control in Singapore*, Basingstoke/London, St Martin's.

READING B: The marketization of public discourse: the universities

Norman Fairclough
(Norman Fairclough is Emeritus Professorial Fellow, Institute for Advanced Research in Management and Social Sciences, University of Lancaster.)

Source: Fairclough, N. (1993) 'Critical discourse analysis and the marketization of public discourse: the universities', *Discourse and Society*, vol. 4, no. 2, pp. 133, 143, 151–3.

[This paper] is a text-based examination of the marketization of discursive practices as a process which is pervasively transforming public discourse in contemporary Britain, with particular reference to higher education ...

The case I shall focus upon is the marketization of discursive practices in contemporary British universities ... by which I mean the restructuring of the order of discourse on the model of more central market organizations. It may on the face of it appear to be unduly introspective for an academic to analyse universities as an example of marketization, but I do not believe it is; recent changes affecting higher education are a typical case and rather a good example of processes of marketization and commodification in the public sector more generally.

The marketization of the discursive practices of universities is one dimension of the marketization of higher education in a more general sense. Institutions of higher education come increasingly to operate (under government pressure) as if they were ordinary businesses competing to sell their products to consumers ...

In what follows I wish to take up the discussion of 'promotional' culture ... I suggest that the discursive practices (order of discourse) of higher education are in the process of being transformed through the increasing salience within higher education of promotion as a communicative function ...

The ... example I want to look at specifically in terms of promotion – and more exactly self-promotion – is an extract from a curriculum vitae (CV). Such data are sensitive for obvious reasons, and I have therefore used an extract from a CV I prepared myself in 1991 for an academic promotions committee. The form of submissions to this committee is controlled by procedural rules which specify the maximum length of a CV and the categories of information it should contain, and require a 'supporting statement' of no more than 'two sides of A4 paper'. The extract I have chosen is a paragraph from the supporting statement. Unlike the CV proper, the content of the supporting statement is not specified in the procedural rules. I had to make informal enquiries to find out what was expected. I was able to look at previous submissions by colleagues, and I received advice from a colleague with experience of the committee. From these sources, I gathered that the supporting statement had to be a compelling account of one's contribution to, if possible, all of the categories of activity in two overlapping schemes of categorization: to research, teaching and administration; and to the department, the university, and the wider community (these categorization schemes are actually spelt out in the procedural rules, though not specifically with reference to the supporting statement). The advice I received was that one had to 'sell' oneself to stand any chance of success. The following extract from an internal memorandum, produced shortly after I had prepared the submission, gives a sense of the prevailing wisdom at the time:

> To succeed, departments have to 'sell' their candidates. One cannot expect merit to gleam with its own halo; the halo has been assiduously polished up! Put differently, this means that one has to hone one's application to give an impression of all-round excellence, preferably over a period of time, with feedback from others.

This easily extends to an emphasis on the need for extended preparation for the well-honed application – for instance, it is helpful to have favourable student feedback on one's courses, ideally over several years. One's future promotability may become a significant factor in the planning of one's current activities. Here is the extract:

Contributions to the Department

I have I believe played a significant role in the academic and administrative leadership of the Department over the past eight years or so. I was Head of Department from 1984 to 1987 and again for one term in 1990, and I have carried a range of other responsibilities including MA and undergraduate programme coordination and admissions. I helped to set up and now help to run the Centre for Language in Social Life. Through my coordination of the Language, Ideology and Power research group and in other activities, I have stimulated research (e.g. on critical language awareness) among colleagues and postgraduate students, and helped form what is now being recognized nationally and internationally as a distinctive Lancaster position on and contribution to study of language and language problems in contemporary British society. I am currently helping to edit a collection of Centre for Language in Social Life papers for publication.

Some of the self-promotional properties of the extract are obvious enough. There is a series of claims realized as clauses with past tense, present perfective and present continuous verbs and *I* as subject and theme. These are mainly claims which are categorical in their modality, positive assertions without explicit modalizing elements, though there is a subjective modality marker in the first clause (*I believe*) which (a) foregrounds the subjective basis of judgement in the whole paragraph in that the first clause is a summary formulation of the paragraph, but also (b) foregrounds (one might say rather brazenly) the self-promotional nature of the activity. (For the analytical terminology used here see Halliday, 1985, and Fairclough, 1992.) Except for one relational process (*I was Head of Department*), all clauses in the extract contain action processes. It would seem that material actional process verbs are consistently being selected even where other process types would be just as congruent with or more congruent with the happenings and relationships reported – for instance, although I am indeed one of the five co-directors of the Centre for Language in Social Life, it receives practically no 'running' from anyone, and I might well (indeed better) have worded this *am now an active member of*. Similarly *played a significant role in* might have been *been a significant part of*, *carried a range of other responsibilities* might have been *had a range of other responsibilities*, *helped to set up* might have been *was a founding member of*, and so forth. These changes would, I think, reduce the sense of dynamic activity conveyed in the extract. A noteworthy lexical choice is *leadership* in the first sentence. The wording of academic relationships in terms of *leadership* belongs, in my view, to a managerial discourse which has come to colonize the academic order of discourse recently, and which I actually find deeply antipathetic. In terms of the characteristics of promotional discourse discussed earlier, the extract is very much a signification/construction of its subject/object rather than just referentially based description, and meaning would seem to be subordinated to effect.

I suppose I saw the preparation of the submission as a rhetorical exercise. By which I mean that I was consciously using language in a way I dislike, playing with and parodying an alien discourse, in order to 'play the game' and convince the committee of my merits. That is rather a comforting account of events, and a common enough one; the self stands outside or behind at least some forms of discursive practice, simply assuming them for strategic effects.

I felt embarrassed about the submission, but that is, I think, compatible with the rhetorical account. There are, however, problems with this account. In the first place, it assumes a greater consciousness of and control over one's practice than is actually likely to be the case. For instance, while I was quite conscious of what was at stake in using *leadership*, I was not aware at the time of how systematically I was 'converting' all processes to actions, although I *could* have been (and perhaps I ought to have been) – unlike most people I have the analytical apparatus. More seriously, the rhetorical account underestimates the incorporative capacity of institutional logics and procedures. Whereas the average academic rarely has contact with promotions committees, contact with other organizational forms whose procedures are based upon the same logics are necessary and constant. Doing one's job entails 'playing the game' (or various connected games), and what may feel like a mere rhetoric to get things done quickly and easily becomes a part of one's professional identity. Self-promotion is perhaps becoming a routine, naturalized strand of various academic activities, and of academic identities.

References for this reading

Fairclough, N. (1992) *Discourse and Social Change*, Cambridge, Polity.

Halliday, M. (1985) *An Introduction to Functional Grammar*, London, Edward Arnold.

7 Making judgements about English

Donald Mackinnon

7.1 Introduction

The most unexpected bestseller of recent years must be a book about punctuation. *Eats, Shoots & Leaves: The Zero Tolerance Approach to Punctuation* by Lynne Truss was published in 2003, and by 2006 had sold over three million copies worldwide. The author was criticising the general standard of punctuation today, but in a light-hearted manner:

> Either this will ring bells for you, or it won't. A printed banner has appeared on the concourse of a petrol station near to where I live. 'Come inside,' it says, 'for CD's, VIDEO's, DVD's, and BOOK's'.
>
> If this satanic sprinkling of redundant apostrophes causes no little gasp of horror or quickening of the pulse, you should probably put down this book at once. By all means congratulate yourself that you are not a pedant or even a stickler; that you are happily equipped to live in a world of plummeting punctuation standards; but just don't bother to go any further. For any true stickler, you see, the sight of the plural word 'Book's' with an apostrophe in it will trigger a ghastly private emotional process similar to the stages of bereavement, though greatly accelerated.
>
> (Truss, 2003, pp. 1–2)

Truss's facetiously exaggerated outrage is not unique among those who write about the English language. Reading it, I was reminded of some of the purple passages in H.W. Fowler's famous handbook, *A Dictionary of Modern English Usage*, published almost eighty years earlier. One memorable example is about what he called 'elegant variation' – that is, replacing a word or phrase with a synonym for no reason other than to avoid repetition:

> It is the second-rate writers, those intent rather on expressing themselves prettily than on conveying their meaning clearly, & still more those whose notions of style are based on a few misleading rules of thumb, that are chiefly open to the allurements of elegant variation ... first terrorized by a misunderstood taboo, next fascinated by a newly discovered ingenuity, & finally addicted to an incurable vice ...
>
> (Fowler, 1926, pp. 130–1)

Fowler and Truss are only two of many who have written books telling their readers how to speak and write better English. On a recent visit to an ordinary public library in Glasgow, I found the following handbooks side by side on the shelves: *The Cassell Guide to Common Errors in English* (Blamires, 1997); *Essential English for Journalists, Editors and Writers* (Evans, 2000); *Improve Your Written English* (Field, 2003); *The King's English* (Amis, 1997); *The Oxford Guide to English Usage* (Weiner and Delahunty, 1993); *The Penguin Writer's Manual* (Manser and Curtis, 2002); *Plain English* (Collinson et al., 1992); and *Quick Solutions to Common Errors in English* (Burt, 2004).

Many of the authors of these handbooks have been highly successful in a variety of fields where language is important. They include a novelist, a playwright, a literary critic, a philosophy professor at Oxford University and the editor of the *Sunday Times*. In writing these handbooks, they are writing about language itself: telling a general audience about the rights and wrongs of English usage. Such a stance is at odds with work by what I would call 'professional linguists', those whose job it is to think and write about English at an academic level. Most linguists are professionally wary of making judgements about language quality. Indeed, many linguists argue that some of the kinds of judgement made about quality in language are radically misguided.

In this chapter, I want to look at the kinds of judgement we can and cannot reasonably make about the quality of people's English – the sorts of judgement that linguists largely avoid and discourage the rest of us from making, but that handbook authors like Fowler and Truss not only do make, but consider very important. In doing so, I shall draw on judgements taken from a variety of sources, but mainly of two types. First, of course, are the prescriptive handbooks themselves. Second are the complaints and worries about English often found in the newspapers. For the latter, I have paid particular attention over the last few years to the *Guardian*, a national newspaper in the UK. I shall use extracts from this newspaper almost as a case study. Whether those who complain about language to the *Guardian* are typical of the population is a moot point. But since the *Guardian* is generally recognised as being on the 'left', 'liberal' or 'progressive' side of present-day British thinking, there is at least no reason to leap to the conclusion that its readers are unusually conservative in their attitudes to language. At any rate, I shall refer to them from time to time as a convenient, if highly imperfect, sample of the views of people who are interested in language but are not linguists. This is a category that I myself belong to. I approach the English language – and judgements and arguments about it – as one trained in English literature and philosophy, not linguistics.

As you have read in earlier chapters in this book, language use is tightly bound up with context, and the types of judgement we make are equally context bound. As my particular background is not linguistics, the style of this chapter will be rather different from those earlier ones. You will not find here a comprehensive survey of, or systematic sampling from, any of the sources from which I draw my examples. Since I am concerned to identify and evaluate some of the different *kinds* of argument used in judging English,

I draw on both academic and popular views about language. These are mostly from British English sources because of my context, though concerns about the quality of English can be found in English-speaking countries throughout the world.

What kinds of judgement, then, do people make about the quality of English?

ACTIVITY 7.1

Allow about
20 minutes

Spend a few minutes thinking about what different *kinds* of favourable or unfavourable judgement can be made about English. Draw up a list and compare it with mine below.

As you do so, try to recall judgements about the quality of English that you have heard, or read, or made yourself. If you have access to any handbooks of English usage – such as Fowler's *A Dictionary of Modern English Usage* from which I quoted or some of the books I listed above – you might find it helpful, as I did, to look at the kinds of judgement they contain.

Comment

Here is the list I came up with. We may judge examples of English to be:

- *correct* or *incorrect* in various ways, such as grammatical structure, spelling, pronunciation or the meanings of words
- *appropriate* or *inappropriate* for some contexts, such as an exam answer, a job interview, a pub conversation or a love letter
- more or less *useful* for some purposes, such as communicating meanings, or expressing feelings
- *beautiful* or *ugly* as with some accents, and some styles of speech and writing, often given labels like 'management-speak' or 'jargon'
- *socially acceptable* or *unacceptable* – a type of judgement less often made openly than it once was, but still to be found
- *offensive* in a variety of ways – swear words are often *obscene* or *blasphemous*; other words and expressions are often judged as racist, sexist or in other ways *discriminatory*
- *controversial* – by this I mean that we may distance ourselves from any of the above judgements, but acknowledge that other people will make them – and perhaps avoid them ourselves and recommend others to avoid them too.

This is rather a long list, and I could not attempt to cover everything in it. What I am going to do in this chapter is concentrate mainly on one of these categories – that of *correctness*, which seems to be at the forefront of many people's judgements of English. But I shall also look more briefly at three related categories. The first is that of *appropriateness*, which seems to have become, in some quarters, a substitute for correctness. The second is that of *social acceptability*, which sometimes seems to lie behind apparent judgements of correctness. Finally, I will also examine how some language comes to be judged *offensive*. The actual judgements that people make, and the arguments with which they support them, do not always fall neatly into just one of my categories, so I shall also be touching on some of the other categories from time to time.

7.2 Correctness

> In your article on international brands I have been quoted as saying that Lacoste has a phobia 'against' bad quality. You can have a phobia 'about' something, not against it. I am sure I said 'about' in the interview. You may consider this a minor detail, we don't.
>
> (Jayant Kochar, President, Sports and Leisure Apparel Limited, New Delhi, *India Today*, 30 September 1994, p. 9)

Jayant Kochar had strong enough views about correctness to go to the trouble of writing to a magazine. Professional linguists, those whose job it is to research, think and write about English, also recognise some things as being wrong, or simply 'not English'. However, they are a lot less ready to condemn what people say or write as incorrect than many other commentators on language. Jean Aitchison, formerly Professor of Language and Communication at the University of Oxford, is a professional linguist who has decried what she calls 'purist' views of language. She set out the case some years ago, in an article for a popular London newspaper, the *Evening Standard*.

ACTIVITY 7.2

Reading A is an edited version of Jean Aitchison's article, 'Why do purists grumble so much?' Please read it now.

As Professor Aitchison acknowledged, many readers and writers outside linguistics do make judgements of the kind she regards as 'moans over trivia'. And Lynne Truss's sales figures leave little doubt that she and her fellow writers are meeting a public demand.

In contrasting professional linguists with handbook writers, I am setting up those who describe language and value its variety in opposition to those who attempt to lay down or prescribe rules which tend to favour one variety over another. This is a simplified picture, of course; professional linguists do sometimes offer prescriptions, as we shall see, and handbook authors do tolerate some change and variety. But, by and large, the contrast does hold.

These two opposed attitudes to judgements about English – the descriptive and the prescriptive – are illustrated, albeit unintentionally, in the book, *Rediscover Grammar with David Crystal* (Crystal, 1996).

ACTIVITY 7.3

Reading B is in three parts, all of which come from David Crystal's book. Part 1 is the publisher's account of the book on its back cover. Part 2 is taken from Professor Crystal's own Introduction, in which he explains his approach. And Part 3 is Crystal's discussion of one of the specific points mentioned in the publisher's account, the use of *will* and *shall*. Please read these now and answer the following questions:

- How well do the two accounts of what the book is about – the publisher's and the author's – match one another? Make a note of similarities and differences.
- For the particular case of *will* and *shall*, how closely does Crystal's discussion correspond to what the publisher seems to expect?

Comment

The accounts in Parts 1 and 2 give rather different impressions of the book. As its title suggests, it is a 'popular' introduction to grammar, not an academic textbook. But Crystal is an academic linguist, and his approach to the subject is characteristic of the discipline. For him, grammar is primarily *descriptive*: it is an attempt to discover and set out explicitly the rules that people actually follow when they speak a language such as English. It is not primarily *prescriptive*: it is not a set of ideal rules against which ordinary speech is to be judged, often found wanting, and corrected. But this does not seem to have been fully appreciated by Crystal's publisher. They seem to regard his book as being more like the prescriptive handbooks which set out to correct common errors and improve their readers' English.

The distinction between the prescriptive approach of the publisher and Crystal's descriptive approach is clearly illustrated in the discussion of *will* and *shall*, where Crystal explicitly contrasts 'traditional grammars' of the more prescriptive sort with his own approach. The traditional grammars recommend a sharp distinction between the two words – and this seems to have been the approach that Crystal's publisher expected from him. But what Crystal does is describe the way the words are actually used today, pointing out that no distinction is now normally made between them, and that *shall* is becoming less common.

Not long after Aitchison urged journalists to discourage 'moans over trivia', the *Guardian* took what might be seen as a step in the opposite direction. In 1997, it appointed a readers' editor (Ian Mayes) with the task of looking at complaints from readers, and correcting 'significant' errors in the newspaper. For this purpose, the paper has a daily 'Corrections and clarifications' section for specific errors, and a weekly column in which Ian Mayes reflects on more general issues. A year after taking up the position, he noted that, from the

6,000 or so letters or emails that he had received, 'The fattest file of all those accumulated ... is the one containing complaints about the way we use, or misuse, the English language in the *Guardian*' (Mayes, 1998). And over subsequent years, this has remained true – though corrections of mistakes in language form only a small fraction of those that he publishes.

From time to time, Mayes has considered whether these complaints are trivial, always concluding that on the whole they are not. Here are two examples of the kind of correction he publishes of his colleagues' English:

> The phrase 'comprised of' has been used in these pages 37 times in the past 12 months ... 'Comprises' is the word required. The New Fowler's Modern English Usage puts it this way: 'The special function of comprise ... is to introduce a list of parts making up the whole that is its subject; that is, it means to consist of or be composed of.' It gives as an example of correct usage: 'A full pack comprises 52 cards.'
>
> (Mayes, 2003a)

> We described children listening to the results of their sports day events as being disinterested, when uninterested was what was meant. From Collins [English Dictionary] – 'Disinterested: free from bias or partiality' ...
>
> (Mayes, 2004a)

As examples like these show, Mayes unhesitatingly judges certain usages to be incorrect. He is making judgements as if there were a fixed and unchanging standard of what is correct. He takes relatively little account, as we shall see, of changes and developments in language use, or even of how clearly a message is communicated. The handbooks I mentioned above are often equally prescriptive.

Handbook authors are not only confident that many expressions used by other people are wrong, they are also often equally confident that expressions condemned by others are perfectly correct. For instance, one type of expression widely condemned is the split infinitive – of which the most famous example must be the Star Trek mission 'to boldly go ...'. In his memoirs, John Simpson, the BBC's world affairs editor, recalls one of his teachers at Cambridge, Arthur Sale, who apparently was 'generally regarded as the best individual teacher of English in the university':

> Years later, after I had come back from a frightening and physically exhausting tour of duty covering the war in Afghanistan, I went to see him. My report had gone out a few days earlier. The high point of it was a piece to camera with fighting going on all round me. Arthur had seen it. He always seemed to see the things one hoped he wouldn't. 'You split two infinitives when the guns were going off,' he said.
>
> (Simpson, 1999, pp. 70–1)

But sixty years earlier, Fowler had mocked the rule against split infinitives as a 'superstition'. And in his handbook, the novelist Kingsley Amis (1997, p. 217) dismisses the same rule as 'the best known of the imaginary rules that petty linguistic tyrants seek to lay upon the English language'.

So how do we – or the authors of handbooks, or teachers at Cambridge, or professional linguists – know when something in English is correct or incorrect? What, indeed, do we mean by saying it is correct or incorrect? And why should we be concerned about this?

To explore these questions I shall begin with the most clear-cut of examples:

> disiple Wrong spelling. See DISCIPLE ...
>
> distroy Wrong spelling. See DESTROY.

(based on Burt, 2004, p. 72)

When Angela Burt says that the spellings are wrong, I imagine that few readers would disagree, and fewer still would say they did not know what calling them 'wrong' means. Nevertheless, let us pursue the questions a little, at the risk of labouring the obvious. What do we mean by saying that *disiple* or *distroy* is a spelling mistake?

It is clearly not a mistake of the same kind as claiming that the Earth is flat or that two plus two equals five. It is more like breaking a rule in football or a convention in dining-table etiquette. The first instances are mistakes concerning facts about the world, or necessary truths. These facts and truths cannot be changed; the truths are true everywhere and the mistakes mistaken everywhere; human beings discover them, but do not make the truths true, or the mistakes mistaken. By contrast, the second instances are breaches of human-made rules and conventions. These rules and conventions can and do vary from place to place and change from time to time.

English spellings have only taken on a relatively fixed form as a result of the decisions made by printers and publishers, and by lexicographers writing dictionaries over the years. Dictionary writers today are at pains to acknowledge that there is still variation, listing alternative spellings and spellings acceptable in certain varieties of English but not others. Of course, particular organisations can define spellings, pronunciations and other usages for their own purposes, as with the 'house style' of a publisher, a newspaper or the BBC; but they have no authority beyond their own walls, even if they sometimes have wider influence.

I studied the public spellings of English words in 1994 in a small town near Bangalore in India (see Figure 7.1). Many of the spellings – in carefully painted shop signs and notices – do not conform to standard British or American spelling; they do not correspond to any standard Indian spelling either. But I do not think it is helpful to characterise these non-standard spellings simply as incorrect. When one shop offers *pluming* services in its main sign, and *plumbing* in the more detailed description underneath, when even a street

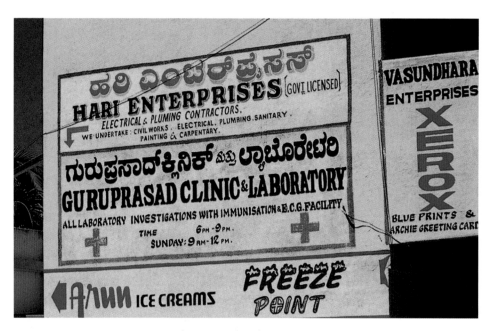

Figure 7.1 Indian shop signs

trolley calls itself a *tiffin centre* on the front and a *tiffen center* on the side, and so on, surely this state of affairs is better described as a relaxed acceptance of variety than as a large number of mistakes. This is a state of affairs that Shakespeare would have felt very much at ease with. After all, even his own name was spelt in a variety of ways in his lifetime – his birth, for example, was registered in the name of *Shakspere* (Wells, 2002).

So how are the rules of English decided? What makes usages correct or wrong?

ACTIVITY 7.4

Allow about
20 minutes

What criteria are used, or might be used, in deciding whether particular English expressions are correct or wrong?

Once again, you may find it helpful to refer to handbooks of English usage to see what kinds of reasons (if any) are given for the judgements they make.

I give my ideas in the rest of this section.

Frequency of occurrence

This seems to play a central part in many people's judgements of correctness, but it is rarely used simply on its own. If it were, then mistakes in spelling, grammar or meaning that became common would automatically turn into correct alternatives. Book titles like *Common Errors in English* would make no sense, and the *Guardian* readers' editor's rebukes to his colleagues for the number of times they make the same mistakes in their English would be self-defeating. Thus, even Mayes occasionally acknowledges unenthusiastically that time and frequency may sometimes change things. When a reader asked if *bored of* is 'one of those things that used to be wrong but is now becoming acceptable because more and more people do it', Mayes replied, 'No it is not acceptable (yet)' (Mayes, 2003b). But just how often the construction would have to be used, or what else would have to happen to make it acceptable, he did not say.

In many modern dictionaries, frequency is used as a criterion. Such dictionaries are compiled on the basis of a 'corpus' – a large sample of actual language use, often stored electronically on a computer, which can be analysed statistically. Frequency is often indicated in quite subtle ways, as Sue Engineer, a lexicographer with Longman Dictionaries, illustrated for me some years ago, with regard to spelling: 'where two variants are common, we give the most frequent first and separate them by a comma, where one is far less frequent than the other (e.g. jail and gaol), we separate them by "also"' (Sue Engineer, 1995, personal communication).

Of course, current use of English is not always uniform, and the processes by which spellings and usages change seem much more likely to be gradual than sudden. So there is often an ambiguous state when certain spellings, meanings and grammatical forms may be in transition from being old mistakes to being newly correct. One current example of this seems to be the choice between *who* and *whom*. Here, the prescriptive handbooks are usually clear and firm: '**who or whom?** The grammatical distinction is that "who" is a subject pronoun and "whom" is an object pronoun' (Burt, 2004, p. 213). But many people nowadays do not seem to use *whom* at all. Indeed, if my own teenage children are typical, *whom* is often considered distinctly pedantic, a word to be avoided in any but school contexts.

The difficulty of steering a 'correct' course is highlighted in the extract below from *The BBC News Styleguide* which reveals how different parts of the same organisation can come to different decisions. In this example, the differences concern whether collective nouns such as *company*, *cabinet*, or *government* should be accompanied by singular or plural verb forms – the company *is* or the company *are*:

> It is the policy of BBC Radio News that collective nouns should be plural, as in *The Government have decided.* Other departments, such as BBC Online, have resolved that collective nouns should always be singular, as in *The Government has decided.* BBC Television News has no policy and uses whichever sounds best in context. The difficulty for writers comes because there is no rule – collective nouns can be either singular or plural.
>
> ...
>
> There is one rule you must follow, though – be consistent. Do not write: *The jury was out for three hours, before they reached their verdict.*

> (Allen, 2003, p. 31)

To which the obvious question arises: why not? As we have seen above, the principle of consistency is as open to challenge as any other.

Appeals to authority

If straightforward frequency of use is not taken as the criterion of correctness, what should be? One obvious and popular alternative is to grant some language users more authority than others.

In the early years of the twentieth century, writers on language were often uninhibited in their elitism. Only certain categories of English speaker or writer were regarded as using the language with any authority. In *A Dictionary of Modern English Usage*, Fowler simply dismissed the usages of 'the uneducated' and 'the more or less illiterate', as he cheerfully referred to some of those he disagreed with (Fowler, 1926).

Few people would write like that today. However, elitism still appears, in more moderate forms. In particular, preference is often still given in the handbooks to the English used by 'educated' people. Even David Crystal has this to say when discussing the apostrophe:

... many people nowadays feel unsure about the correct use of the apostrophe, and add it before plural endings and verb endings: *We sell fresh pie's, Everyone like's our chips.* This usage is universally condemned by educated writers.

(Crystal, 1996, p. 127)

Why educated people in general should have more authority than others over language usage is not obvious. Those educated in language, the professional linguists discussed earlier, may indeed be in a better position than others to say what the conventions are. But where there are different and conflicting conventions, why should people educated in language (or anything else) carry any special authority over which ones should be preferred and followed?

One answer might be: because they care about clarity. In discussing apostrophes, the *Guardian* newspaper *Style Guide*, after explaining the rules, goes on to say:

> And if anyone tries to tell you that apostrophes don't matter and we'd be better off without them, consider these four phrases (listed in Steven Pinker's The Language Instinct), each of which means something completely different:
>
> my sister's friend's investments,
>
> my sisters' friends' investments,
>
> my sisters' friend's investments,
>
> my sister's friends' investments.

(*Guardian*, 2005a)

However, I fear that the *Guardian* is here fighting a battle that has already been lost. Given that many people no longer seem to make or recognise the distinction between *'s* and *s'*, it is surely unwise for writers to rely on the position of the apostrophe to make their meaning clear. If there were any doubt about how many sisters or friends were involved, I myself would always write something like, *friends of my sister, a friend of my sisters*, and so on. And of course that is what we have always had to do in speech. Even to people who distinguish between *'s* and *s'* in writing, all four phrases listed above by *The Guardian Style Guide* sound the same when spoken.

Disapproval

As we have seen, something on which everyone agrees is that some usages are widely disapproved of. Modern handbook authors often point this out while expressing their own disapproval; and the linguists often report disapproval as part of their description of the way a word, an expression or a grammatical structure is used. *The Oxford Guide to English Usage* (Weiner and Delahunty, 1993), for example, uses a 'bullet' (•) whenever it wants to warn that a common usage may be unacceptable in some circles. This seems to be a relatively new attitude. The writers of older handbooks – and certainly the Fowler brothers (1906) – always seemed to speak firmly and unapologetically in their own voice, condemning certain usages no matter how many people allowed them.

The consequences of disapproval can sometimes be severe, of course, especially if it comes from people regarded as having authority with respect to language, or people with power of other kinds – such as teachers, examiners and employers. Even if we are not convinced that other people's disapproval makes certain usages incorrect, it may sometimes be sensible for us to avoid them.

Logic

Handbook writers often treat English as though it ought to have the rigour and precision of propositions in formal logic or mathematics. Angela Burt's treatment of double negatives is an example of this (even down to the = signs):

> The effect of two negatives is to cancel each other out. This is sometimes done deliberately and can be effective:
>
> I am not ungenerous. (= I am very generous.)
>
> He is not unintelligent. (= He is quite intelligent.)
>
> Frequently, however, it is not intentional and the writer ends up saying the opposite of what is meant:
>
> I haven't had no tea. (= I have had tea.)
>
> You don't know nothing. (= You know something.)

(Burt, 2004, p. 73)

By contrast, some linguists treat the latter type of double negative as intensifying the negation. Jean Aitchison points out that it is following a pattern found in the English of Chaucer and in other languages, where 'the more negatives you have the more negated it is' (Grove, 1993). This seems convincing to me, and I doubt if, in context, the two types of double negative are often confused. I cannot believe anyone ever genuinely misinterpreted Pink Floyd's lyrics *We don't need no education* as proclaiming, 'We need education.' And when the father of the bride in the film *My Big Fat Greek Wedding* wails a multiple negative, 'I don't know nothing because nobody don't tell me nothing', everybody in the cinema understands at once what he means. There is no need to count his negatives, cancel them off in pairs and see whether what is left at the end of the sum is negative or positive.

Conservative or innovative

David Crystal has little sympathy for linguistic conservatism:

> Not everyone likes it when they notice the emergence of different grammatical patterns from the ones they have themselves used since childhood. Some people get angry, condemn the changes, and protest about them to anyone who will listen. Change is invariably considered to be for the worse. But no one has ever managed to stop the course of grammatical change ...

> (Crystal, 1996, p. 21)

As he acknowledges, though, many readers and writers outside linguistics do make judgements about language of the kind that he sees as straightforward dislike of change. Sometimes the handbook writers and the *Guardian* correction columns seem to regard new usages almost automatically as straightforward mistakes, calling for correction, not argument. But sometimes they do give arguments in favour of conservatism in language. The literary critic Harry Blamires is resigned, as a realist, to accepting without resistance many changes that he regrets – but not all: 'What seem to me to be really damaging are changes which deprive us of a useful word or which blur useful distinctions of meaning. Such, for instance is the current failure now to distinguish the verb "avoid" from the verbs "prevent" and "forestall"' (Blamires, 1997, p. 5).

I am with Blamires in regretting the blurring of distinctions of meaning – perhaps not so much in the particular example he mentions, but in others like *disinterested* (which used to mean *impartial*, not *uninterested*) and *refute* (which used to mean *disprove*, not *deny*). However, I cannot agree that either of these changes is 'really damaging'. For one thing, the number of words whose meanings are blurred in this way is probably small. For another, the simple and obvious solution to any problems caused is to use different words – such as the near-synonyms I have just quoted, *impartial* and *disprove*. In general, even if useful words lose or change their meanings, I am sure we can always find alternative words to express our meanings or make the distinctions we want. At any rate, I do not know any examples of a meaning or distinction that once could be expressed in English but no longer can be.

In addition (as Crystal would not be surprised to find), Blamires does not even consider another possibility – that a change in language might give us a *new* useful word, or make a *new* useful distinction of meaning. Ironically, examples of this abound, especially because of recent developments in science and technology. To take an obvious one, a few years ago we did not have the word 'internet', let alone a need to distinguish it from the 'World Wide Web', because we did not have the things to which they refer.

Sometimes the extreme view seems to be taken that abandoning a rule of traditional grammar leaves us with no grammar at all. Here is the *Guardian* readers' editor again:

> One of our columnists wrote recently, '... he followed my husband and I home ...' This brought cries of indignation. 'I know the meaning is perfectly clear but it is rubbish grammar and [the writer] should know better.' One reader offered a useful piece of advice. 'As my English teacher dad used to tell us, when in doubt, separate out the pronoun. You wouldn't say "He followed I" would you?'
>
> The New Fowler's Modern English Usage, revised by RW Burchfield (Oxford) is unusually sharp on this point, putting the use of I 'as the second member of an objective phrase, eg "He drove Kirsten and I home"' in the same category as the dire, 'Between you and I.' 'Anyone who uses it now,' says Fowler, 'lives in a grammarless cavern in which no distinction is recognised between a grammatical object and a subject.'
>
> (Mayes, 2000)

How convinced are you by these claims? Is 'separating out the pronoun' a useful method of testing whether an expression like those quoted above is grammatically correct? Is anyone who uses 'I', as in these examples, living 'in a grammarless cavern in which no distinction is recognised between a grammatical object and a subject'? I am not convinced on either point.

As regards the first, why should 'separating out the pronoun' tell us what to say when the pronoun is not separated out? Current English usage treats the two situations differently. Many people use and accept expressions like 'He drove Kirsten and I home', whereas none would say or accept 'He drove I home'. If we make actual usage our criterion for correctness, the latter is wrong but the former is correct. In practice, people seem to be following a perfectly coherent rule that can be expressed in Burchfield's terms like this: 'I' cannot on its own be the object of a sentence, but it can be the second member of an object phrase. (Similarly, 'me' cannot, on its own, be the subject of a sentence, but it can be the second member of a subject phrase. We would not say, 'Me went home'; but that does not mean it is wrong to say, 'Kirsten and me went home'.)

As regards the second point, I do not suppose Burchfield imagines that the speakers criticised are literally 'grammarless'. This seems to be another of the exaggerations enjoyed by people complaining about changes in English language usage (like Fowler and Truss), and I shall say no more about it. But the more moderate part of the accusation – that these speakers do not recognise a distinction between a grammatical object and a subject – is not convincing either. Burchfield seems to have forgotten that, in English, grammatical case is shown more by the position of words in a sentence than by the form of the words. Indeed, in English only a few pronouns have different forms for different cases.

When I studied Latin many years ago, one of the illustrations I was given of the differences between Latin and English was the pair of headline 'sentences' MAN BITES DOG and DOG BITES MAN. In English, the order of the words tells us what is subject and what is object, and gives the two sentences different meanings, even though the form of all the words is the same. By contrast, in Latin, as in many other languages, it is predominantly the form of the words that determines which is subject and which is object, as Steven Pinker has explained more recently:

> ... in Latin, the nouns for man and dog, *homo* and *canis*, change their endings depending on who is biting whom:
>
> Canis hominem mordet. [not news]
>
> Homo canem mordet. [news]
>
> Julius Caesar knew who bit whom because the noun corresponding to the bitee appeared with -*em* at the end. Indeed, this allowed Caesar to find the biter and bitee even when the order of the two was flipped, which Latin allows: *Hominem canis mordet* means the same thing as *Canis hominem mordet*, and *Canem homo mordet* means the same thing as *Homo canem mordet*.

> (Pinker, 1994, p. 115)

Burchfield seems to be treating English as though it were more like Latin than it is, with only the forms of the words differentiating subject and object. In reality, the word order is surely more important. Where there is a conflict in English between the word forms (according to traditional grammar) and the word order, it is the order that will determine the meaning for virtually everyone.

The extract from Mayes's column above also provides an ironic example of how subjective such judgements about language often are. One of the writers who complains about the use of 'my husband and I' as the object of a sentence calls it 'rubbish grammar' (Mayes, 2000) – a phrase likely to annoy at least as many traditionalists as the one complained about, as *rubbish* is not traditionally used as an adjective in front of a noun.

Conflicts between those who resist and those who welcome change in English are far from new, but they have been given a new urgency by the spectacular developments of recent years in the technology of communication. Linguistic conservatives often disapprove, for example, of the English used on the internet. Here is part of a review of the film *About a Boy* that Lynne Truss found posted on the Amazon website:

> I watched this film ... a few days ago expecting the usual hugh Grant bumbling ... character Ive come to loathe/expect over the years. I was thoroughly surprised. This film was great, one of the best films i have seen in a long time. The film focuses around one man who starts going to a single parents meeting, to meet women, one problem He doesnt have a child.

> (quoted in Truss, 2003, p. 17)

And this is Truss's comment on it.

> Isn't this sad? People who have been taught nothing about their own language are (contrary to educational expectations) spending all their leisure hours attempting to string sentences together for the edification of others. And there is no editing on the internet!

> (Truss, 2003, p. 17)

Some of this must again be deliberate exaggeration for comic effect (words like 'nothing' and 'all' are probably not to be taken literally in Truss's writings). But even allowing for that, she does seem to be claiming that the review demonstrates ignorance of English and an inability to write it as a result of inadequate teaching.

I am not convinced. It is true that the review does not consistently follow all the normal rules of English prose. The first person singular pronoun and proper names are sometimes written without a capital letter, sentences do not always end in a full stop, and apostrophes are omitted altogether. But this hardly justifies Truss's extravagant claims. On the contrary, the review contains clear evidence that its author does know and can use the rules that he or she sometimes breaks.

Thus the first person singular pronoun is written once as *i*, but three times as *I*. Hugh Grant's first name is written with a lower case *h*, but his surname has its capital *G*. The closing sentences are not conventionally (or helpfully) punctuated, but the earlier ones are. Only the apostrophes required by traditional grammar are missing throughout. What this suggests to me is that the author of the review knows very well how English prose 'should' be written, and normally writes that way; but when they make mistakes in typing, they do not go back to correct them.

Why should this be? One explanation might be laziness, but there is a more plausible alternative. It is illustrated by the following extract from an email sent by a professor of artificial intelligence to a novelist friend who is a newcomer to this method of communication:

> ... you're going to have to loosen up your prose style for email. speed is the essence for instance dont bother with caps because they take up time unnecessarily, two keystrokes instead of one and dont bother correcting typos.

(Lodge, 2001, p. 184)

Admittedly this email, like its sender and recipient, is fictional, taken from a novel by David Lodge. But it can stand as an example of one strand from a vast and intricate web of rules, conventions and etiquette that has been formed around internet communication. And as such, it offers a plausible explanation of why the author of the review quoted by Truss might write on the internet the way he or she does.

Predictably enough, Lodge makes the novelist who receives this advice reject it saying she 'can't lose a lifetime's habit of correct spelling and punctuation' (Lodge, 2001, p. 184). This indicates another factor – age. One reader of an early draft of this chapter, an English teacher, commented that she writes emails, text messages, and so on, in full with careful punctuation, but her teenagers, who are 'A' grade students, do not; however, their handwritten essays are carefully punctuated.

However, the internet and other forms of electronic communication, such as mobile phone texting, are still only at the beginning of their development. As yet, we cannot even guess what their overall influence on the English language will be.

Etymology

A huge number of words in English are derived from words in other languages, and it is sometimes assumed that these origins determine the correct meaning of the English words today. This view seems particularly strong when the languages of origin are the prestigious ones of Ancient Greek and Latin. For example, the word 'synthetic' is said to come from the Greek *syn*, together, and *tithemi*, place. So, by this criterion, it must mean 'placed together', not 'false'. I found this example in the handbook by Harold Evans, the former *Sunday Times* editor, where it appeared in a list of 'some of the words commonly misused in newspapers' (Evans, 2000, pp. 57, 62).

A Latin example comes from an entry in the *Guardian* 'Corrections and clarifications' section, where again the supposed errors of journalists are being corrected:

> ... on two occasions yesterday the word forensic was incorrectly used as meaning an autopsy or a detailed examination. ... [On] page 5, a police

investigator is quoted as saying that identification of the bodies 'may need to be done forensically'. On page 7 ... we say 'investigators carried out a forensic examination of the points'. Collins English Dictionary defines the word as 'related to, used in, or connected with a court of law ... from Latin forensis public, from FORUM.' So 'forensic', in the scientific sense, is not a specific method but describes the use of science or technology in the investigation and establishment of facts or evidence in a court of law.

(*Guardian*, 2002a)

ACTIVITY 7.5

Allow about
10 minutes

Look for, or think of, some example sentences using *synthetic* and *forensic*. Are the meanings similar to their Greek or Latin origins? Is referring to the origins of a word a good way of deciding how to use it?

Comment

The meaning that Evans gives to *synthetic* – 'placed together' – is surely not one recognised by ordinary English usage today. If I prepared a salad by placing lettuce and tomatoes together on a plate, would the result be called synthetic? I don't think so. I agree with Evans, however, that the word does not mean 'false'. The ordinary meaning of *synthetic* today is surely *artificial*, a meaning related to its Greek origins – though quite distantly now. (The Latin origins of *artificial* itself are quite close to its present-day meaning, but this is just a happy chance.)

As with *synthetic*, the meaning of *forensic* in modern English usage seems to me to be only distantly related to its Latin origins. It surely refers nowadays to the scientific methods used in criminal investigations, and by extension to the kind of scientific methods characteristic of criminal investigations, even when they are used for investigations of other types. Both the occurrences of the word in the *Guardian* that the newspaper later 'corrected' seem to be in line with this meaning.

For a more modern example, you might like to consider the uses of the word *flak* in comparison with its original meaning in German. Try searching for *flak* using an internet search engine.

The correct *forms* of words, as well as their meanings, are sometimes thought to be determined by their origins in other languages. The *Guardian* 'Corrections and clarifications' column published the following corrections of supposedly mistaken plurals that appeared in the paper in one week in October 2002:

'The main criteria is' ... ; 'that criteria' ... – criterion is the singular; 'agent provocateurs' should be 'agents provocateurs' ... ; 'a fast-growing algae' – alga is the singular ...

(Guardian, 2002b)

However, I am not convinced that these plurals are quite as straightforwardly wrong as this suggests. When words from other languages are taken into English, they often acquire English habits as time passes. 'Agent provocateur' is a well-established English term by now. To form the plural in speech, the obvious way is to add an 's' sound at the end, in the normal English fashion. To represent this in writing, 'agent provocateurs' seems perfectly reasonable.

The case of 'criteria' (or 'data', 'bacteria', etc.) is not quite the same, but there too, the singular form ending in 'a' is now well-established usage in English, regardless of what happened in the Greek or Latin from which they were taken long ago. To be sure, 'criterion' is still also in current use in English, as are 'bacterium' and perhaps even 'datum'. But 'alga' is surely on the borderline between the pedantic and the absurd. All in all, I cannot see any reason – in these cases or in general – for allowing etymology to override usage in our judgements of what is correct in modern English.

This section has set out a few of the criteria that are used to judge correctness. Other criteria that you might have suggested include: *usefulness, consistency* and *dialect*. Does the appearance of new words or meanings add useful distinctions to our language or blur existing distinctions? If we allow that people have choice over which person of the verb should accompany a collective noun, must whichever they choose be used consistently? Do we need to distinguish between a non-standard usage that forms part of a *dialect* and a purely personal and idiosyncratic departure from Standard English?

To sum up, I want to turn to an article that raises many of the questions I have been considering. Reading C is taken from one of the weekly columns in the *Guardian* to which I have referred, in which the readers' editor, Ian Mayes, usually looks at some general issue or issues raised by recent errors in and complaints to the newspaper. This one is about the acceptability of *alright* as an alternative spelling of *all right*.

ACTIVITY 7.6

Please read 'A rule without reason' by Ian Mayes (Reading C). What different types of argument are used here, both in favour of and in opposition to the acceptability of *alright*? How convincing do you find them? Is *alright* acceptable?

Comment

Many of the criteria of correctness that I discussed above (and others too) are deployed in this column, either by Mayes himself or by the writers he quotes. I identified the following.

- **Frequency of usage**   Mayes reveals that his colleagues on the *Guardian* have used *alright* nearly 700 times in the preceding year or two. This, of course, does not make it correct for him ('common errors are still wrong').
- **Reference to authority**   Joyce West, one of Mayes's correspondents, quotes the authority of a dictionary in support of her use of *alright*, but seeks the approval of the *Guardian* too. Mayes declines to give this approval though, acknowledging two much admired novelists, Chinua Achebe and Anita Desai, as providing exceptions to his rejection of *alright*.
- **Conservatism**   Ms West reveals that on many other language issues, she is conservative, and finds the *Guardian* supporting her in resisting change. Mayes's own linguistic conservatism shows an interesting complication here. An old usage does not lend support to a modern expression if there has been a big gap in its use. Thus the fact that *alright* was used in the twelfth and thirteenth centuries does not count, as it seems to have been abandoned after that until the late nineteenth century.
- **Usefulness**   One of Mayes's colleagues argues that *alright* marks a useful difference in meaning from *all right* – meaning something like *acceptable* rather than *all correct*. But other colleagues reply that that distinction can already be adequately made by the context in which the phrase *all right* is used. The latter is a type of argument more often used *against* conservatives when they claim that a new usage (such as 'disinterested' meaning uninterested) blurs a useful distinction.
- **Consistency**   This, Mayes concludes, is the *Guardian*'s 'elusive object', but why should it be so desirable? If, as he has acknowledged, the term *all right* has two meanings, it is at least arguable that giving these different spellings is useful in making clear which is intended. Besides, as I mentioned earlier, consistency of spelling has not always been so highly valued in British English, nor is it always so highly valued today in other parts of the world.

Mayes quotes some other criteria that go beyond correctness, and involve some of the other sorts of judgement about English that I identified at the beginning of the chapter. Thus, Burchfield, in preparing the updated version of Fowler's *Modern English Usage* (1998), makes *social* judgements about the background, upbringing and education of people who use the word (judgements, incidentally, that are not present in the discussion of *alright* in Fowler's original 1926 text). These and other kinds of judgement will be considered below.

7.3 Appropriateness

Some linguists seem to treat appropriateness as a substitute for correctness, and it plays a similar role in their writings to the one played by correctness for the more conservative handbook writers. '[V]ariety is the norm,' Aitchison tells us, 'and appropriateness the key: the right words and style for the right occasion, and ... no one "style" is correct at all times' (Aitchison, 1994). This is not complete tolerance, however. The obvious implication is that particular styles are correct (and wrong) at *some* times.

Similar ideas can be found in some of the less conservative handbooks. *The Oxford Guide to English Usage* has this to say: 'Much that is sometimes condemned as "bad English" is better regarded as appropriate in informal contexts but inappropriate in formal ones. The appropriateness of usage to context is indicated by the fairly rough categories "formal" and "informal", "standard", "regional", and "non-standard", "jocular" and so on' (Weiner and Delahunty, 1993, p. x). The most general distinction of this sort made by linguists is that between *formal* and *informal* styles. Frequently, the rules and conventions that linguists describe as applying in practice in formal contexts correspond quite closely to those prescribed as correct in the handbooks.

I am not convinced that replacing correctness with appropriateness solves many of the problems associated with correctness; for there is disagreement about what is appropriate for different contexts, just as there is disagreement about what is correct. And over the years, opinions change about what is appropriate for particular contexts, exactly as opinions change about what is correct.

So why should we consider certain language varieties or styles to be inherently appropriate or inappropriate for certain contexts? Denying that there is a single standard of correctness that applies across all contexts has not taken us very far if we then allow that there is a single standard of correctness that applies within each context. It seems to me, on the contrary, that judgements about appropriateness raise again, this time in a range of different contexts, all the questions and problems we have looked at in the previous section.

It may seem sensible enough to say that different varieties of English are 'appropriate' for the office or the street; for the rock concert or the pulpit; for the seminar or the pub; and for wine makers in Johannesburg or surfers in Sydney. But why? What criteria should speakers use to decide what is appropriate in any of these contexts? Is it frequency of usage? Do some speakers carry more authority than others? And so on, down a list very similar to the one we looked at for correctness. And besides, why are there any differences in appropriateness between the contexts? Why should it be appropriate to say 'Jim and me went to a movie' in one context, but 'James and I went to the cinema' in another?

All in all, I find the identification of the problems with 'correctness' made by Jean Aitchison and the *Oxford Guide* more convincing than their solutions in terms of 'appropriateness'. Appropriateness seems to me to be just as problematic an ideal, and to demand just as critical an approach.

7.4 Social judgements

Some of the judgments of English usages that we have looked at seem to be not so much about the language as such as about the social position and standing of the person using the language. A striking example that we have already seen in Reading C is Burchfield's contention that an inability to see anything wrong with *alright* 'reveals one's background, upbringing, education etc, perhaps as much as any word in the language' – a judgement that Mayes will not be alone in finding 'snooty' (Reading C).

Such judgements probably stand out from the others on the list, in that these are of a kind many people today would not readily admit to making themselves, while suspecting that they sometimes lurk behind the judgements that other people make.

ACTIVITY 7.7

Allow about
10 minutes

Here is part of a letter which appeared a few years ago in *The Times*, complaining about the quality of British primary school teachers.

> The real problem lies in the very poor level of entrant to teacher training ... We are well into the generation of semi-literate teachers. Three years ago, in a comprehensive school in the south, I 'dared' to point out spelling and grammatical errors to a resentful and stupid girl struggling with A-level English literature. 'It don't ma't'er,' came the retort. 'I'm gonna be a ninfant teacher. You only needs two Es.'
>
> (*The Times*, 19 June 1994)

While criticising the spelling and grammar of the girl she was teaching, the writer introduces some odd spellings of her own into her quotation of what the girl said. What do you think these are meant to convey? How convinced are you by this representation of the girl's speech?

Comment

One possibility is that the unusual spellings are there to convey something of the girl's pronunciation. It is quite a common practice for writers to indicate accents other than Received Pronunciation (RP) by non-standard spellings (even though standard spelling is far from being a written representation of RP). The word *gonna* seems a fairly clear example of this. I assume that *ma't'er* is of a similar character, though I can only guess what feature of pronunciation it was meant to indicate – perhaps a glottal stop. But *a ninfant teacher* goes further. What could possibly be conveyed about pronunciation by writing this instead of *an infant teacher*?

What we have here derives, I would suggest, from a literary tradition. In many English novels of the nineteenth and early twentieth centuries, the speech of working-class people, uneducated people or (sometimes) children is written with misspellings that convey nothing about pronunciation. Somewhere in P.G. Wodehouse, when the servants talk about the *ennui* suffered by their aristocratic employers, the word is spelt as *onwee*. Since 'onwee' is probably as close as most English people from any social class ever get to the French pronunciation, I assume that the misspelling is there as a marker of the social and educational inferiority of the servants, who are unaware that *ennui* is a French word. In the same way, I would guess, *The Times* letter is meant to convey that a would-be infant teacher would not even be able to spell 'infant'.

In response to attitudes like these, some writers recommend paying attention to spelling for very practical purposes. At the end of 2004, both the BBC and Independent Television broadcast highly publicised spelling tests, *Hard Spell* and *The Great British Spelling Test* respectively. The former was a 'massive countrywide spelling contest', for children aged between 11 and 14, in which a champion was found from 100,000 initial contestants (Rackham, 2004, p. 88). As part of the publicity for these programmes, the magazine *Radio Times* sought the views of a number of authorities about spelling. One of them was notably frank:

Does correct spelling really matter any more?

Yes, especially for the young, according to *Hard Spell* consultant and senior lecturer in English at Cambridge University Laura Smith ... 'It's a shorthand way of saying, "I am educated, take me seriously." ...'

(Lay, 2004, p. 39)

Smith is being constructive rather than critical, but the underlying attitude is the same as that of the writers quoted just above: in Britain spelling is important for what it conveys about the social and educational standing of the speller.

This is, I suspect, the nub of the issue. Judgements are being made not about clarity or ability to communicate, but about social status. There is no real worry that bad spelling will seriously interfere with communication. At any rate, I cannot actually recall ever being seriously puzzled or misled by misspellings. Even the pupil in my school teaching days in Glasgow who wrote about 'the chooky embra' was easily intelligible in context. (The context was 'the queen and the chooky embra' – the Duke of Edinburgh). By contrast, I am often puzzled and sometimes totally defeated by bad handwriting, including increasingly my own as I get older. But for some reason handwriting in Britain (though not everywhere in the world) attracts much less complaint than spelling, and bad handwriting seems not to be taken as a sign of poor education. I have read countless books over the years whose acknowledgements include unblushing thanks to a secretary for deciphering the author's bad handwriting. I have yet to read even one where a secretary or editor is thanked for correcting the author's bad spelling.

7.5 Offensive language

One of the strongest judgements that people can make about language is that it is offensive. In this section I explore: why some people find particular categories of language offensive; why such words and expressions are offensive to some people and not to others; and whether the offence is inherent in the language or depends on the intent of the user. I should perhaps add a warning at this point: in this section, I will be quoting some of the words that people find offensive; this is inevitable if it is to be clear what is being discussed.

ACTIVITY 7.8

Allow about
10 minutes

Before I go on to give you my thoughts on offensive language, think about recent occasions in which you have read or heard language you found offensive. Are there different categories of offensive language? Consider why you found the language used offensive.

Comment

One major category of words that many people are likely to have thought of as offensive is 'swear words'. In British society today these words are often to do with sex, excretion or religion. A second major category contains language that is discriminatory; for example, it may be racist, sexist or homophobic. Again, this list reflects a particular society, social group and historical time. Views of what constitutes offensive language vary between different age groups and communities, both within and between different countries and cultures.

For the purposes of this discussion, I want to keep to the two broad categories – swear words and discriminatory language. Both these categories of language contain words that offend, but the level of offence taken varies – both between words, and between listeners or readers. Why is this? Is the offensiveness tied to a particular *word*, or is it the *intent* of the user that makes them offensive? I want to start by discussing swear words; these seem to me to provoke the widest range of responses.

Swear words

Tom Wolfe, in a novel about American college life, coined the term 'fuck patois' for the dialect used by many of the young characters. Their dialogue is peppered with previously taboo words, but there is no sense of these having any specific meaning:

> 'You know how much that fucking guy weighs?' said Vance, who was sitting back in an armchair on the base of his spine, holding a can of beer. 'Three-hundred and twenty-five fucking pounds. And he can fucking move.'

> (Wolfe, 2004, Chapter 4)

This dialogue contains swear words that seem to have been stripped of any offensive intent. Indeed, in the final sentence the swear word is used positively to convey approval of the sportsman being discussed. For these, admittedly fictional, characters then, swear words used in this way are not to be considered offensive, they simply add emphasis to what is said. This is not to say that readers of the book will not find them offensive.

Of course, this type of speech is much older than 2004, and much more widespread than American colleges. My own most vivid memory of my first holiday job as a student – as a fisherman in north-east Scotland, nearly forty years ago – is of the incessant use of the word 'fucking', with no offence intended or taken.

Swear words used in anger or hostility, however, contain other meanings, as the expression 'sod off' below illustrates:

> WHEN 35 Greenpeace protesters stormed the International Petroleum Exchange (IPE) yesterday they had planned the operation in great detail.

> What they were not prepared for was the post-prandial aggression of oil traders who kicked and punched them back on to the pavement.

> ... Behind him [a protestor], on the balcony of the pub opposite the IPE, a bleary-eyed trader, pint in hand, yelled: 'Sod off, Swampy.'

> (Peek and Chong, 2005)

Perhaps this is one of the fundamental distinctions – whether or not swear words are used with aggressive or hostile intent. This might suggest that it is not the words themselves that are offensive, but how they are used. However, this view does not explain the frequent use of abbreviations and euphemisms which appear to be more acceptable. 'Fuck', for example, can become 'f**k', 'eff' or 'the f-word'. Few readers or hearers can be in any doubt about which word is meant, but offence is apparently avoided. However, further complications creep in when someone actually uses an abbreviation or euphemism with aggressive intent, for example 'Eff off!'

Different newspapers have different policies on printing swear words, and are also sensitive to the *prominence* given. A front-page story in the *Observer* reported the claim that the US Secretary of State, Colin Powell, had referred to some of his more belligerent colleagues in President Bush's administration as 'fucking crazies'. The f-word was printed in full in the text of the story, but the headline used a common euphemism: 'Colin Powell in four-letter neo-con "crazies" row' (Bright, 2004).

ACTIVITY 7.9

Allow about
5 minutes

The Guardian Style Guide on the subject of swear words says: 'never use asterisks, which are just a copout' (*Guardian*, 2005b).

Do you agree with the *Guardian*'s editorial guidelines that asterisks (and presumably also euphemisms like *the f-word* and *four-letter words*) are 'just a copout' and should never be used? Or are there circumstances where you would use asterisks or euphemisms?

Comment

I don't agree with the *Guardian* here. I can easily think of circumstances where asterisks or euphemisms serve a useful purpose. Many people feel that swear words are never acceptable and a euphemism can enable me, for example, to tell a story that depends on the words without offending them. Even people who would prefer not to read the word 'fucking' might be interested to learn that the US Secretary of State had been moved to use it in describing his colleagues.

By using 'fucking' in the text but 'four-letter' in the headline, the *Observer* seems to assume that its own readers are able to cope with the word, but that some other people, such as customers in newsagents' shops, might be offended if they saw the word in large print and out of context. This seems entirely sensible to me.

However, I should report that the majority of *Guardian* journalists take a different view – only ten of about a hundred whose views the readers' editor obtained favoured asterisks:

> The overwhelming opinion ... was strongly against the use of asterisks. 'Fuck is one of the commonest words in British demotic speech. Asterisks are silly and genteel and merely make the paper look fussy ...' About half of the respondents to my email said the use of asterisks would be retrograde, patronising and coy. One said: 'The paper should reflect the way people use language in the real world.'

> (Mayes, 2004b)

Having said that I can see good reasons to make use of euphemisms or asterisks, I do not find all such uses sensible. Sometimes it is not obvious why some words are considered offensive enough to need disguising while others are not. When British Prime Minister Tony Blair's former press secretary, Alastair Campbell, was interviewed for the magazine *Radio Times*, he expressed his disapproval of various things by using colloquial words for body parts and functions. Two of these, 'balls' and 'crap', were considered respectable enough to be printed in full, but a third, 'arse' appeared as 'a**e'

(Duncan, 2004, pp. 28, 29). I find this puzzling, as I imagine that most people reading the magazine would find all three words equally offensive – or inoffensive.

What these various examples show is that there is a great deal of subjectivity in our response to language, which cannot be explained by just considering the meaning of the words themselves. Reactions to swear words are more likely to reflect an interplay of social factors such as gender, age, race, sexual orientation, religious sensibilities, and so on. Ismail Talib (2002, p. 37) identifies positive reactions to swear words such as 'fuck' in contemporary Scottish literature, calling this 'an emblem of a more extensive dialectal usage ... inheritance'. He illustrates this with the Scottish novelist, James Kelman, who 'claims only to have been aware of the original meaning of the word "fuck" when he was in his twenties: hitherto, the word had had a hundred other meanings, a thousand different uses' (quoted by Bell, 1994, p. 161, in Talib, 2002, p. 38). What we consider offensive language, then, is strongly linked to the social taboos or tolerances of our society and our own social circle.

Discriminatory language

Like swear words, language that is considered discriminatory will vary over time and from group to group. I will start with an example from Britain of an utterance generally agreed to be discriminatory, racist and unacceptable that illustrates some shifts in social attitudes. In early 2004, a well-known television football commentator, wrongly believing himself to be off the air, described a black footballer as 'what is known in some schools as a fucking lazy, thick nigger'. When his words were broadcast, there was widespread disgust, and to no one's surprise he left his job soon afterwards. It was his use of 'nigger' rather than 'fucking' that caused the revulsion and led to his resignation, whereas not very many years ago it would probably have been the other way round.

The changing attitude to the word 'nigger' when used by white people to refer to black people is a demonstration of how a word can move from being on the border between acceptable and offensive in many people's eyes to being highly offensive to almost everyone, in less than fifty years. We can get an insight into how this process takes place by looking again at the *Guardian* online *Style Guide*:

[R]acial terminology

Avoid the word 'immigrant', which is very offensive to many black and Asian people, not only because it is often incorrectly used to describe people who were born in Britain, but also because it has been used negatively for so many years that it carries imagery of 'flooding', 'swamping', 'bogus', 'scroungers' etc

> The words black and Asian should not be used as nouns, but adjectives: black people rather than 'blacks', an Asian woman rather than 'an Asian', etc

(*Guardian*, 2005c)

Two reasons are given for avoiding the word 'immigrant': first because it is often an incorrect description, but more interestingly, because the words it is often associated with have given it strong negative connotations. This suggests that it is not the word itself that is offensive, but the offensive intent that may surround its use. Some words then, such as 'nigger', move into the offensive category when they are so imbued with the historical baggage of offensive intent that their use is nearly always perceived as unacceptable.

There is one more group of words that have offensive potential and these again are words that tend to group people by their characteristics such as sexual orientation, gender, or disability. Words that in my parents' generation would have been perfectly acceptable, such as 'cripple', 'slow', 'backward', are now avoided as highlighting a disability rather than focusing on the individual as a person. This reflects a change in society's attitudes to such people and an awareness that the language used to describe them has powerful connotations.

This brings us back to the question of what makes some words offensive? What the words refer to is obviously part of it. For swear words, those generally held to be most offensive are related in some way to sex: sexual acts or parts of the body associated with sexual acts. A second category – generally held to be less offensive – refers to excretion, and the parts of the body associated with it. And a third category consists of a range of religious terms used outside their religious context. These last are nowadays generally considered very mild indeed; modern authors are unlikely to write 'd—n' for 'damn', as their Victorian predecessors did. But although what the words refer to is obviously relevant to their offensiveness, it appears to be the *words* themselves – their sound in speech or their appearance in writing – that are offensive to some people, as is shown by the respectability of asterisked versions that are easily decipherable.

Further evidence is the fact that the swear words in the first two categories all have perfectly respectable synonyms or near-synonyms. 'Fuck' may be offensive, but 'copulate' is not. And there are several polite alternatives for 'arse': even the *Radio Times* would hardly need asterisks for words like 'bottom'.

So, are all these words *inherently* offensive? I can only give a personal response. Where words like 'fuck' are used with deliberate abusiveness, I do find them offensive. Admittedly, for me, most of the offensiveness lies in the abusive intent, not in the words themselves. But there seems to me to be an added offence in the association of the sex act or parts of the body with the intention to abuse.

However, that these words *as such* are offensive – their sound in speech or their appearance on the page – is not something I can accept. Like many other words, they can be used offensively, and many of us may want to avoid them in contexts where they will give offence – but that does not require us to agree that they are inherently offensive. They are words that often pepper the speech of many people, acting perhaps as a marker of identity with a particular group, as, for example, on the building site discussed in Chapter 5. Their use between friends is attested to by the frequency with which swear words are heard on the street or on public transport during friendly conversations. Can we say, therefore, that in the case of swear words, they are offensive only if the intention behind them is aggressive and offensive? For me, this is the case. I would not be offended if I were told jovially to 'fuck off'; I would be if I were told aggressively to 'go away'. It is the intention that matters, not the words in which it is expressed. However, I know that this is not the case for everyone, and that some people do consider such words inherently offensive and regret their frequency in current usage.

The situation is different, I believe, with discriminatory words. It is not because there is anything inherently offensive in the sounds of the words or their appearance on the page any more than with swear words. It is because the history and current usage of a word such as 'nigger' make it difficult to believe that it could be used with anything other than malevolent intent. (This is so at least as used by white people about black people. The fact that, like a number of discriminatory words, it has been adopted as a gesture of defiance and self-assertion by some members of the groups to whom it is malevolently applied by others, does not affect the present issue.)

7.6 Conclusion

In this chapter, I have been looking at some of the kinds of judgement we can and cannot reasonably make about the quality of people's English. As we have seen, linguists tend to be sceptical about such judgements, whereas non-linguists who are interested in language often make them and accept them with enthusiasm. And as you will know by now, although I am not a linguist, I find myself mostly on the linguists' side. Indeed, where I disagree, this is often because I am more sceptical, not less. (For example, I think 'appropriateness', many linguists' preferred substitute for 'correctness', is often just as problematic.)

This is not to say that linguists never judge anything to be incorrect English. Of course they do. But they make these judgements using what English speakers would ordinarily say and accept as their standard of correctness. What the linguists do not usually do is judge ordinary English usage against some external set of standards and find it wanting and in need of correction. Here again, I follow in the linguists' footsteps.

I find myself on the side, then, of Professor Aitchison against the purists who grumble so much. I have little sympathy with those who insist on correctness in grammar, spelling and meaning – without recognising that correctness depends totally on how language is actually used, that usages vary and change and, above all, that even genuine mistakes are usually of little or no importance.

READING A: Extracts from 'Why do purists grumble so much?'

Jean Aitchison
(Jean Aitchison was formerly the Rupert Murdoch Professor of Language and Communication at the University of Oxford.)

Source: Aitchison, J. (1994) 'Why do purists grumble so much?', *Evening Standard*, 27 April.

Humpback whales alter their songs every year, and a song thrush was heard to incorporate the chirp-chirp of a modern phone into its melody. No one has complained. So why do so many people grumble about change in the English language?

Language is not decaying due to neglect. It is just changing, like it always did.

...

Language lamenters mostly haven't understood how language works. In language change, new variants grow up alongside existing ones, often as stylistic alternatives. Usually each variant is relevant in a particular situation. You might say 'tara' on leaving a pal in the Midlands, but goodbye to one in London. The past tense of 'shoot up' is 'shot up' in 'The cat shot up the tree', but 'shooted up' of drugs: 'Someone passed me this syringe ... and I shooted up' ...

... The media can help combat prejudices against regional accents and stylistic variations by pointing out that variety is the norm and appropriateness the key: the right words and style for the right occasion, and that no one 'style' is correct at all times. But, above all, journalists could discourage moans over trivia. Such complaints divert attention from a far more serious language threat, the manipulation of people's lives by the dishonest use of language. Take the 'surgical' speech in the Gulf War. There was talk of air-strikes with 'pinpoint accuracy', and 'precision' bombing. These phrases misled many people into believing that the war was primarily an attack on buildings, and that humans were mostly unharmed. It may be more important to detect manipulation of this type than to worry about whether the word 'media' is singular or plural.

READING B: Extracts from *Rediscover Grammar with David Crystal*

David Crystal
(David Crystal is Honorary Professor of Linguistics at the University of Wales, Bangor.)

Source: Crystal, D. (1996) *Rediscover Grammar with David Crystal* (revised edn), Harlow, Longman, from back cover; pp. 6, 8, 11; p. 101.

Part 1: From the publisher's description on the back cover

Rediscover Grammar with David Crystal

Do you know?

- when to use shall and when to use will?
- where to put the apostrophe?
- how to spot split-infinitives – and what to do about them?

This lively and entertaining book sets you on the path to better English. A leading language expert explains English Grammar in a way that everyone can understand. Whether you read it straight through or use the detailed index to look up tricky points, *Rediscover Grammar* will provide a wealth of easy-to-follow advice on a subject we all find difficult from time to time.

...

Rediscover grammar – an easy guide to getting it right.

Part 2: From the author's introduction

Grammar is the business of taking a language to pieces, to see how it works. ...

Everyone reading these sentences, and understanding them, already knows the grammar of the English language ... We can see this from the way we speak. We put words together in the right order, with the right endings, and only occasionally make a mistake. We have evidently learned the rules, and we recognise when somebody breaks them. It is 'not English' to say *Cat the on a mat sitting was*. Everyone who speaks English **knows** grammar, intuitively and unconsciously.

But not everyone who speaks English **knows about** grammar. 'Knowing about' means being able to talk about what we know. It means being able to describe what we do, when we string words together, and being able to work out what the rules are. ... It is a conscious process, and it does not come naturally.

...

This book describes the basic features of the way grammar is used in English. It deals with a wide range of spoken and written usage, and includes data on formal, informal, regional, literary and other styles. ...

The information is presented objectively. I indicate areas where people need to be careful about informal usage if they wish to avoid criticism. But there is no condemnation of regional or informal usage. I take the view that all varieties of the language have an intrinsic value and interest, while recognising that one of these varieties – formal standard English – carries more social prestige and has more universal standing than any other.

Part 3: From the author's discussion of *will* and *shall*

Some traditional grammars insist on a sharp distinction between the use of *will* and *shall*.

- To express **future time**, they recommend the use of *shall* with first persons ... and *will* with second and third persons: *I/we shall go, You/he/she/it/they will go.*
- To express an **intention to act** ..., they recommend *will* with the first person and *shall* with the others: *I/we will go You/he/she/it/they shall go.*

On this basis, sentences such as *I will be 20 soon* are condemned as wrong, because, it is said, we cannot 'intend' to be a certain age. However, modern spoken usage does not observe the *will/shall* distinction, and it has largely disappeared in several varieties (notably, American, Scottish, and Irish English). It is now rare to find *shall* in the second and third person ... except in the most formal of styles, and it is becoming less common in the first person. *Will* is today the dominant form.

READING C: 'A rule without reason'

Ian Mayes
(Ian Mayes is the Guardian *Readers' Editor.)*

Source: Mayes, I. (2004) 'A rule without reason', *Guardian* [online], 27 March, http://www.guardian.co.uk/comment/story/0,,1179067,00.html (Accessed 11 November 2005).

At the end of my last column on the Guardian's use of English, I commented on the alright/all right controversy, quoting the Guardian style guide: 'All right is right; alright is not all right' – and I suggested that the 'alright' form may have arisen from confusion with already (which is all right).

There was an immediate flurry of correspondence from readers anxious to speak up for 'alright'. One reader [Joyce West] wrote: 'I have been innocently using alright for years as in "Are you hurt? – No, I'm alright." I looked in my Chambers dictionary, which told me that alright was an alternative, less acceptable spelling of all right.

'I would, of course, use all right as in "today his sums were all right," where the meaning seems to me to be entirely different.' On the comparison with 'already', the reader suggests: 'This would seem to be a good model for alright. "We are all ready" has a completely different meaning from "She already knows".'

This reader ended with a plea: 'It is well recognised that the language is constantly changing, and some of us resist some of these changes fiercely, often with strong backing from the Guardian. However, I intend to go on using alright as I have done in the past, and it would make me really happy if the Guardian were to tell me that it was all right.'

Let us get the disappointment out of the way immediately. The Guardian, which has been revising its style guide, soon to be published in book form, has every intention of sticking to the definition with which this column opened: all right is right; alright is not all right.

The 1933 edition of the Oxford English Dictionary described the word 'alright' as obsolete, having meant 'just, exactly'. It quoted only two examples, one from c1175 and the other from c1230. By the time of the 1972 supplement, the dictionary was at least prepared to concede the reappearance of the word as 'a frequent spelling of all right'. Its earliest quoted example was from the Durham University Journal, 1893: 'I think I shall pass alright.' This quotation highlights a distinction of meaning that a colleague, agreeing with my correspondent, believes might be usefully served by preserving 'alright': 'Your examination answers do not have to be all right for the result to be alright.' Others to whom 'alright' is an abhorrence argue that even in such a sentence as that the context makes the distinction in meaning apparent: 'Your examination results do not have to be all right for the result to be all right.'

...

A ... recent edition of Fowler, the New Modern English Usage, revised third edition, edited by RW Burchfield (Oxford 1998) reserves one of its snootier notes for the subject: 'The use of "all right", or inability to see that there is anything wrong with "alright", reveals one's background, upbringing, education etc, perhaps as much as any word in the language ... It is preferred, to judge from the evidence I have assembled, by popular sources like the British magazines The Face, the New Musical Express ... the Socialist Worker ... and hardly ever by writers of standing.' Quoted exceptions are Chinua

Achebe, 1987: 'You'll be alright, love'; and Anita Desai, 1988: '"Yes, they visit tombs and live in ashrams alright," Farrokh sneered.'

Within the Guardian, despite its own rule, 'alright' has a persistent presence, with almost 700 examples coming up in an electronic search from the past year or two. Figuring prominently among the users of 'alright' is Guardian Unlimited [the newspaper's website version], particularly in sport and popular music: 'Great entertainment and the cricket's alright as well'; 'It's sensational stuff, alright!' But it crops up in other areas too: 'I read it alright and I know it's got your name on it, but who wrote it?' (Review)

Kingsley Amis, in The King's English (HarperCollins 1997), wrote: 'I still feel that to inscribe "alright" is gross, crass, coarse and to be avoided, and I say so now.' But why it is all those things no one seems to know.

Kingsley Amis again: 'Its interdiction is as pure an example as possible of a rule without a reason, and in my case may well show nothing but how tenacious a hold early training can take.' In the Guardian's case consistency is the elusive object.

References

Ahl, F. (1988) 'Ars est celare artem (art in puns and anagrams engraved)' in Culler, J. (ed.) *On Puns: The Foundation of Letters*, Oxford, Blackwell.

Aitchison, J. (1994) 'Why do purists grumble so much?', *Evening Standard*, 27 April.

Allen, J. (2003) *The BBC News Styleguide* [online], http://www.bbctraining.com/pdfs/newsstyleguide.pdf (Accessed 10 December 2005).

Amis, K. (1997) *The King's English*, London, HarperCollins.

Atkinson, J.M. (1984) *Our Master's Voices: The Language and Body Language of Politics*, London, Methuen.

Bakhtin, M.M. (1981) *The Dialogic Imagination* (trans. M. Holquist, ed. C. Emerson and M. Holquist), Austin, TX, University of Texas Press.

Barton, D. (1994) *Literacy: An Introduction to the Ecology of Written Language*, Oxford, Blackwell.

Barton, D. and Padmore, S. (1991) 'Roles, networks and values in everyday writing' in Barton, D. and Ivanic, R. (eds) *Writing in the Community*, London, Sage.

Baynham, M. (2001) 'Reading the weather', *Journal of Research in Reading*, vol. 24, no. 3, pp. 307–12.

Baynham, M. and Maybin, J. (1996) 'Literacy practices in English' in Maybin, J. and Mercer, N. (eds) *Using English: From Conversation to Canon*, London, Routledge/Milton Keynes, The Open University.

Beattie, G. (1983) *Talk: An Analysis of Speech and Non-Verbal Behaviour in Conversation*, Buckingham, Open University Press.

Blamires, H. (1997) *The Cassell Guide to Common Errors in English*, London, Cassell.

Blume, R. (1985) 'Graffiti' in Van Dijk, T. (ed.) *Discourse and Literature*, Amsterdam, Benjamins.

Bowans, G. (ed.) (1964) *Penguin Book of Japanese Verse* (trans. G. Bowans and A. Thwaite), Harmondsworth, Penguin.

Bright, M. (2004) 'Colin Powell in four-letter neo-con "crazies" row', *Observer*, 12 September 2004.

Brown, D.E. (1991) *Human Universals*, New York, McGraw-Hill.

Brown, P. and Levinson, S. (1987) *Politeness: Some Universals in Language Usage*, Cambridge, Cambridge University Press.

Bruner, J. (1986) *Actual Minds, Possible Worlds*, Cambridge, MA, Harvard University Press.

Burt, A. (2004) *Quick Solutions to Common Errors in English: An A–Z Guide to Spelling, Punctuation and Grammar* (3rd edn), Oxford, howtobooks.

Bush, G. (2004) Extract from 'Transcript: first presidential debate', http://www.washingtonpost.com/wp-srv/politics/debatereferee/debate_0930.html (Accessed 18 May 2005).

Cameron, D. (1995) *Verbal Hygiene*, London, Routledge.

Cameron, D. (1997) 'Performing gender identity: young men's talk and the construction of heterosexual masculinity' in Meinhoff, U. and Johnson, S. (eds) *Language and Masculinity* Oxford, Blackwell.

Cameron, D. (2000) *Good to Talk? Living and Working in a Communication Culture*, London, Sage.

Cheepen, C. and Monaghan, J. (1990) *Spoken English: A Practical Guide*, London, Pinter.

Chouliaraki, L. and Fairclough, N. (1999) *Discourse in Late Modernity – Rethinking Critical Discourse Analysis*, Edinburgh, Edinburgh University Press.

Coates, J. (1996) *Women Talk: Conversation Between Women Friends*, Oxford, Blackwell.

Coates, J. (2003) *Men Talk: Stories in the Making of Masculinities*, Oxford, Blackwell.

Collinson, D., Kirkup, G., Kyd, R. and Slocombe, L. (1992) *Plain English* (2nd edn), Buckingham, Open University Press.

Connor, U. (1999) '"How like you our fish?" Accommodation in international business correspondence' in Hewings, M. and Nickerson, C. (eds) *Business English: Research into Practice*, Harlow, Longman.

Cook, G. (2000) *Language Play, Language Learning*, Oxford, Oxford University Press.

Corner, J. (1995) *Television Form and Public Address*, London, Edward Arnold.

Cruickshank, K.E. (2001) 'Parallel lines: Arabic-speaking teenagers' literacy and schooling', PhD thesis, Faculty of Education, University of Technology, Sydney.

Crystal, D. (1996) *Rediscover Grammar with David Crystal* (revised edn), Harlow, Longman.

Crystal, D. (1998) *Language Play*, Harmondsworth, Penguin.

Duncan, A. (2004) 'The running man', *Radio Times*, 11–17 September, pp. 28–30.

Eckert, P. and McConnell-Ginet, S. (2003) *Language and Gender*, Cambridge, Cambridge University Press.

Ervin-Tripp, S.M. (1969) 'Sociolinguistics' in Berkowitz, L. (ed.) *Advances in Experimental Social Psychology*, New York, Academic Press.

Evans, H. (2000) *Essential English for Journalists, Editors and Writers* (fully revised by C. Gillan), London, Pimlico.

Fairclough, N. (ed.) (1992) *Critical Language Awareness*, London, Longman.

Fairclough, N. (1993) 'Critical discourse analysis and the marketization of public discourse: the universities', *Discourse and Society*, vol. 4, no. 2, pp. 133–68.

Fairclough, N. (1994) 'Conversationalization of public discourse and the authority of the consumer' in Keat, R., Whiteley, N. and Abercrombie, N. (eds) *The Authority of the Consumer*, London, Routledge.

Fairclough, N. (1995) *Critical Discourse Analysis,* London, Longman.

Fairclough, N. (1995) *Media Discourse*, London, Edward Arnold.

Fairclough, N. (1996) 'Border crossings: discourse and social change in contemporary societies' in *Change and Language*, BAAL 10, Clevedon, Multilingual Matters.

Fairclough, N. (2000) *New Labour, New Language?* London, Routledge.

Field, M. (2003) *Improve Your Written English* (4th edn), Oxford, howtobooks.

Fowler, H.W. (1926) *A Dictionary of Modern English Usage*, Oxford, Clarendon.

Fowler, H.W. (1998) *The New Fowler's Modern English Usage* (3rd revised edn) (revised by R.W. Burchfield), Oxford, Clarendon Press.

Fowler, H.W. and Fowler, F.G. (1906) *The King's English*, Oxford, Clarendon.

Fowler, R. (1991) *Language in the News*, London, Routledge.

Freire, P. and Macedo, D. (1987) *Literacy: Reading the Word and the World*, London, Routledge & Kegan Paul.

Freud, S. (1952 [1905]) *The Complete Psychological Works*, London, Hogarth/Institute of Psychoanalysis.

Goddard, A. (2002) *The Language of Advertising* (2nd edn), London, Routledge.

Goddard, A. (2004) '"The way to write a phone call": multimodality in novices' use and perceptions of interactive written discourse (IWD)' in LeVine, P. and Scollon, R. (eds) *Discourse and Technology: Multimodal Discourse Analysis*, Washington, DC, Georgetown University Press.

Goddard, A. (2006) 'Discourses Я us: intertextuality as a creative strategy in interactive written discourse (IWD)' in Maybin, J. and Swann, J. (eds) (2006) *The Art of English: Everyday Creativity*, Basingstoke, Palgrave Macmillan/Milton Keynes, The Open University.

Goffman, E. (1967) *Interaction Ritual*, Harmondsworth, Penguin.

Goodin, R.E. (1980) *Manipulatory Politics*, New Haven, CT, Yale University Press.

Goodman, S. (1996) 'Market forces speak English' in Goodman, S. and Graddol, D. (eds) *Redesigning English: New Texts, New Identities*, London, Routledge/Milton Keynes, The Open University.

Goodwin, M.H. (1990) 'Tactical use of stories: participation frameworks within girls' and boys' disputes', *Discourse Processes*, vol. 13, no. 1, pp. 33–71.

Gowers, E. (1948) *Plain Words: A Guide to the Use of English*, London, HMSO.

Grove, V. (1993) 'Of dipsticks and the joys of a double negative', *The Times*, 17 November.

Guardian (2002a) 'Corrections and clarifications', *Guardian* [online], 14 May, http://www.guardian.co.uk/corrections/story/0,,715124,00.html (Accessed 13 December 2004).

Guardian (2002b) 'Corrections and clarifications', *Guardian* [online], 24 October, http://www.guardian.co.uk/corrections/story/0,,817802,00.html (Accessed 16 January 2005).

Guardian (2005a) 'Apostrophes' in Marsh, D. and Marshall, N. (eds) *The Guardian Style Guide* [online], http://www.guardian.co.uk/styleguide/page/0,5817,184844,00.html (Accessed 10 December 2005).

Guardian (2005b) 'Swearwords' in Marsh, D. and Marshall, N. (eds) *The Guardian Style Guide* [online], http://www.guardian.co.uk/styleguide/page/0,5817,184832,00.html (Accessed 11 November 2005).

Guardian (2005c) 'Racial terminology' in Marsh, D. and Marshall, N. (eds) *The Guardian Style Guide* [online], http://www.guardian.co.uk/styleguide/page/0,5817,184831,00.html (Accessed 10 December 2005).

Halliday, M.A.K. (1973) *Explorations in the Function of Language*, London, Edward Arnold.

Halliday, M.A.K. (1978) *Language as Social Semiotic: The Social Interpretation of Language and Meaning*, London, Edward Arnold.

Halliday, M.A.K. (1985) *Spoken and Written Language*, Deakin, Victoria, Deakin University Press.

Halliday, M.A.K. (1987) 'Spoken and written modes of meaning' in Horowitz, R. and Samuels, S.J. (eds) *Comprehending Oral and Written Language*, Orlando, FL, Academic Press.

Hearst, D. (1994) 'It loses something in the translation', 'Moscow Diary', *Guardian*, 25 July.

Hewitt, R. (1987) 'White adolescent creole users and the politics of friendship' in Mayor, B. and Pugh, A.K. (eds) *Language, Communication and Education*, London, Croom Helm.

Hochschild, A.R. (1983) *The Managed Heart*, Berkeley, CA, University of California Press.

Hodgens, J. (1994) 'How adult literacy became a public issue in Australia', *Open Letter*, vol. 2, no. 2.

Holmes, J. (2001) *Introduction to Sociolinguistics* (2nd edn), London, Longman.

Howard, J. (2004) Extract from the transcript of the 'Address to the Victorian Liberal Party State Council meeting in Hawthorn, Melbourne by the Prime Minister, John Howard', http://www.australianpolitics.com/news/2004/04/04-04-03.shtml (Accessed 18 May 2005).

Kell, C. (1994) 'An analysis of literacy practices in an informal settlement in the Cape Peninsula', MPhil dissertation, Cape Town, Faculty of Education, University of Cape Town.

Kerry, J.F. (2004) Extract from 'Transcript: first presidential debate', http://www.washingtonpost.com/wp-srv/politics/debatereferee/debate_0930.html (Accessed 18 May 2005).

Koester, A. (2004) *The Language of Work*, London, Routledge.

Koester, A. (2006) *Investigating Workplace Discourse*, London, Routledge.

Kress, G. and van Leeuwen, T. (2001) *Multimodal Discourse: The Modes and Media of Contemporary Communication*, London, Edward Arnold.

Labov, W. (1972) *Language in the Inner City*, Philadelphia, PA, University of Pennsylvania Press.

Lakoff, R. (1975) *Language and Women's Place*, New York, Harper & Row.

Lay, P. (2004) 'Casting a spell', *Radio Times*, 27 November–3 December, p. 39.

Lodge, D. (2001) *Thinks...*, London, Secker & Warburg.

Malinowski, B. (1923) 'The problem of meaning in primitive languages' in Ogden, C.K. and Richards, I.M. (eds) *The Meaning of Meaning*, London, Routledge & Kegan Paul.

Manser, M. and Curtis, S. (2002) *The Penguin Writer's Manual*, London, Penguin Books.

Marley, C. (2002) 'Popping the question: questions and modality in written dating advertisements', *Discourse Studies*, vol. 4, no. 1, pp. 75–98.

Marriott, H. (1995) 'Deviations in an intercultural business negotiation' in Firth, A. (ed.) *The Discourse of Negotiation: Studies of Language in the Workplace*, London, Pergamon.

Maybin, J. (2006) *Children's Voices: Talk, Knowledge and Identity*, Basingstoke, Palgrave.

Mayes, I. (1998) 'Open doors: a letter to Laura and co', *Guardian* [online], 12 November, http://www.guardian.co.uk/Columnists/Column/0,,324865,00.html (Accessed 11 November 2005).

Mayes, I. (2000) 'Trivial pursuit', *Guardian* [online], 8 July, http://www.guardian.co.uk/saturday_review/story/0,,340929,00.html (Accessed 3 April 2006).

Mayes, I. (2003a) 'Corrections and clarifications', *Guardian* [online], 11 October, http://www.guardian.co.uk/corrections/story/0,,1060801,00.html (Accessed 13 December 2004).

Mayes, I. (2003b) 'A headline too far', *Guardian* [online], 17 May, http://www.guardian.co.uk/Columnists/Column/0,,957976,00.html (Accessed 11 November 2005).

Mayes, I. (2004a) 'Corrections and clarifications', *Guardian* [online], 26 July, http://www.guardian.co.uk/corrections/story/0,,1268940,00.html (Accessed 13 December 2004).

Mayes, I. (2004b) 'Life without the asterisk', *Guardian* [online], 8 May, http://www.guardian.co.uk/Columnists/Column/0,,1213458,00.html (Accessed 11 November 2005).

Maynard, D. (1992) 'On clinicians co-implicating recipients' perspective in the delivery of diagnostic news' in Drew, P. and Heritage, J. (eds) *Talk at Work: Interaction in Institutional Settings*, Cambridge, Cambridge University Press.

McNair, B. (2003) *An Introduction to Political Communication* (3rd edn), London, Routledge.

Mercer, N. (1996) 'English at work' in Maybin, J. and Mercer, N. (eds) *Using English: From Conversation to Canon*, London, Routledge/Milton Keynes, The Open University.

Merchant, G. (2001) 'Teenagers in cyberspace – an investigation of language use and language change in internet chatrooms', *Journal of Research in Reading*, vol. 24, no. 3, pp. 293–306.

Nash, W. (1993) *Jargon: Its Uses and Abuses*, Oxford, Blackwell.

Orwell, G. (1987) *Animal Farm*, London, Secker & Warburg.

Pandharipande, R. (1992) 'Defining politeness in Indian English', *World Englishes*, vol. 11, no. 2/3, pp. 241–50.

Peek, L. and Chong, L. (2005) 'Kyoto protest beaten back by inflamed petrol traders', *Timesonline*, 17 February, http://www.timesonline.co.uk/article/0,,2-1487741,00.html (Accessed 10 December 2005).

Pinker, S. (1994) *The Language Instinct: The New Science of Language and Mind*, London, Allen Lane.

Poncini, G. (2002) 'Investigating discourse at business meetings with multicultural participation', *International Review of Applied Linguistics*, vol. 40, pp. 345–73.

Psathas, G. (1995) *Conversation Analysis: The Study of Talk-in-Interaction*, London, Sage.

Rackham, J. (2004) 'Hard Spell', *Radio Times*, 27 November–3 December, p. 88.

Rampton, B. (2005) *Crossing: Language and Ethnicity Among Adolescents* (2nd edn), Manchester, St Jerome Press.

Redfern, W. (1984) *Puns*, Oxford, Blackwell.

Rees, N. (1980) *Graffiti 2*, London, Unwin.

Rees, N. (1981) *Graffiti 3*, London, Unwin.

Roberts, C. and Sayers, P. (1988) 'Keeping the gate: how judgements are made in interethnic interviews' in Knapp, K. et al. (eds) *Analysing Intercultural Conversation*, The Hague, Mouton.

Romaine, S. (1990) 'Pidgin English advertising' in Ricks, C. and Michaels, L. (eds) *The State of the Language*, London, Faber & Faber.

Sacks, H., Schegloff, E. and Jefferson, G. (1974) 'A simplest systematics for the organization of turn-taking in conversation', *Language*, vol. 50, no. 4, pp. 696–735.

Saussure, F. de (1960 [1916]) *Course in General Linguistics* (trans. W. Baskin), London, Fontana.

Sebba, M. (1993) *London Jamaican: Language Systems in Interaction*, London, Longman.

Seidlhofer, B. (2001) 'Closing the conceptual gap: the case for a description of English as a Lingua Franca', *International Journal of Applied Linguistics*, vol. 11, pp. 133–58.

Shuman, A. (1993) 'Collaborative writing: appropriating power or reproducing authority?' in Street, B. (ed.) *Cross-Cultural Approaches to Literacy*, Cambridge, Cambridge University Press.

Shuy, R. (1993) *Language Crimes: The Use and Abuse of Language Evidence in the Courtroom*, London, Blackwell.

Simpson, J. (1999) *Strange Places, Questionable People*, London, Pan.

Street, B. (2005) 'Applying new literacy studies to numeracy as social practice' in Rogers, A. (ed.) *Urban Literacy: Communication, Identity and Learning in a Development Context*, Hamburg, UNESCO Institute of Education.

Swales, J. (1990) *Genre Analysis: English in Academic and Research Settings*, Cambridge, Cambridge University Press.

Talib, I.S. (2002) *The Language of Postcolonial Literatures: An Introduction*, London and New York, Routledge.

Tannen, D. (1984) *Conversational Style: Analyzing Talk Among Friends*, Norwood, NJ, Ablex.

Tannen, D. (1989) *Talking Voices: Repetition, Dialogue and Imagery in Conversational Discourse*, Cambridge, Cambridge University Press.

Tannen, D. (1992) 'How is conversation like literary discourse? The role of imagery and details in creating involvement' in Downing, P., Lima, S.D. and Noonan, M. (eds) *The Linguistics of Literacy*, Amsterdam, John Benjamins.

ten Have, P. (1999) *Doing Conversation Analysis: A Practical Guide*, London, Sage.

Tollefson, J.W. (1991) *Planning Language, Planning Inequality*, London, Longman.

Truss, L. (2003) *Eats, Shoots & Leaves: The Zero Tolerance Approach to Punctuation*, London, Profile Books.

Ulmer, G. (1988) 'The puncept in grammatology' in Culler, J. (ed.) *On Puns: The Foundation of Letters*, Oxford, Blackwell.

Volosinov, V.N. (1973) *Marxism and the Philosophy of Language*, New York, Seminar.

Vygotsky, L.S. (1978) *Mind in Society: The Development of Higher Psychological Processes*, London, Harvard University Press.

Walsh, K. (1994) 'Citizens, charters and contracts' in Keat, R., Whiteley, N. and Abercrombie, N. (eds) *The Authority of the Consumer*, London, Routledge.

Warschauer, M. (2002) 'Languages.com: the internet and linguistic pluralism' in Snyder, I. (ed.) *Silicon Literacies: Communication, Innovation and Education in the Electronic Age*, London and New York, Routledge.

Weiner, E.S.C. and Delahunty, A. (1993) *The Oxford Guide to English Usage* (2nd edn), Oxford, Oxford University Press.

Wells, S. (2002) *Shakespeare for All Time*, London, Macmillan.

Wernick, A. (1991) *Promotional Culture*, London, Sage.

Wolfe, T. (2004) *I Am Charlotte Simmons*, New York, Farrar, Straus and Giroux.

Wolfson, N. (1982) *CHP: The Conversational Historical Present in American English Narrative*, Cinnaminson, NJ, Foris.

Wooffitt, R. (1996) 'Rhetoric in English' in Maybin, J. and Mercer, N. (eds) (1996) *Using English: From Conversation to Canon*, London, Routledge/ Milton Keynes, The Open University.

Yell.com (2006) http://www.yell.com (Accessed 12 March 2006).

Acknowledgements

Grateful acknowledgement is made to the following sources:

Text

Pages 31–5: Eades, D. (1991) Communicative Strategies in Aboriginal English, extracts from pp. 84–93, Romaine, S. (ed.) *Language in Australia*, Cambridge University Press; pages 36–41: © Copyright Jane Sunderland; pages 53–4: The official transcript is available from the Australian Government web page: http://www.pm.gov.au/news/speeches/speech1293.html. Permission to reproduce any other material that is not part of the official transcript should be sought from australianpolitics.com; pages 73–4: Fairclough, N. (2000) Introduction, *New Labour, New Language?*, p. 953, Routledge, www.tandf.co.uk & www.eBookstore.tandf.co.uk; pages 94–5: Sam Cooke, Lou Adler and Herb Alpert, ABKCO Music & Records, Inc.; page 105: GNER (Great North Eastern Railway); pages 113–16: Tan, M. 1993, Language play in Dick Lee's songs – the Singapore element, BA Thesis submitted to the National University of Singapore; pages 116–21: Reprinted by permission of Sage Publications Ltd from O.G. Nwoye, Social Issues on the Walls: Graffiti in university lavatories, *Discourse and Society*, Copyright © Sage Publications, 1993; pages 136–7: Baynham, M. (2001) Reading the Weather, Hamilton, M., & Barton, D. (eds), *Journal of Research in Reading*, pp. 308–11, UKLA (The United Kingdom Literacy Association); pages 153–9: Scollon, R. and Wong Scollon, S. (2003) Place semiotics: Code preference, *Discourses in Place – Language in the Material World*, pp. 116–124, Routledge, www.tandf.co.uk & www.eBookstore. tandf.co.uk; pages 241–4: Reproduced by permission of Sage Publications, Thousand Oaks, London and New Delhi, from Fairclough, N., Critical discourse analysis and the marketization of public discourse, *Discourse and Society*, Volume 4, #2, p177–180, Sage Publications, 1993; page 259: Mayes, I. (2000) Trivial Pursuit, Copyright Guardian Newspapers Limited 2000; pages 262–3: Mayes, I. (2002) Corrections & Clarifications, Copyright Guardian Newspapers Limited 2002; page 276: Aitchison, J. (1994) Why do purists grumble so much?, *Evening Standard*, 27 April 1994, Solo Syndication Ltd; pages 277–8: Crystal, D. (1996) Extracts from: *Rediscover Grammar with David Crystal*, Pearson Education Ltd; pages 278–80: Mayes, I. (2004) A Rule Without Reason, Copyright Guardian Newspapers Limited 2004.

Figures

Page 46: Jawaharlal Nehru University; page 47: Reproduced with kind permission from The University of Singapore; page 48: Courtesy of The University of Waikato, New Zealand; page 63: North East Says No Ltd; page 68: GNER (Great North Eastern Railway); page 71: By kind permission of L'Oreal (Malaysia); page 95: Photo supplied by BBH. The Select Model Agency; page 102: © Art of the State; page 102: © Art of the State; page 114: Warner Music Singapore;

page 135: (top left, middle left and centre): John Yuen; (middle right and bottom left): Joan Swann; (top right and bottom right): Literary Research Group, Lancaster University; page 138: By kind permission of Marjorie Suedekum; page 139: Colour Mean Sea Level Pressure Analysis weather map, from the Bureau of Meteorology website. Copyright Commonwealth of Australia reproduced by permission; page 148: By kind permission of Borneo Linnells Solicitors; page 172: ACE STOCK LIMITED/Alamy; page 176: Stone/Getty Images; page 178: Connor, U. (1995) Business Communication, *Business English: Research into Practice*, Pearson Education Ltd, 1999; page 217: La Redoute UK; page 219: *5 A DAY – Just Eat More (fruit & veg)* (2003) Department of Health. Crown copyright material is reproduced under Class Licence Number C01W0000065 with the permission of the Controller of HMSO and the Queen's Printer for Scotland; page 221: Bugis Junction advertisement, appearing in *The Straits Times*, April 1995. By kind permission of Bugis City Holdings Pte Ltd; page 222: Minimum Sum Scheme advertisement, April 1995, Central Provident Fund Board; page 224: Minimum Sum Scheme advertisement, April 1995, Central Provident Fund Board.

Illustrations

Page 20: Image100/Photolibrary; page 32: A.I.A.T.S.I.S.; page 256: © David Austin.

Every effort has been made to contact copyright holders. If any have been inadvertently overlooked the publishers will be pleased to make the necessary arrangements at the first opportunity.

Index